THE
COSMOLOGICAL
MILK SHAKE

• THE •
COSMOLOGICAL
MILKSHAKE

•

A
SEMI-SERIOUS
LOOK
AT THE
SIZE
OF
THINGS

•

ROBERT EHRLICH
Illustrated by Gary Ehrlich

Library of Congress Cataloging-in-Publication Data

Ehrlich, Robert, 1938–
    The cosmological milk shake : a semi-serious look at the size of
things / Robert Ehrlich ; illustrated by Gary Ehrlich.
        p.   cm.
    Includes bibliographical references and index.
    ISBN 0-8135-2045-2 (cloth) — ISBN 0-8135-2046-0 (pbk.)
        1. Physics—Miscellanea.   2. Physics—Study and teaching.
    3. Astrophysics—Miscellanea.   4. Size judgment—Miscellanea.
    I. Title.
    QC75.E37   1993
    530—dc20   93-28135
                                                                         CIP
                                                                          r93

British Cataloging-in-Publication information available

●

Dedicated to my father,
WILLIAM EHRLICH

Contents

HOW HEAVY OR MASSIVE IS IT?

●

HOW HOT OR COLD IS IT?

●

HOW FAST IS IT?

●

HOW OLD IS IT?

●

Preface

IT'S A WILD, wonderful, wacky universe we live in. Did you know that the Sun might have stopped burning 100,000 years ago—but we might not be able to tell, because the light generated at the Sun's core takes that long to get to the surface?[1] Or that every so often, for unknown reasons, the north and south magnetic poles of the Earth switch places? Or that the galaxies are spread throughout the universe in a kind of cosmological milk shake?

The milk shake metaphor can apply to this book as well: it's meant to be a smooth blend of diverse ingredients that leaves you smiling and well fed—but not bloated. Our scope is literally the entire universe, from the innards of atoms to the farthest quasars. Our focus is on the size of stuff: how big, how small, how massive, how far, how fast, how hot, how old. In this lighthearted romp through the cosmos, we will stop to look at real, down-to-earth things as well as off-the-wall expressions of the scientific imagination— from the tallest possible tree and largest possible mountain to the biggest possible planet that could be shaped like a cube.

Facts about size, distance, temperature, and so on can be interesting in themselves. But things are often the size they are for a reason, and figuring out that reason can be intellectually exhilarating—whether you are a toddler just figuring out that small things can hide in bigger things or a Newton figuring out how gravitational force and distance are related. That's why the essays talk a lot about how we know what we know and how we can figure out what we don't know, no matter whether the questions are serious (how far away are the stars?), or possibly practical (how fast should you drive to be able to stop your car in a given distance?), or absurd (what's the right nail spacing for a pain-free bed of nails?), or downright grotesque (how long a noodle could you be turned into?).

I invite you to read this book in whatever order you like. Glance down the table of contents or flip through the pages and start reading the first essay or cartoon to

---

1. Light inside the Sun takes that long to reach the Sun's surface because it kind of staggers along a "random walk"—like that of a drunk—rather than following a straight-line path. Were the light to follow a straight-line path instead of a random walk, it would reach the surface in just over 2 seconds, rather than 100,000 years.

capture your curiosity. The 135 essays and their cartoons fall under five broad headings, and within a heading the topics form loose sequences. But you don't have to read them that way. There's no continuity of scientific fields from one essay to another—the book as a whole will give you a taste of disciplines as different as nuclear physics and microbiology. Each essay is meant to be pretty much self-contained, so you can dip in here and there. If you find yourself puzzled by the meaning of a term, try backtracking an essay or two.

Trust your everyday understanding of words like force, energy, or speed, even if they have formal scientific definitions. Don't worry, either, if your math feels shaky. Although talking about the sizes of things implies a bit of manipulation of numbers or formulas, this is an example of the level of mathematical reasoning you can expect to find:

Suppose Professor Longfellow has a theory that sex appeal is proportional to the square of a person's height. If your height doubled, then how much, according to Longfellow's theory, would your sex appeal increase? (Answer: it would quadruple. If your height goes from 1 unit to 2 units, its square goes from 1^2 to 2^2—from 1 to 4—heartthrob units.) Now, what if Longfellow's rival, Professor Small, claims that Longfellow is all wrong: sex appeal varies inversely as the square of a person's height. What would Small predict would happen to your sex appeal if your height doubled? (Answer: it would be $1/4$—$1/2^2$—its original value.) Based on their theories about the connection of sex appeal and height, what would you guess about the relative statures of Longfellow and Small? (Scientists are not immune from the human tendency to devise theories that make them and their group look good.)[2]

In any case, you can always skip over the math, get the train of the argument, and come back to the formulas later, if you want.

Over and over again, the essays will appeal to your own experience of things in the world—sipping soda through a straw, stepping on a tack, wringing out a wet towel. Many essays suggest easy experiments and demonstrations you can try out at home.[3] In connecting ordinary life with the abstractions of science, these "homely" experiments remind you that great insights have often grown out of noticing and musing over commonplace phenomena. While it's true that for some topics—subatomic physics or relativity—no simple experiments are possible, we can still rely on lively combinations of imagined experiments, analogies, and experiments in related areas. Even when you can't perform the actual experiments in esoteric fields yourself, you can get the idea of the experiment and what it shows.

If you read the whole book, you'll have the equivalent of an unconventional introductory course in physics. (Teachers who assign the book to their classes can obtain kits of problem sets/answers, illustrations, and review questions by writ-

2. When is the last time you heard of a study done by scientists of one race or nationality claiming that another race or nationality is actually the most intelligent, or a study claiming that dolphins are actually more intelligent than people?

3. For a collection of simple demonstration experiments using mostly things you can find around the house, see my book *Turning the World Inside Out and 174 Simple Physics Demonstrations*, published by Princeton University Press.

ing to the publisher.) But far more important than the particular physical facts, laws, and theories you encounter here is the chance you get to try thinking like a scientist. May you find it as much fun as I do!

Finally, a word about the cartoons: the essays are often a bit zany, but the cartoons are deliberately weird. And some of them may strike you as "for adults only" or politically incorrect—though tastefully done, of course. (On the other hand, you may consider them to be sick, degenerate filth. In that case you should be sure not to look at the cartoons for essays 1, 66, 74, and 125.) Unfortunately, as a rule, you won't get a cartoon unless you've read the accompanying essay. Think of it as dessert.

Acknowledgments

MANY PEOPLE kindly supplied feedback on drafts of this book. I would particularly like to thank Juan Carlos Chavez, J. M. Anthony Danby, Robert Ellsworth, Harvey Gould, Evelyn Kiley, Richard Kouzes, Eugenie Mielczarek, Judy Ng, Craig Pennington, John Risley, Suzanne Slayden, James Trefil, Jarek Tuszynski, and Charles Whitney. I especially thank my sister, Millie Ehrlich, whose editing encouraged me to slough off my dry professorial husk and reveal a zany (corny?) interior, my wife, Elaine Ehrlich, for not laughing at stuff that wasn't very funny, and my excellent copy editor, William Hively.

HOW
BIG
OR
FAR
IS IT?

1.   Whose Foot Is a Foot Long?

FEET, FURLONGS, femtometers, and fermis are just a few of the many units of distance or size. Once a unit of distance is defined in terms of a standard, any given distance can be expressed as a multiple or fraction of that standard. For example, long ago some ruler(!) must have decreed the length of his foot as *the* foot. (Probably, he did so after having reached maturity.) The foot is still a unit of distance in common use in the United States, but practically everywhere else in the world the metric system is in use. The metric system is universally used by scientists, although some are fussier than others about forgoing all other units. This book is "metrically incorrect," in that it uses both metric and nonmetric units.

The meter, originally defined in eighteenth-century France as one 10-millionth the distance from the equator to the north pole, is equivalent to 39.37 inches, or just over a yard in length. The big advantage of the metric system is its use of powers of ten to represent all length units in terms of the meter. For example, three of the more common units (with their abbreviations) are the millimeter (mm), centimeter (cm), and kilometer (km). These can be expressed as $\frac{1}{1,000}$ of a meter, $\frac{1}{100}$ of a meter, and 1,000 meters, respectively. Powers of ten also make it easy to convert areas and volumes from one metric unit to another. For example, consider a cube 1 meter on a side, whose volume is 1 cubic meter. Given that 1 meter equals 100 centimeters, we can express the cube's volume equivalently as 100 cm × 100 cm × 100 cm, or 1 million cubic centimeters. Likewise, the area of one of the six faces of the cube is 1 square meter, which equals 100 cm × 100 cm, or 10,000 square centimeters.

The meter is no longer defined in terms of the distance from the equator to the north pole, a definition that seemingly presents an awkward problem: do you subdivide that distance using a long piece of string? A more serious objection is the lack of precision with which the distance can be known, given our inability to locate precisely either the north pole or the equator. A more recent definition of the meter was the distance between two fine scratches on a platinum bar kept in a vault in Paris (where else?). That definition, like the definition of the foot based on some ruler's foot, seemed less "natural" than a definition based on the size of the Earth, but at least it could be accurately measured, and it was internationally recognized. In contrast, the unit called the foot had slightly different lengths in different countries—presumably based on the size of the feet of each ruler who defined it.

The current definition of the meter is no longer based on the distance between scratches on a bar, because we have found it possible to measure something with much greater accuracy: the time or frequency of atomic vibrations. The idea of defining a distance in terms of a time interval should be as familiar as the use of driving time to measure a trip's distance, assuming a standard speed. The speed of light in vacuum is a natural choice for the standard, because unlike other speeds, such as the speed of sound, that of light is believed to be absolutely constant. The meter is now defined as the distance a beam of light would travel during the fraction $1/299,792,458$ of a second.[1] Why that particular number? Because it allows everyone to keep using their old meter sticks. When the meter was defined as the distance between two scratches on a bar, the speed of light was measured as 299,792,458 meters per second.

FIGURE 2. *The ruler on the planet Grong decreed the unit of distance to be the length of his snork.*

Achieving the high accuracy implied by these definitions may not be important in everyday measurements, but obviously it is in certain kinds of scientific and technical work. Whatever units we use, when we say that the length of a distance or time interval is 3 meters or 3 seconds, we are saying it is three times as long as the distance or time interval we define as the standard.

1. The unit of time we call the second is no longer defined in terms of the length of the day; instead it is defined as the time required for a certain number of vibrations of the cesium atom.

2. How Long a Hot Dog Would You Make?

LET'S SUPPOSE you are working in a hot dog factory, and a *very* unfortunate accident occurs. How long a hot dog do you think your body would make? To figure this out, we first need to estimate your volume. There are all sorts of formulas for volume, none of which apply to a shape as irregular as you. If we just want an approximate value, we can assume that you barely float in water, implying that gram-for-gram you take up roughly the same volume as water. In fact, the gram was originally defined as the mass of 1 cubic centimeter of water, which implies that a kilogram of water occupies a volume of 1,000 cubic centimeters. So if you weigh 150 pounds (equivalent to around 70 kilograms), your volume is roughly seventy times that of 1 kilogram of water, or 70,000 cubic centimeters.[1] This estimate for the volume of a 150-pound person is unlikely to be off by more than a few percent, since most people float with only a few percent of their body above water.

So, how long a hot dog would you make? A typical hot dog has a thickness (diameter) of about 2 centimeters and a radius of 1 centimeter. Thus, its cross-sectional area (equal to πr^2) is about $\pi = 3.14$ square centimeters. A hot dog made from you would therefore need to have a length of about 22,000 centimeters (220 meters), so that when the length is multiplied by the cross-sectional area, we obtain the required volume. This calculation ignores the fact that your body has some hollow interior spaces, so that your volume when all ground up would actually be a bit less than your intact volume. Let's take an even more ridiculous scenario (if that is possible) and suppose you work in a noodle factory. The thickness of a noodle is perhaps only a tenth that of a hot dog, and so its cross-sectional area is only a *hundredth* as great. As a result, if you fell into the noodle-maker, the noodle that would come out would be a hundred times as long as the hot dog, or 22,000 meters (nearly 14 miles)! Finally, suppose we assume that your body is made into the "ultimate noodle"—one molecule thick. By estimating the number of molecules in your body and multiplying by the approximate size of a molecule, we get a value of 66 light-years (about sixteen times the distance to the nearest star).

---

1. In general, the mass of a body in kilograms is related to its volume by the rule *mass = density × volume*, where density refers to the mass of 1 cubic meter of the material. The important difference between a body's mass and weight will be discussed later. If your density is the same as water, your volume is just the volume of water that weighs as much as you do.

Notice, incidentally, that even though your volume would be nearly the same if you were made into a hot dog or a noodle, your surface area would be drastically greater. How can we find your intact surface area? One way is to assume your body has the shape of a rectangular parallelepiped (a box), which is a better approximation for some people than others. Let us assume that you are roughly 2 meters high by 0.25 meter wide by 0.25 meter deep. We can then find the surface area of each of the four sides plus the top and bottom, which gives a total of just over 2 square meters. Of course, we get only a very approximate value this way. If you need a more accurate value for your surface area, one method would be to see how much paint was needed to paint your entire body, and then see how large an area of wall space that same amount of paint covered. You probably are not interested enough in finding your surface area to go to this trouble, especially considering that you would need to shave your entire body to get a reliable value.

FIGURE 3. *The one profession that usually approximates people by rectangular parallelepipeds.*

You may think that scientists are always interested in obtaining the most accurate value possible for a given quantity, but just the reverse is true. Scientists generally want to measure things only to a precision necessary for the purpose at hand, *and no greater*, because measuring things to a higher precision often requires greater expense, time, and trouble. If you do have a need to know your surface area or volume, it seems likely that the parallelepiped approximation will be sufficient for most purposes.

3. What Is the Maximum Nail Spacing for a Comfortable Bed of Nails?

IN ORDER TO SHOW their abilities to withstand pain and to perform magic, some Eastern mystics have been known to lie on a bed of nails. You may also have seen this feat performed by some slightly strange science teachers wishing to demonstrate the "magic" of physics. Although the teachers probably did not wish to subject themselves to pain, they may have felt that the idea was not altogether displeasing to their audience. But in fact, lying on a bed of nails need be no more painful than lying on your own bed, provided that the nail spacing is small enough, so that the fraction of your weight supported by any one nail is not too large.

If you want to find the proper spacing between nails, you first need to see how hard a nail can press against your skin without causing pain. One easy way to make this estimate is to press a nail against a bathroom scale with the point of the nail against your finger until it just begins to hurt a bit. You may want to try it with nails whose tips have been dulled with a file. Obviously, the scale reading will depend on the nail sharpness, as well as on your sensitivity to pain. Let's say that the scale reads 2 pounds when your finger just begins to hurt. If you weigh 160 pounds, this means that you want no fewer than 80 nails supporting your body, assuming the nails will all support the same fraction of your weight—which would be true only if you were perfectly flat. Since you are

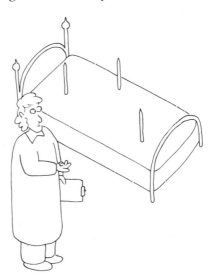

FIGURE 4. *Dr. Jones rechecks his calculations on proper nail spacing before lying down on the bed of nails.*

probably not flat, you might want a larger number of nails, because some will support more weight than others.

What nail spacing will ensure that at least 80 nails support your weight? In posing this question, we have actually found a need to know your surface area, or at least the surface area of a portion of your anatomy. You might think that the relevant number is the surface area of your back or side, but most people sit on a bed before they lie on it, so the area of your body in contact with the nails while sitting will be considerably less than while lying down. In other words, had we found the maximum nail spacing to support your weight without pain while lying down, you probably would find your bed quite painful when you rested your full weight on your bottom, which would have fewer nails supporting it. Suppose your bottom fits on an area 8 by 10 inches, or 80 square inches. In order to fit 80 nails on an area of 80 square inches, the proper spacing between nails is obviously 1 inch.[1] Even though your bottom is not flat, the 80 nails should probably be sufficient, since part of your weight will rest on your feet while you sit. So, given our assumptions, the proper nail spacing should be no more than 1 inch.

If you have any inclination to make yourself a bed of nails to sit or lie on—they say it's better than magic fingers—be sure to check the preceding calculation yourself, so as to verify all the assumptions, especially the amount of force you can bear without pain as you press a dull nail against your finger, and the surface area of your bottom. It will take quite a large number of nails to make a bed big enough to lie on with a 1-inch nail spacing: for example, for a 70-inch by 20-inch bed you would need 1,400 nails. This does seem like a lot of trouble, so you may instead just want to make an area large enough to sit on. You very likely would not want to stand on the nails, because I suspect that the area of the bottom of your feet is less than the area of your bottom.

4. What Is the Smallest Suction Cup You Could Use to Walk on the Ceiling?

INSECTS HAVE no difficulty walking on the ceiling, but humans seem incapable of this feat. Perhaps, if people had either very sticky hands and feet or, better yet, suction cups whose grip could be re-

1. In general, if the number of nails is N and the area is A, the square area associated with any one nail is N/A, and the side of the square (the maximum distance between nails) is the square root of that number.

6

leased at will, ceiling walking might yet become the latest fad—at least for the more physically fit element of the population. Let's consider how suction cups actually work. Suction cups are based on the idea that if all the air is pushed out of the rubber cup, the outside atmospheric pressure pushes the cup against the surface to which it is attached. Atmospheric pressure at sea level is around 15 pounds per square inch, meaning that the atmosphere exerts a 15-pound force on every exposed square inch of surface. The source of this atmospheric pressure is simply the weight of the atmosphere. In other words, the vertical column of air above 1 square inch of the Earth's surface weighs 15 pounds.

If you climb a mountain, there is less atmosphere above you and therefore lower atmospheric pressure, so suction cups don't hold quite as well. In space they don't work at all. How large a suction cup attached to the ceiling would you need to hold your weight? At 15 pounds per square inch atmospheric pressure, a person whose weight is 150 pounds would therefore need 10 square inches of suction cup area to support her. Actually, a larger cup would probably be needed, since suction cups don't make a perfect seal. The same 15 pounds per square inch that holds up the suction cup also presses from all directions on every square inch of your body. We saw earlier that your body has a surface area of around 2 square meters (about 3,000 square inches). So if we multiply 3,000 square inches by 15 pounds for each square inch, we see that the atmosphere presses on your body from all directions with a total force of about 45,000 pounds! The reason you don't instantly collapse is that unlike the suction cup, which has atmospheric pressure pushing only against one side, in your case there is usually air both inside and outside your body at normal pressure.

In Magdeburg, Germany, in 1654, a famous demonstration was given of the tremendous force atmospheric pressure can exert. In this demonstration the air was pumped out of the space inside a pair of joined hollow steel hemispheres held together only by the outside air pressure. When two teams of eight horses were hitched to the two hemispheres, they were unable to pull them apart, which is not surprising since the Magdeburg hemispheres had a cross-sectional area of 1,200 square

FIGURE 5. *Jim's design for suction loafers suffered from a fatal flaw.*

inches; the horses would have had to pull with a force of $15 \times 1,200 = 18,000$ pounds to overcome atmospheric pressure. A modern-day demonstration of the great force that air pressure can exert is provided by the design of the Minneapolis Metrodome, whose 290-ton roof is held up by the mere 0.03-pound-per-square-inch excess pressure created by large fans inside the dome. Presumably, in the event of a power failure the human "fans" might be called on to use their lung power for more than cheering their team on![1]

Using an empty aluminum soda can, you can easily demonstrate the crushing power of atmospheric pressure. Put a little water in the can and heat it on the stove until steam comes out of the hole, signifying that the steam has largely driven the air out of the can. Grab the can with tongs or a towel and quickly turn it upside down, immersing it entirely in cold water. The can will collapse, because the steam in the can has mostly displaced the air, and a partial vacuum will result when cooling causes the steam to condense quickly. Water cannot enter the can quickly enough, and so the can collapses. The reverse situation of low outside pressure can cause things to explode rather than to collapse. You may have seen one of those gory scenes in science fiction movies where an astronaut with a leaky space suit is thrust into space.

5. What Are the Longest and Narrowest Straws You Could Suck Through?

WHAT DOES IT mean to suck? Normally, we think of sucking through a straw as *pulling* the liquid up, but actually the liquid is being *pushed* up the straw. In other words, when you lower the air pressure at the top of the straw by sucking, the greater pressure of the atmosphere on the exposed surface of the liquid outside the straw pushes the liquid up the straw. Sucking a liquid up a straw would not be possible on the airless surface of the Moon. On Earth the pressure of the atmosphere is equivalent to that created under a depth of about 10 meters of water, so ideally you could suck water up a height of 10 meters if you created a vacuum at the top of a straw. Although I am unaware of any world records for sucking, it is clear that most people can suck water only a small fraction of this distance. It is not surprising that you cannot create a very large pressure drop by sucking, since this ability evidently evolved to

1. That's just a joke. You can easily convince yourself that a person could not create enough force by blowing to sustain "his" area of the roof, which we can assume is around 1,000 square inches. The force required would be around 30 pounds.

allow mammals to nurse. An ability of infants to create near vacuum pressures by sucking would not seem to have any evolutionary advantages!

If you want to find out how big a sucker you are, just tape some straws together and see how high a distance you can suck water up. For best results use plastic straws, which are less likely to collapse than paper straws, and tape the straws together using cellophane tape, being careful to avoid air leaks. I found that while standing on a chair, I could suck water vertically upward through nine straws taped together—a distance of about 1.8 meters. The pressure drop created by sucking was, in this case, presumably 18 percent of an atmosphere, since as noted above, a full one-atmosphere pressure drop (perfect vacuum) would have raised the water to a height of about 10 meters.

In the preceding example we assumed that the width of the straw has no bearing on how high a given sucking pressure can make water rise, which is roughly correct for normal-width straws. But for very narrow straws we need to take into account the attraction of the liquid for the walls of the straw.[1] In order to raise the liquid in the straw, the sucking pressure needs to overcome not only the weight of the liquid but also its attraction to the walls of the straw—a force that depends on the inner surface area of the straw in contact with the liquid. For narrow straws this surface force becomes much more important than the weight of the liquid, because the ratio of the lateral surface area of a cylinder to its volume increases the narrower the cylinder gets. For example, suppose the surface force is just equal to the weight of the liquid in a particular

FIGURE 6. *On being welcomed to hell, all arrivals are given a free drink with a straw too narrow to suck on.*

straw. In a straw of half the width, the surface force would equal twice the weight of the liquid—which explains why sucking up is hard to do with narrow straws.[2]

1. One indication of the attraction of water for the walls of a straw is the meniscus, or curved surface, that is formed at the top of the water column—the liquid is literally "climbing the walls" of the straw. Different surfaces attract (or repel) water molecules with different strengths, and they cause meniscuses of different curvatures as a result. There is a certain liquid (helium-II), known as a "superfluid," whose molecules find walls so much more attractive than one another that they spontaneously climb out of their container and the fluid flows over the walls!

2. If the liquid weight and surface force are equal for a straw of a particular height (h), in

9

6. How Tall Can Trees Grow?

WHEN A TALL TREE falls in a forest, there is literally a race for survival among saplings nearby to see which will be the first to fill the open space created. Trees have a strong reason to grow as tall as possible in order to maximize the sunlight their leaves receive at the expense of their neighbors. Some redwood trees, in fact, grow to the extraordinary height of 110 meters. To see why this height may be near the maximum possible, we need to understand how trees work.

In order to photosynthesize the sunlight incident on its leaves and create chlorophyll, a tree needs to be able to pump water up from the roots to the leaves. How can tall redwood trees accomplish this trick? The water flows upward through very narrow channels (capillaries) in the tree. Even if the tree could create a vacuum at the top of a capillary, you might think it could lift the water a distance of only 10 meters—equivalent to one atmosphere of pressure. But this height limitation applies only to water being pushed up the capillary by atmospheric pressure (much as water is pushed up a straw by the outside atmosphere when you reduce the pressure at its top by sucking).

No such 10-meter height limitation applies to water being *pulled* up a capillary. In fact, the attractive forces between water molecules are so strong that if there were a way to pull one end of a freestanding water column, it could be pulled up to a height of 2.8 kilometers (about 1.8 miles) before the column would break due to its weight. Essentially, as long as water in a capillary forms a continuous cylinder without breaks, we may think of the water as comprising a rope. The notion of a rope of water seems rather bizarre, since under ordinary circumstances pulling on a rope of water seems as inconceivable as pushing on an ordinary rope. But water can be pulled upward, as happens in a siphon, for example. One other such mechanism for pulling water upward is so-called capillary action.

If you want to observe an example of capillary action, hold the bottom of a piece of white cloth in some colored liquid. You will observe the liquid slowly move upward through the fibers of the cloth. Capillary action works because for a very narrow capillary the surface attraction of the water molecules to the capillary wall often exceeds the attraction of the water molecules to each other. In fact, as explained in essay 5, the narrower the capillary, the greater the ratio of the surface attraction to the weight of the fluid, and hence the higher the liquid will spontaneously rise. But capillary action does have its limits. For example, for an

---

a straw of half the radius (r), the lateral area ($2\pi rh$) would be reduced by half, while the volume ($\pi r^2 h$) would be reduced to a quarter of its previous size. Thus the surface force would be twice the weight in the half-width straw.

extremely narrow (0.1-millimeter diameter) capillary, water will rise spontaneously only about 15 centimeters. Clearly, capillary action alone is insufficient to raise water to the 110-meter height of the tallest trees, since a prohibitively narrow capillary would be required.

The source of energy that *pulls* water up the capillaries of a tree is provided by sunlight. When sunlight shines on the uppermost leaves, water at the top of the capillaries evaporates—meaning that water molecules spontaneously leave the tree from the top of the water column. Given the extremely strong cohesion between

FIGURE 7. *One tree floats a proposal to head off an all-out "limbs race."*

water molecules, the molecules that leave the top of the water column during the act of evaporation pull the entire column of water upward slightly to take their place.[1] The higher a tree gets, the greater is the work needed to raise water from the roots to the top leaves. As a result, for a given amount of energy supplied to the leaf of a tall tree and a short tree, the tall tree will be able to raise less water up to the leaf than the short tree in the same amount of time. Apparently, much above 100 meters, trees just cannot get it up fast enough to satisfy the needs of photosynthesis.

1. You might think that very strong attractive forces between water molecules would prevent them from evaporating. But as explained later, the molecules in a liquid or gas have a range of speeds, and molecules that happen to have speeds statistically much higher than the average are moving fast enough to break free.

7. What Is the Largest Possible Creature?

THE LARGEST LAND ANIMALS known to have roamed the Earth are some of the dinosaurs, the largest of which, ultrasaurus, weighed as much as six African elephants. Could there exist a creature ten or a hundred times larger than ultrasaurus? The larger a land animal gets, the thicker its legs need to become in order to support its weight. The reason large creatures have chunkier legs is because, for a given shape, the creature's weight is proportional to the *cube* of its height, while the cross-sectional area of its leg bones is proportional only to the *square* of its height.[1] This means that if you doubled the height of a creature and kept its proportions constant, its weight would increase *eightfold* (2 cubed), while the cross-sectional area of its legs would increase only *fourfold* (2 squared). So the leg bones of the enlarged creature would bear twice as much weight per unit area, and they would be likely to fracture. Obviously, as creatures get larger, there comes a point where their legs need to get so thick and bulky that they become virtually immobile. At that point such a creature's best solution to the problem of movement might be to evolve into the shape of a sphere and get where it wanted to go by rolling—assuming it lived in a fairly level environment![2]

Another solution to a large creature's problem of supporting its weight is to stay close to the ground—growing laterally rather than up. Snakes and alligators have followed this course of evolution. What sets the limit to how long snakes can grow? There are hazards for a snake getting too long chiefly in keeping track of and controlling what all its parts are doing. Consider a hypothetical kilometer-long snake. Nerve impulses traveling at a typical speed of 10 meters per second would take 100 seconds to travel the length of the creature. No such creature could move around and avoid getting its rear end eaten if it took 100 seconds for

---

1. To see why a creature of a given shape must have a weight or volume proportional to the cube of its height, imagine that the creature is made from a very large number of tiny cubes. If the creature's height and all other dimensions were to double, this would have the effect of doubling the dimensions of each tiny cube. The volume of each cube and the creature itself would therefore increase eightfold.

2. Apparently, certain species of snakes do form their bodies into hoops and roll down hills.

its brain to find out what was happening and another 100 seconds to do something about it.

Sea creatures have solved the problems of gravity with buoyancy. It is no accident that the world's largest animal is therefore found in the sea: the blue whale, which weighs as much as twenty-four African elephants (around 120 tons). The main size limit for sea creatures is probably due to the need to find nourishment. The blue whale feeds primarily on huge quantities of krill, or small shrimp, which it swallows through its open mouth as it swims. A creature ten times as large as the blue whale would have a thousand times its volume and mass, and if it had the same metabolism, it would need to eat a thousand times as much. A given feeding area could therefore support only a thousandth as many such creatures—far too few for the species to survive. The preceding analysis is somewhat oversimplified because the metabolism of mammals lessens with increasing size (large mammals tend to be more sluggish). Even so, the food consumption of a sea creature ten times the size of the blue whale almost certainly would keep its numbers below those needed for the species to survive.

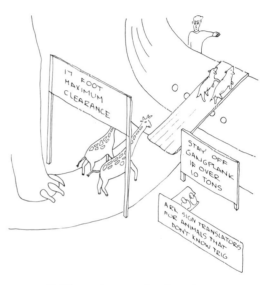

FIGURE 8. *The real reason for there being a maximum-size animal.*

If we speculate about life elsewhere in the universe, creatures on planets with much less gravity than Earth could obviously grow much larger, but they would be limited in size by the available food. The best solution to both the gravity and food problems might be for a creature to live in space. Gravity would then be no constraint at all, and the creature could solve the food problem if it had a way to convert sunlight into energy (and if it could prevent water and other volatile materials from escaping into space). It is unclear what, if anything, would limit the ultimate size of a space creature, although a creature of sufficient size would collapse under its own gravity and become a star!

8. What Is the Smallest Living Thing?

HAVE YOU EVER FOUND yourself apologizing to a lamppost you bumped into? In everyday life we usually have little difficulty distinguishing living from nonliving things. But when scientists try to define exactly what constitutes life, the matter is far from clear-cut. The biggest gray area is occupied by the viruses. Viruses, the smallest of which have diameters in the range 2 to 10 nanometers (billionths of a meter), can't quite "make up their minds" whether they are alive or not. For example, when they are outside a living "host" cell, viruses seem no different from many other nonliving complex molecules synthesized by chemists. But inside a living cell, viruses take on all the essential properties of living entities, including the ability to reproduce.

The smallest organisms that are clearly alive and capable of self-replication outside a host cell are believed to be the mycoplasmas, which have a diameter of 300 nanometers, or 12 millionths of an inch. Let us consider what factors make it difficult for living systems of a size appreciably smaller than a mycoplasma to survive. A sphere of 300 nanometers in diameter is only about 2,000 atoms across, and consists of a total of about 10 billion atoms. More relevant, however, than the total number of atoms are the numbers of atoms of trace elements essential to life, such as molybdenum and cobalt. A

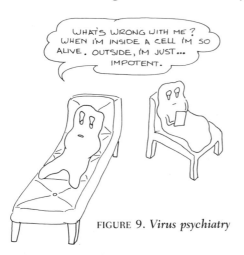

FIGURE 9. *Virus psychiatry*

mycoplasma bacterium has only a few dozen of these atoms, each of which is suspected of being a needed component of a specific enzyme. In a hypothetical bacterium much smaller than the mycoplasmas, it would therefore seem statistically likely that some key enzymes and the functions they control would often be absent, making life highly unlikely.

The atoms of all living matter are organized in highly complex structures with high information content, in contrast to the much lower information content of inanimate matter. A crystal structure, for example, can be specified by a few parameters: the identity of the atoms, their spacing in each dimension, and the type of crystal symmetry. Under certain circumstances, crystals share with living systems the ability to grow and reproduce. But unlike living systems, crystals reproduce according to a rigidly determined plan, and they are incapable of undergoing mutations that can be passed on to their progeny. Inheritable mutations are essential to living creatures. Although the vast majority of mutations are harmful, the small fraction that are not allow a species to adapt to its ever changing environment. All living systems, from microbes to people, pass on the recipe for their construction—mutations and all—in their genes or DNA molecules.

The length of the DNA molecules or the total number of "nucleotide" molecular building blocks they contain is a measure of the complexity of an organism, since the DNA encodes the organism's entire structure. A mycoplasma cell contains DNA that is 700,000 nucleotides long. In contrast, the DNA in human cells is 3 billion nucleotides long. The amount of DNA in mycoplasmas contains enough information to build an estimated 600 different proteins, which can be used to initiate or control 600 different chemical processes. According to some biologists, it is difficult to conceive of a self-reproducing autonomous system that could function on much fewer than 600 such processes. (Many chemical processes are needed to generate and act on such internal "messages" as "Try that, it might be food," "I'm lonely, I think I'll split," "Take out the trash," etc.) If the biologists are right, this would be further grounds for placing mycoplasmas near the smallest possible size of living systems.

9.   How Sky-high Is the National Debt?

ONE WAY TO APPRECIATE the meaning of a very large number is to create a vivid mental image. For example, we can better understand the astronomical size of the U.S. national debt—currently about 4 trillion 1992 dollars—by seeing how high a stack of dollar bills that would be. Let us first estimate the thickness of a dollar bill—perhaps about the same as the thickness of one of the pages of this book. You should find that the thickness of 100 pages is roughly 1 centimeter. So, the height of a stack of 4 trillion bills would be 40 billion centimeters, or 400,000 kilometers, which would reach all the way to the Moon. The U.S. national debt has quite literally reached astronomical proportions. Given the present rate of increase in the national debt, the top of the stack of dollar bills is rising at about 40 centimeters per second—the speed of a slow walk.

For another image to convey the huge size of the U.S. national debt, let us see how large an area it would cover. Taking the product of the length and width of a bill in centimeters, we find an area of roughly 100 square centimeters. So the number of dollar bills equal to the national debt would cover an area equal to 400 trillion square centimeters—equivalent to a square 200 kilometers (125 miles) on a side—or about twice the area of New Jersey. How large a warehouse would be required to store the national debt? The volume of a dollar bill is roughly 1 cubic centimeter (found by multiplying its area, 100 square centimeters, by its estimated thickness, $1/100$ centimeter). So the national debt in dollar bills can be stored in a volume of 4 trillion cubic centimeters. To visualize a volume this size, you might picture a football field whose dimensions are approximately 10,000 by 5,000 centimeters (100 by 50 meters), piled with bills to a height of 80,000 centimeters—about half a mile. On the other hand, if we use bills of $100,000 denomination, they would fit in a cube only 3.4 meters (11 feet) on a side, or the interior volume of a typical room—which is one way of reducing the national debt to "manageable" proportions.

FIGURE 10. *Putting concerns about attracting tourists ahead of the laws of physics, the architects design their tower.*

When we find the height of a stack of dollar bills whose value equals the national debt, we are of course referring to theoretical stacks of bills. A real stack of dollar bills would probably topple long before it got to be a meter high. In general, a stack of bills (or anything else) remains upright as long as the center of gravity—that point about halfway up the stack where all the weight appears to be concentrated—stays vertically aligned over the base, but topples as soon as the center of gravity sways out beyond the base. As you can see by trying various stackable items such as books or pennies, the higher the center of gravity and the narrower the supporting base, the less stable the stack. Pennies might be particluarly good choice for stacking, since no damage is done when the stack topples. Notice how, as each penny is added, the stack becomes less and less stable as small disturbances bring the center of gravity closer to the edge of the bottom penny.

10. How Far Can the Top Brick in a Pile Project Out?

I ONCE WORKED for a professor who was such a procrastinator about reading his magazines that he allowed them to accumulate unread until the pile became unstable and toppled. Sometimes, to impress visitors, he made the pile lean forward by an alarming amount. Suppose that our goal is to build a stack of uniform objects whose top projects forward the greatest possible distance relative to the bottom object without the stack toppling. Let's imagine using bricks instead of magazines, so as to avoid the complications associated with flexible objects. The way to find the maximum forward extension of the top brick in a pile is literally to start from the top and work your way down.

Clearly the top brick can extend at most half its length forward over the one below—any farther and its center of gravity will be beyond the edge of the brick below, and it will fall.[1] How about the second brick down—how far can it project over the one below? The combined center of gravity of the top two bricks is midway between the individual centers of gravity. So by requiring that the combined center of gravity of the top two bricks not extend beyond the edge of the one below, it is easy to see that the second brick can extend forward no more than a *quarter* of its length, as illustrated

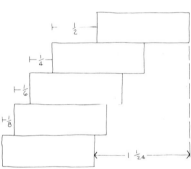

FIGURE 11. *Ideally, the top brick in a pile of five can extend forward more than one brick length without toppling.*

in the diagram. If we use the same reasoning for each brick in turn, we find that the maximum extensions in units of brick length, starting with the top brick, are just the reciprocals of the even integers: $\frac{1}{2}, \frac{1}{4}, \frac{1}{6}, \frac{1}{8}, \dots$.

In order to find the *total* extension of the top brick, you need to sum the preceding series. For example, for five bricks we find a total projection of $\frac{1}{2} + \frac{1}{4} + \frac{1}{6} +$

---

1. Recall that the center of gravity of an object is that point at which all its weight appears to be concentrated. For a single uniform brick the center of gravity is located at the center of the brick.

$\frac{1}{8} = \frac{25}{24}$, or $1\frac{1}{24}$ brick lengths. You may find it surprising that the maximum projection can exceed 1 brick length when there are only 5 bricks in the pile. Even more surprising is the fact that if we sum the series for an arbitrary number of bricks, we find that the total projection can increase without limit as the number of bricks increases! But to achieve very large projections, you need astronomical numbers of bricks. For example, to achieve a projection of 10 brick lengths requires a stack of 240 million bricks, and to achieve a projection of 100 brick lengths requires more bricks than there are atoms in the entire universe—a number that has been estimated as 10^{80} (a 1 followed by 80 zeros).

If you try making a stack yourself to see how large a projection you can get, you will probably find that the stack will not be stable unless you make the projections slightly less than those indicated above, which were found assuming perfectly flat, uniform bricks. For example, you will probably find that contrary to the preceding calculation, you will need a stack of 6 rather than 5 bricks to achieve a projection greater than 1 brick length. Just be sure to start with the top brick and work your way down.

FIGURE 12. *Some librarians enjoy playing practical jokes.*

In other words, the projection at each level is maximum if you sense that any greater amount will cause the bricks above to topple. Even though we have been referring to bricks, you might find it easier to use other flat, stackable items such as playing cards, books, cassette tape boxes, or meter sticks.[2]

2. Meter sticks or flat rulers are also particularly good, since you can easily see how far each is projecting forward, but beware: meter sticks don't necessarily all have the same weight!

18

11. How Big Is the Doomsday Rock?

A FAVORITE science fiction scenario for mankind's demise is the prospect of Earth being hit by a large metcorite—the "doomsday rock." But most people are not overly concerned about the possibility of being individually struck and killed by a meteorite. Such nonchalance is understandable, since there is to date only one documented case of such a death. The chances of a very large meteorite striking Earth are even more remote than for a small one. Yet paradoxically, your chances of being killed by a large meteorite are much greater than for a small one, since the very large meteorite is likely to kill you (along with everyone else) no matter where it hits, whereas the more common small meteorite is likely not to kill anyone except with a direct hit.

In fact, small meteorites usually burn up in the atmosphere and are seen as shooting stars—as many as one per minute can be seen in the night sky at some times of the year. The larger, much rarer meteorites known as asteroids easily survive the fiery trip through the atmosphere and hit the Earth with great energy, throwing up huge amounts of debris. The records of these impacts are craters such as those seen on the Moon. On Earth the crater record is much less evident because of weathering and other geological processes, but well over a hundred large impact craters have been confirmed. The largest one, located in Ontario, Canada, is 124 miles in diameter.

Aside from these actual impacts of meteorites or asteroids, there are many near misses of Earth, which are observed by telescope. One near miss of a ½-mile-wide asteroid occurred in 1989, when it crossed the Earth's orbit a mere six hours before the earth occupied that spot. Had the asteroid hit the Earth, the calculated energy of impact would have been equivalent to one thousand 1-megaton nuclear bombs[1]—an estimate based on the asteroid's mass and speed relative to Earth. A large asteroid's ability to affect life on Earth catastrophically is obviously related to its size. The explosive force of the impact would not be the primary source of our extinction, however, but rather the profound climate change caused by the dust the impact would put into the atmosphere. This dust could obscure sunlight for a prolonged time, causing a pronounced global cooling. Just such an event is believed to have caused the extinction of the dinosaurs (but fortunately, not our ancestors) about 65 million years ago.

An asteroid made of rocky materials having a diameter of 1 mile would weigh about 6 billion tons. If only 10 percent of a 1-mile-diameter asteroid were vapor-

---

1. A 1-megaton bomb has the explosive force of 1 million tons of TNT.

ized on impact and thrown up into the atmosphere, the resulting worldwide dust cloud would probably block enough sunlight to cause a catastrophic climate change. Even though all the dust would be thrown up at one place on the Earth's surface, it would likely be injected to such a high altitude (into the stratosphere) that during the ensuing months and years it would spread around the entire globe. The resulting worldwide dust cloud would therefore probably lead to near darkness and severely reduced temperatures for months or years.

How often do 1-mile-diameter asteroids hit the Earth? Based on the record of near misses and the number of craters seen on the Moon, the estimate is as high as once every 300,000 years. This means that in a person's entire lifetime, the chances of such an impact are roughly one in six thousand. If you don't think that's a large enough risk to worry about, consider that your chances of being killed in an airplane crash are about three times lower! Given the stakes involved, some scientists have suggested trying to prevent the next asteroid impact by intercepting and deflecting the asteroid from its course. Unfortunately, asteroids are tiny nonluminous bodies that are extremely difficult to spot—although they do follow regular orbits about the sun and can be tracked once they have been spotted. If an asteroid on a collision course with Earth were spotted by large telescopes while it was far away, a rocket could be launched to intercept it, and a nuclear explosion detonated to nudge it off its course. Incidentally, even a large asteroid would have no effect whatsoever in knocking the Earth out of *its* orbit, given the much larger size of the Earth. A 1-mile-diameter asteroid colliding with the Earth would be comparable to a gnat colliding with an elephant.

FIGURE 13. *"Fly the unfriendly skies with us—it's three times safer than staying on the ground."*

12. How Close Could You Get to Ground Zero and Survive?

ONE OF THE few good things you can say about nuclear weapons is that their consequences are so horrible that their nonuse since Hiroshima and Nagasaki may be attributable precisely to that fact. For this reason you may be among those who find a discussion of the effects of nuclear weapons repugnant, since it tends to bring these weapons out of the category of the ultimate doomsday weapons and into the category of weapons actually useful to fight wars. Even worse, such discussions may evoke some defense planner's calculations of war-fighting scenarios. Despite one's feelings regarding nuclear weapons, however, the fact is that their effects are reasonably well understood—at least for the short term. (See essay 114 for a description of their long-term effects.)

The three primary short-term lethal effects of a nuclear weapon are its air-pressure blast, its nuclear radiation, and its thermal radiation or heat—the last two categories being particular to nuclear weapons, which create much higher temperatures than conventional explosives. The heat and light from the fireball spreads out in all directions as an expanding sphere, so if you were twice as far away they would be spread over a sphere of twice the radius and four times the surface area. The heat deposited on each square meter of the sphere is therefore *inversely* proportional to the square of the distance from the detonation. Even at a distance of 10 miles, you could receive third-degree burns from the heat emitted by a 1-megaton detonation.

Although the only direct experience we have of the effects of nuclear weapons on people is with the two "small" bombs the United States dropped on Japan, we know—based on the aboveground nuclear testing of the 1950s and 60s—how the effects of nuclear weapons vary with their size and with distance from ground zero. The nuclear weapons testers of that era actually went to the trouble of building houses, and filling them with furniture and dummies, to see what the bomb effects would be at a given distance. In the event of a nuclear detonation, your overall survival chances would depend on many factors besides your distance from ground zero, including whether you were indoors or outdoors, lying down or standing, out of the line of sight of the fireball or in it, whether the air was smoggy or clear, and whether the bomb was detonated on the ground or in the air. Your best survival chances would occur for the first of each of the preceding pairs. Taking a typical 1-megaton bomb in today's arsenals, which is seventy times larger than the bomb dropped on Hiroshima, you would stand a fifty-fifty chance of surviving the short-term effects if you were 4.2 miles from ground zero.

Should you care about your survival chances following a nuclear blast? Many people probably couldn't care less, given such widespread beliefs as (a) nuclear war is unlikely to happen, especially now that the cold war is over; (b) if it does happen, there are so many nuclear weapons that one is likely to land not too far away; (c) if the prompt effects don't get you, the long-lasting radiation and other effects will; and (d) at the rate scientists change their minds about things, we'll soon learn that nuclear war is actually good for you!

FIGURE 14.

At various times during the nuclear age, the United States and other countries have contemplated building a defense against nuclear attack. Presently some billions of dollars continue to be spent in the United States on researching the feasibility of such a defense. Ultimately, whether such a defense is built will depend as much on political as technical factors, and the issue of whether it truly "works" may remain an unsettled question. Let us hope that one's survival chances after a nuclear war remain forever an unsettled issue, in the absence of the definitive "experiment."

13.   How Long Is Britain's Coastline?

SUPPOSE YOU are given the task of measuring the length of Britain's coastline. One technique you might try is to send a helper exactly 1 mile down the coast, using surveying instruments to get the distance right. The two of you could then march down the coast in 1-mile intervals. This method would miss indentations and projections in the coastline much smaller than 1 mile, so you might try using smaller intervals. Clearly, you would find longer and longer values for the coastline as you decreased the interval size and took into account smaller indentations. But no matter what size interval you used, you would miss still smaller indentations. Even using a short piece of string to make the measurement, you would miss indentations smaller than the width of the string.

You might think that your measurement of the coastline's length will not be off by much when you miss only very small indentations, but that is not the case. Coastlines, Britain's included, are natural examples of shapes known as fractals, which by definition reveal complexity when viewed under any magnification. We shall see that closed shapes having this property can have an *infinitely* long perimeter. If we try to match their boundary using finer and finer strings, we find that the length of string required grows without limit as the string width approaches zero. In order to demonstrate this surprising result, we shall construct a simple fractal shape by a limiting process and show that its perimeter increases without limit.

Let's start with an equilateral triangle and divide each side into thirds. Next, remove the middle third of each side and erect a 60-degree "tent" in its place, as shown in the diagram. The resulting figure has the shape of a six-pointed star. Its perimeter is ⁴⁄₃ that of the original equilateral triangle, since the three equal segments of each side have been replaced by four. Now, starting with the six-pointed star, again divide each line segment into thirds and erect a 60-degree "tent" in place of the middle third of each segment, leading to a further increase in perimeter by a factor of ⁴⁄₃. By repeating this process N times, you will find that the resulting figure has a finer and finer structure at each step, and its perimeter at the Nth step is given by $(⁴⁄₃)^N$. In order to create a true fractal, you would need to let N be-

FIGURE 15. *The first three stages in the development of a "fractal snowflake."*

come infinite, so that the same tentlike structure would be seen under any magnification. In this case the perimeter of the figure would be infinite, because the result of raising ⁴⁄₃ to the power infinity (multiplying ⁴⁄₃ by itself an infinite number of times) is infinite.

So, does Britain *really* have an infinite coastline? Well not really, since a true fractal requires that we let the parameter N, which designates the number of subdivisions, become infinite. In the physical world it makes no sense to continue the subdivision of line segments beyond atomic size. For example, Great Britain is very roughly the shape of a triangle having a 2,000-kilometer perimeter. Following the process described earlier of erecting 60-degree tents, we can reduce the length of line segments that make up the perimeter to $\frac{1}{3}$ their previous length at each step. Starting with a 2,000-kilometer perimeter, it takes only about thirty-two subdivisions before the line segments have atomic dimensions (about one 10-billionth of a meter). Thus, the earlier formula for the perimeter $(\frac{4}{3})^N$ can be evaluated using $N = 32$ to obtain a result of 10,000—meaning that the perimeter at the 32d subdivision is 10,000 times longer than the original triangle. If the fractal shape of coastlines actually obeyed this formula, Britain's coastline would be 20 million kilometers long—a far cry from infinity.[1] Incidentally, even though the perimeter of a true fractal is infinite, its area is clearly finite, since the shape fits inside a circle containing the original equilateral triangle. This raises the absurd prospect of needing an infinitely long string to match the figure's perimeter, while a finite piece of fabric can cover its surface area. Do you see a way to resolve this paradox?

FIGURE 16. *For the queen, the thought that Britain had an infinitely long coastline offered some compensation for the loss of its empire.*

---

1. The figure often cited in almanacs for the perimeter of Britain's coastline is about 10,000 kilometers—a result we would get using the $(\frac{4}{3})^N$ formula with N equal to about 6, corresponding to line segments about 1 kilometer long.

14. What Is an Automobile's Stopping Distance?

SOMETIMES minimizing the stopping distance of your car can be a matter of life or death, in terms of avoiding an accident. Conversely, the big problem with accidents is that they cause the stopping distance of a car to be *too* short, resulting in nasty consequences for the car and its occupants. Apart from the condition of the car, driver, and roadway, a car's stopping distance (by braking) depends principally on its speed. We can see what that dependence is by imagining the speed of a car being doubled and asking how its stopping distance changes. If we ignore the driver's reaction time and assume tire friction reduces a car's speed at a constant rate (constant deceleration), doubling the car's speed means that friction takes twice as long to bring the car to rest. Therefore, if the car's speed is doubled, the stopping distance is *quadrupled*, because the stopping distance is just the average speed times the stopping time, and both the average speed and the stopping time have been doubled. In other words, if a car stops in 100 feet at 30 miles per hour, it should stop in 400 feet at 60 miles per hour. As we see from this example, stopping distance must be proportional to the *square* of a car's speed. Police are often able to use this relationship to infer the speed of a car from the length of tire skid marks.

This relationship between stopping distance and initial speed should hold not only for cars but for any situation where a constant force like friction brings a body to rest. Here is a simple experiment you can do on your kitchen table, using a ruler and a number of pennies, to test the dependence of

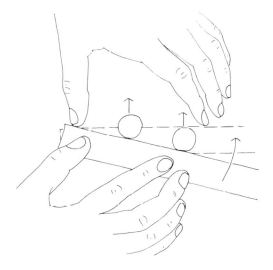

FIGURE 17. *As the ruler pivots about its left end and then suddenly stops at the place indicated by the dotted lines, one coin flies off with twice the speed of the other.*

stopping distance on initial speed. Put two pennies against the ruler's edge and quickly shove the ruler forward a few inches along a direction perpendicular to the ruler, so as to launch the two pennies with a common speed. If the pennies travel different distances before coming to rest, one of them must have slightly different friction with the table than the other. Try using different pairs of pennies until you find a pair that have a common stopping distance when launched two or three times in succession.

Once you select two pennies that have the same friction, you need to launch them simultaneously so that one has twice the speed of the other. To do this, simply place the two pennies against the ruler's edge and pivot the ruler about one end. You can keep one end of the ruler fixed using your left thumb as the pivot and move the other end of the ruler forward suddenly with your right hand, as illustrated in the drawing. If one of the two pennies is placed against the ruler's edge at a point twice as far from the pivot as the other, this penny will fly off the ruler twice as fast as the other when the ruler is suddenly stopped. If you then measure the distance traveled by each penny on leaving the ruler, you should find that the faster penny travels *four* times as far as the other, confirming the relationship between speed and stopping distance.

The situation for cars is slightly more complicated than we have described above, because in practice we cannot neglect the driver's reaction time, which causes a car's stopping distance to depend only partly on the square of its speed. The extra distance traveled by the car during the time before the driver steps on the brake is proportional to the car speed and not its square, so the total distance traveled is not quite proportional to the square of a car's initial speed. We should therefore expect that when the speed of a car doubles, its stopping distance increases by a factor of less than four. For example, according to drivers' manuals, cars going 30 miles per hour can be stopped in around 80 feet, while cars going 60 miles per hour can be stopped in around 255 (not 320) feet.

FIGURE 18.

Incidentally, stopping distances listed in the manuals are roughly independent of tire width, because unless you "burn rubber" like a drag racer, tire friction does not depend on contact area with the road. You can easily verify this surprising result using two identical non-cubic blocks of wood on your kitchen table. Push the two blocks forward with a ruler so that they leave the ruler with the same velocity, just as you did earlier with the pennies. Now rotate one block so that it rests on a smaller face than the other. You should find that the blocks have roughly the same stopping distance even when one of the blocks slides on a face that has much smaller area than the other.

● ● · ● ●

15. How Far Does an Object Fall in One Second?

IT SEEMS SILLY to ask *the* distance objects fall in a second when it is obvious that objects fall at different rates: just compare the fall of a feather and a hammer, for example. But sometimes we can learn much about our universe by concentrating on the essential aspects of phenomena and ignoring those which are nonessential. Of course, the hard part is figuring out what can be safely ignored in a given situation. For thousands of years, for example, it was generally believed that heavy objects fall faster than light ones. But in fact, if air resistance is ignored, all objects fall from rest the same distance in a given time. You can easily test Galileo's seventeenth-century observation to this effect by dropping pairs of objects from chest level and seeing whether their impacts with the ground are simultaneous.

You may be surprised that even a very light object such as a Ping-Pong ball hits the ground at nearly the same time as a baseball. Of course, if you do the experiment by dropping the balls a much greater distance, the Ping-Pong ball will be delayed appreciably relative to the baseball, since air resistance becomes more important the greater the distance objects fall, and the faster they move. Air resistance is also quite important if objects are very light: dropped feathers or tissues fall more slowly than elephants. In carrying out these observations, even if only in your mind, you will be following in the footsteps of Galileo, who literally began the seventeenth-century scientific revolution. Galileo was the first scientist to understand the need to appeal to experiment rather than philosophy to test a theory. Apparently, prior to Galileo, the idea of simply dropping two balls side by side to see whether, in fact, heavy objects fall faster than light ones was evidently not relevant to the matter.

Galileo, in his pioneering work on the motion of falling bodies, had a severe handicap: the nonexistence of mechanical clocks to make his measurements. Lacking a true clock, Galileo measured time by the amount of water flowing out of a hole in a large water-filled can. Since this "clock" could give only a crude measure of time, Galileo found he needed to "dilute" gravity in order to get time intervals that were long enough to measure accurately. He didn't mix some levity with gravity!

Rather, he studied the motions of balls rolling down an inclined trough, then extrapolated his results to the case of a vertical incline. Galileo concluded that if air resistance is negligible, all objects that fall from rest increase their speed with time, that is, they *accelerate*. For freely falling objects on Earth, the acceleration is such that an object increases its speed by 32 feet per second (9.8 meters per second) each second it falls. For example, ignoring air resistance, an object that starts from rest has a speed of 32, 64, and 96 feet per second at the end of 1, 2, and 3 seconds respectively, assuming it does not hit the ground first.

How can we use the measured acceleration of gravity (which is 32 feet per second) to find the distance an object falls from rest in a given time? The easy way is first to find the average speed. For example, if an object falls for 1 second, the average speed is clearly 16 feet per second (the average of zero and 32), so it is easy to see why objects therefore fall 16 feet in one second. Let's go through the same reasoning for an object that falls for half a second starting from rest. An object that gains speed at 32 feet per second, every second, will reach a speed of 16 feet per second after ½ second if it starts from rest. And hence the object's average speed for that ½ second will be 8 feet per second (the average of zero and 16). The distance an object falls from rest in ½ second will therefore be 4 feet, which is the product of its average speed of 8 feet per second and the time of fall, ½ second.

You can easily check this last result experimentally if you have a digital watch with stopwatch capability. Just mark a 4-foot height on a wall and drop a coin from this point. You will probably find that the time of fall is pretty close to ½ second—especially if you visually follow the fall of the coin and anticipate the moment of impact. Given that an object falls 4 feet in ½ second and 16 feet in 1 second, we see that the distance an object falls from rest quadruples when the time of fall doubles. In other words, the distance an object falls from rest is proportional to the *square* of the time of fall. The general rule is stated as a proportionality because actual distances depend on the local strength of gravity. On the Moon, for example, where gravity is one-sixth its strength on Earth, objects fall only one-sixth as far in a given time interval. Astronauts during a visit to

FIGURE 19. *In observing that things fall slower on the Moon, Jim concludes that the Moon has stronger levity rather than weaker gravity.*

the moon actually dropped a hammer and a feather side by side, and showed that they reached the ground at the same time—thereby confirming Galileo's belief that when air resistance is negligible, all objects fall with the same acceleration.

16. How Big Should Movie Models Be?

WHEN FILMMAKERS want to show scenes of crashing trains or planes, or ships being blown up, they generally rely on scale models—usually making the models as large as economically feasible. Of course, given the budgets of some of today's films, there is less need to economize on scale models than there used to be. Larger models permit greater detail, but there are equally important *physical* reasons why movie scale models are usually not the small scale models of hobbyists. Consider the appearance of falling objects, for example.

Scenes involving falling objects such as trains going off cliffs would not look realistic if filmed at regular speed, but they can easily be made realistic by filming at a speed appropriate to the scale of the model. For example, objects fall 16 feet in one second and 4 feet in ½ second, so slowing time by a factor of two corresponds to a *fourfold* decrease in distance scale if a fall is to look realistic. In other words, if you are filming a quarter-size scale model, film it at twice as many frames per second as you show the film, so that the action will appear slowed by half and the fall will look realistic.

As the above example illustrates, scenes involving only falling objects do not require especially large scale models, since the rate of fall can be easily compensated for. This is not the case, however, if the scene involves both falling and exploding objects, because the speed of filming needed to make an explosion look realistic is not the same as that needed to make a fall look realistic. A quarter-size exploding model should be filmed at

FIGURE 20. *The crew had to reshoot when Earl surfaced to get a better view.*

one-quarter speed for realism, but if it is falling it should be filmed at half speed, which is a problem if it is falling *and* exploding. In fact, an explosion of a very small scale model will never look quite realistic no matter what the filming speed, because the small mass of the exploding pieces causes them to slow due to air resistance much more rapidly than the fragments of a full-scale explosion.

Scale models of ships also appear quite different from real ships, as do the appearance of water waves, so the larger the scale model the better. Here, too, some scale differences can be compensated for by adjusting the speed of filming or the speed of the model. For example, a ship model that is a hundredth scale would need to travel at a tenth the speed of a full-scale ship for the wave patterns produced by the model and the full-scale ship to look the same.

Perhaps one of the most important reasons for using scale models as large as possible is the limitation imposed by depth of field—the photographic term for the range of distances over which elements of a scene remain in focus. Small scale models will inevitably be filmed at closer distances, where the depth of field is less, leading to parts of a scene being out of focus, which used to be seen in some low-budget action-adventure movies. Nowadays, many of the problems of scale models can be avoided by photographing the model against a plain blue background and then later combining the images of the model with the rest of the scene, often by computer.

17. Where Would the Body Land?

PHYSICISTS ARE not consulted by attorneys too often, but I was once approached by a prosecutor in a murder case. A body had been found some distance from the foot of a tall building, and the prosecutor wanted to know whether the victim had jumped or been pushed, based on the distance. Presumably, his theory was that jumpers don't make running jumps but just let themselves drop.

Let's see how we can predict the landing point of an object thrown horizontally off a tall building or a cliff. The key to solving this problem is the observation that the length of time objects stay in the air does not depend on their horizontal motion. This means that a horizontally projected object will hit the ground at the same moment as a second object released from the same height at rest, assuming they were launched simultaneously. You can easily verify this observation using two coins, one of which is placed on a table inches from the edge and the other held at table height. If you manage to sweep one coin off the table at the same time you drop the other coin, you should find that the two coins hit the floor at nearly the same time.

Based on the preceding observation, the time of flight of a stone thrown *horizontally* off a cliff should depend only on the height of the cliff, and not on the stone's initial speed. One way of explaining this fact is to say that gravity increases the downward component of the stone's speed by 32 feet per second every second independently of any horizontal motion the stone may have. If the cliff is, for example, 16 feet high, a horizontally thrown stone will be in the air for one second, just as if it were dropped from rest. Suppose the stone is thrown at, say, a speed of 50 feet per second. It will have to

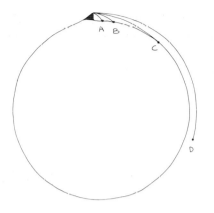

FIGURE 21. *Stones A, B, C, and D are thrown off a tower with increasing horizontal speed, which in the case of stone D is enough to put it into orbit.*

land 50 feet from the base of the cliff if it is in the air for one second, because the horizontal component of the stone's motion is not influenced by gravity. Had we assumed the stone was thrown with a higher horizontal speed, the horizontal distance traveled would have been proportionally greater. Above some speed (7.9 kilometers per second), as the diagram shows, the stone's horizontal range would be so great that it would follow the curvature of the Earth, and be in orbit!

There are occasions when being able to predict the range of a horizontally thrown projectile can be a matter of life and death. Imagine, for example, that you and your friend are on the roof of a burning building with flames closing in. Firemen are holding a net on the ground below and are encouraging you to jump. How fast should you jump forward if you estimate that the center of the net is 20 feet from the building? You should first drop an object to see how long it takes to reach the ground. If it takes 4 seconds, for example, then you would know that you need to move horizontally by 20 feet in those same 4

FIGURE 22. *Through careful scientific analysis of old cartoons, Rita was able to delay her vertical descent until the moment she became aware of the fact that the ground was no longer under her feet.*

31

seconds of fall, or that you need to leave the roof with a horizontal speed of 5 feet per second—about the speed of a fast walk. Of course, it wouldn't hurt to have your friend jump first just to check your calculations.

Oh, by the way, we never were able to use the laws of physics to say anything definitive about whether the victim in the murder case was pushed or fell.

18.   What Is the Length of a One-Second Pendulum?

WHILE IDLY gazing at a swinging chandelier in church one day, Galileo made what he thought was an original discovery about pendulums—a discovery that has had a profound impact on civilization.[1] If you want to make this discovery for yourself, make a pendulum from a piece of string tied to a large hardware nut and see how its period—the time for one complete (back and forth) swing—depends on the size of the swing. In order to measure the period accurately, you will need to measure the time for a large number of consecutive swings (say twenty) and divide by that number. You should find that as long as the size of the swing is not too large—less than around 30 degrees—the period is nearly the same for all sizes of swings. Apparently, the higher speed during a larger swing just compensates for the increased angle of swing. The fact that a pendulum's period is nearly independent of the size of its swing is what allows it to be used as the central timekeeping element of clocks. In fact, before Galileo made his discovery, only fairly primitive means of keeping track of time existed, such as sundials and water clocks. Even today, when far more accurate clocks are available, the stately grandfather clock with its pendulum can be found in many homes.

Although the period of a pendulum is nearly independent of the size of its swing (and also its mass), it does depend on the pendulum's length. For this reason, pendulums in clocks have a screw at the bottom that can be adjusted to change the effective length, in case the clock runs a little fast or slow. Try to discover the relationship between pendulum length and period yourself by measuring the period for several different lengths. You might use two string lengths in the ratio of one to four, say ¼ meter and 1 meter. You should find that the period of the longer pendulum is about 1 second and that of the shorter one is about ½ second, which shows that when you quadruple the length of a pendulum you

1. Actually, the tenth-century Arab astronomer Ibn Yunus appears to have made the same discovery over five hundred years earlier, and who knows how many others discovered it before Yunus?

double its period. In other words, the *square* of a pendulum's period is proportional to its length.[2]

One other quantity that the period of a pendulum depends on besides its length is the strength of gravity—the "restoring force" that continuously pulls the pendulum back toward the vertical position. In the absence of gravity, there would be no "down," and the pendulum would not swing at all, so it would have an infinite period. Clearly, the closer gravity gets to the zero value, the longer the pendulum period is. Since the strength of gravity varies slightly from place to place, you could in fact use the observed period of a pendulum to measure the local strength of gravity—a method that geologists actually use.

Now it happens that the period of a pendulum depends on the *ratio* of the pendulum length to the strength of gravity. As a result, the change in the period of a pendulum is very nearly the same whether you increase its length by some small percentage or decrease the strength of gravity by that same percentage. So based on the grandfather clock example in footnote 2, if a pendulum is found to have a period at location A that is 0.1 percent longer than its period at location B, then the strength of gravity at location A is 0.2 percent less than that at B. Thus, we can think of pendulums as devices for measuring either time or gravity, depending on which of the two is known. Believe it or not, the same is true of any clock, because the strength of gravity affects the rate of passage of time (see essay 81). But it would not be feasible to use your watch as

FIGURE 23. *Young Galileo gave his landlady fits by swinging on the chandelier, even though she knew he was verifying an important scientific discovery.*

a "gravity meter," given the smallness of the effect—unless, of course, you made a pendulum from it and timed the swings.

---

2. For example, suppose you had a grandfather clock that lost 1 second every 1,000 seconds, making its period 1.001 seconds instead of one second. The length of the clock's pendulum must therefore be 1.001^2, or about 1.002 times the proper length for a 1-second pendulum. To correct this clock, you would need to adjust the screw at the bottom of the pendulum so as to decrease its effective length by 0.2 percent.

19. How High Can You Jump?

THE SIGHT OF a high jumper gracefully arching backward over a bar taller than she is can be a wonder to behold. The current world record in the high jump is 2.44 meters (8 feet). High jumpers today can jump much higher than in past years due to the technique of going over the bar headfirst and backward pioneered by Dick Fosbury. This method allows the body to clear the bar with the lowest possible center of gravity, which therefore requires a significant decrease in the expenditure of energy compared with the earlier feetfirst method.[1]

Of course, the height you can jump depends on the strength of gravity. If future Olympics are held on other planets, the "world" records will have to be adjusted for each planet's gravity. If you are able to generate a given speed on takeoff, the height you can jump is inversely proportional to the strength of gravity. For example, on the Moon, where gravity is one-sixth its value on Earth, you would be able to jump six times as high if you were able to take off with the same speed. Apart from the need to wear a bulky space suit, you probably could not take off from the Moon with the same speed as from the Earth, since your muscles are adapted to Earth's gravity.

Thus, even if the future interplanetary Olympic rules attempted to compensate for the strength of gravity on a particular planet, competitors who were native to the planet would have a great advantage over competitors from worlds with very different strengths of surface gravity. For example, 6-foot-high creatures that evolved on a planet with gravity

FIGURE 24. *The high jump competition was quite stiff in the first interspecies Olympics.*

1. In some cases the jumper's center of gravity actually passes *under* the bar if her back is sufficiently arched.

34

much stronger or weaker than that of Earth would almost certainly have evolved to be either much chunkier or much spindlier than humans, respectively. Both types of creatures would be at a severe disadvantage to humans if it were Earth's turn to host the Olympics. The spindly creature might find that its bones fractured under its own Earth weight, and the chunky creature would have the same problems in jumping as an overly muscular human jumper.

Jumping off a very small planet or asteroid would allow you to reach tremendous heights. In fact, for a sufficiently small asteroid, you could jump off with enough speed to escape permanently into space. The main problem you would face in jumping off a small asteroid would be remaining in contact with the asteroid long enough to push off against it, since the slightest force would cause you to leave the ground. Presumably, you would need to push off against a small asteroid in much the same way a swimmer pushes off against the wall of a pool while making a turn in order to maximize your time of contact with the ground during your push-off.

Returning to Earth, you might wonder how the heights that different creatures can jump depend on their size. Despite the enormous difference in size between humans and fleas, for example, a flea can jump to a height of close to 1 meter, while the average human probably cannot jump much higher. The reason that creatures of vastly different sizes are capable of jumping almost the same height is easy to understand. Muscle tissue in both fleas and people is capable of generating roughly the same amount of energy per unit weight. The energy needed to cause a creature to jump to a certain height is proportional to the creature's weight, but then so is the muscle energy available. Fleas, which have perhaps a millionth of your muscle power, have only a millionth the weight to lift, and so they can jump about as high as you. Likewise, a 6-foot-high flea would not be able to jump any higher than you.

20.   How Big
Can a Water Droplet Get?

RAINDROPS COME in a wide range of sizes, from the tiny drops of a fine drizzle to the large drops of a real "cats and dogs" downpour. What accounts for the size of raindrops, which form from the water vapor in clouds? Droplets grow when water molecules from the vapor land on their surface, and they shrink when water molecules on the surface evaporate. When these two processes are in equilibrium, water droplets stay a constant size.

It turns out there is a critical droplet size above which droplets grow, and below which they shrink. The reason for a critical size is that very small droplets have a much greater fraction of water molecules on their surface in a position to leave through evaporation.[1] Of course, if very small droplets always shrink, then they would never get to be big ones, so there must be some way to get past the critical size. This can happen as a result of droplets merging or droplets coalescing on tiny dust particles, which is why high-altitude jets create vapor trails with their engine exhaust particles.

But what keeps water droplets from growing indefinitely once they pass the critical size? One factor is the depletion of water molecules in the vapor out of which the droplets condense, causing more droplets to "compete" for fewer vapor molecules. How big the droplets get depends on the temperature, the vapor density, and how much time the droplets have to grow during their descent. The main obstacle to the formation of really big water droplets forming is the tendency of droplets to fission, or split, under the action of disturbing influences such as turbulent airflow or gravity.

For example, if you turn your kitchen faucet on very slightly, gravity will cause droplets to grow and break off before they get very large. In the absence of gravity, however, really huge droplets can form. You may have seen movies of astronauts playing around with gigantic water droplets formed after they "poured" water out of a glass and the water glob assumed its natural spherical shape. You cannot really "pour" water in a weightless environment, but you can get water out of a glass by quickly pulling the glass out from under the water. When the floating giant water globs are given a poke, they quiver and oscillate—and possibly fission if poked hard enough.

FIGURE 25. *Fission is the primary hazard to large water droplets.*

One simple tabletop experiment that shows how very large droplets can form in a simulated weightless environment requires only a large jar, some rubbing alcohol, and some vegetable oil. Pour the alcohol into the jar after it is first half-filled with water. Next, gently pour about an ounce of the vegetable oil into the center of the jar. The vegetable oil, which has a density intermediate between

1. In a droplet consisting of a very small number of molecules, they could *all* be on the surface (like a bunch of grapes). But for larger droplets, the vast majority of molecules are inside, rather than on the droplet's surface.

that of water and alcohol, should form a single large droplet or glob that floats at the boundary between the water and alcohol.

Might it be possible to form really big droplets of liquid? Presumably it would even be possible to have a planet-size water droplet, assuming an appropriate source of water vapor existed. A planet-size water droplet would be in little danger of fissioning, since it would be held together by its own gravity as well as surface tension. In fact, the larger a planet-size water droplet, the more stable it would be, because the strength of gravity grows in proportion to the droplet's size.

21. How Far Does Sound Travel in One Second?

FROM THE flapping of a moth's wings to the vibration of your vocal cords, all sounds arise from the same basic mechanism: vibrating objects successively compressing and decompressing the adjacent air, creating a fluctuating pressure. If the number of pressure fluctuations per second (the frequency) is in the range of about 20 to 20,000, the sound will be audible. If the frequency is higher than 20,000 pressure fluctuations per second, the sound will probably be inaudible to you but perhaps not to your dog, and it is referred to as ultrasound. The pressure fluctuations in sound (or ultrasound) are communicated outward from the point of origin as a result of collisions between molecules. The effect is similar to the way a disturbance can propagate along a line of people if some rowdies at the end of the line give a hard push, so as to create a "people wave." People waves, unlike sound waves, can also propagate without any physical contact between people-molecules, as in the case of "the wave" in a stadium crowd, but both types of waves require a medium in which to travel. Conceiving of a sound wave traveling through a vacuum is as unthinkable as a people wave without people, or a water wave without water.

Here is an easy way you can measure the speed of sound with the aid of a friend. Stand 100 meters away from your friend, and have her start clapping hands (or hitting two sticks together) at a regular beat of around 3 claps per second. A good way to do this would be to have her keep time to a metronome. Walk toward or away from her until you see her hands making contact at the precise moment you hear each clap. At this distance, you are actually hearing the sound from the previous clap, which takes a time of exactly one beat to reach you. To find the speed of sound, all you need to do is divide the distance to your friend by ⅓ second, which is the time between claps or the time it takes sound to reach you. In order to get something close to the accepted value of 330 meters per second, or about 1 mile every 5 seconds, your distance should be around 110 meters.

Just as we can measure the speed of sound by seeing how long it takes to travel a known distance, we can reverse the process and measure distances if we take the speed of sound as given. This is the basis of digital tape measures that create an ultrasonic pulse, detect the echo from a wall, and then compute the wall distance from the round-trip travel time. Bats use ultrasonic echoes to navigate in complete darkness. Apparently, bats can construct an audio image of their environment, much as hospitals use ultrasound to make images for diagnostic purposes.

Still another application of using sound speed to measure distance is the well-known rule for finding your distance from a lightning strike. Since sound takes 5 seconds to travel a mile, you can find the distance in miles by counting the seconds between seeing the lightning and hearing the thunder, then dividing by five. This rule, of course, correctly assumes that the light from the lightning takes a negligible time to reach you.

FIGURE 26. *"Judging by the distance to that mushroom cloud, I think we have time for one more hand."*

To take a more gruesome example, you could use exactly the same principle to find your distance from a nuclear bomb detonation. The light from the fireball would reach you almost instantly, but the blast wave, which travels at roughly the speed of sound, would take 5 seconds to cover each mile. For a bomb detonated 10 miles away, you would have nearly a full minute to contemplate your fate, seek shelter, or finish your card game before the blast wave arrived.

22. How Far Does Light Travel in One Second?

LIGHT TRAVELS about a million times faster than sound, so measuring the speed of light is much more difficult than measuring the speed of sound. In one early attempt at measuring the speed of light, Galileo and an assistant positioned themselves on mountaintops some miles apart. Galileo uncovered a lantern, and his assistant uncovered his lantern at the moment he saw the light from Galileo's lantern. Galileo hoped to use the measured time interval between uncovering his lantern and seeing the light from his assistant's lantern to get the round-trip travel time for a light beam. Unfortunately, the time Galileo sought to measure was much less than the two observers' reaction times, and it could not be measured by such a crude method. Galileo, being no fool, was aware of this problem, because when he repeated the measurements with his assistant farther away, he found the same time as originally.

The first successful measurement of the speed of light relied on the trick of recording the time for light to travel an enormous distance, thereby producing a long enough time interval to measure. The planet Jupiter eclipses one of its moons each time the moon ducks behind the planet, once each lunar orbit. The seventeenth-century Dutch astronomer Olaus Roemer noticed that the elapsed time between successive eclipses of Io, one of Jupiter's moons, became shorter as Earth approached Jupiter and longer as it receded from Jupiter. The variation in time between eclipses was presumably due to the changing distance the light had to travel for us to see Io, as shown in the diagram. Roemer noted the

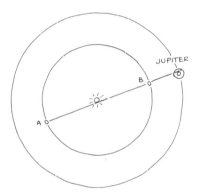

FIGURE 27. *Light from an eclipse of one of Jupiter's moons travels farther to reach us when the Earth is at A than at B—the extra distance being approximately the diameter of Earth's orbit.*

time of an eclipse when the Earth was nearest Jupiter, and by observing how often eclipses occurred with Earth at this close distance from Jupiter, he predicted when one would occur when the Earth was on the far side of its orbit from Jupiter. His predicted time was about 1,000 seconds late, which must represent the

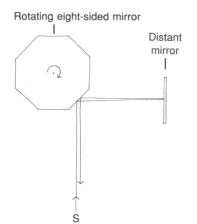

Rotating eight-sided mirror

Distant mirror

S

FIGURE 28. *For just the right rotational speed of an eight-sided mirror, a light beam is reflected off a distant mirror and back to the source* S *as though the rotating mirror were at rest.*

time light takes to travel across Earth's orbit. The diameter of Earth's orbit was known in Roemer's day to be about 300 million kilometers. Roemer therefore concluded that the speed of light must be roughly 300,000 kilometers per second in order to travel the 300 million kilometers across Earth's orbit in 1,000 seconds.

Many other techniques have been used to find the speed of light since Roemer's measurement. One such method is similar in concept to the hand-clapping technique I suggested earlier for measuring the speed of sound. An eight-sided box with mirrored faces is rotated with a high-speed motor, and a light beam is reflected off the box toward a distant stationary mirror (see the diagram above). The reflected light beam then bounces back and hits the rotating mirrored box once again. In general, the returning ray hits a side of the rotating box at a different angle than it did originally. If the speed of rotation of the eight-sided box is gradually increased, at some point it will rotate exactly an eighth of a revolution in the time it takes the light beam to make a round-trip to the distant stationary mirror. In this case the light beam will reflect off the box back to the original source *just as if the box were at rest.* Thus, by increasing the rotational speed of the mirrored box until the light beam first reflects back along its original direction, you can determine the light beam's round-trip travel time. The speed of light is then equal to the round-trip distance the light travels to the distant mirror divided by the time for an eighth of a revolution of the eight-sided box.

FIGURE 29. *Galileo knew his method for finding the speed of light would work, if only he could find an assistant with a fast enough reaction time.*

40

Nowadays, still other methods can be used to measure the speed of light. For example, by pulsing a laser and detecting the emitted light pulse a few feet away, you can use an oscilloscope to measure the elapsed time between the emitted and received light pulse. You would find that the delay was about a nanosecond (a billionth of a second) for every foot increase in the light path. Traveling at this speed, the light from Galileo's lantern would have reached an assistant 2 miles away in mere 10-millionths of a second. The assistant would have needed a reaction time ten thousand times faster than normal to measure the speed of light.[1]

23. What Is the Greatest Distance Anything Can Go in One Second?

ONE OF THE stranger facts about our universe is the existence of a fastest possible speed: the speed of light. This idea of a fastest speed seems bizarre at first, because of all the ways you might think of getting beyond that speed limit. But first let's think about trains. If you walk at 3 miles per hour down the aisle of a train moving at 60 miles per hour, your speed relative to the ground is either 63 or 57 miles per hour, depending on which direction you walk. Using exactly the same idea, you might think you could exceed the "light barrier." For example, while traveling in a spaceship at 99 percent the speed of light (.99c), you could shine a light beam in the forward direction at speed c. You might expect that the light beam would then have a speed 1.99c (the sum of c and .99c), but amazingly its speed would not be altered by the ship's motion, and it still would have its original value, c! Empirically, we find that nothing can alter the speed of light in vacuum—light always travels at a speed c, which is both an absolute constant as well as a universal speed limit.

We cannot yet do the preceding imagined experiment to check the constancy of the speed of light using spaceships, but we can make the equivalent observations using stars. Consider, for example, a pair of identical stars in orbit around each other (they would circle a point midway between them). Let's suppose you are looking at the plane of their orbit edge-on, and the stars are both moving

1. If you ever futilely tried to catch a dollar bill after someone dangling it between your outstretched fingers suddenly dropped it, you probably realize that your reaction time is about 1/10 second, based on the distance the bill falls, before you can pinch your fingers closed.

41

around a circle at opposite ends of a diameter at one-thousandth the speed of light (.001*c*). Twice each orbit there will be a moment when one star is heading directly toward you and the other star directly away. If speeds combined the way we normally expect them to, you would predict that the light from the star heading toward you approaches Earth at 1.001*c*, and the light from the receding star approaches Earth at 0.999*c*. The light from the two stars would therefore take different times to reach us, and the stars would not appear to be at opposite ends of a diameter (equal distances from you). The fact that *no such effect is ever seen* means that light's speed is unaffected by a star's motion.

The reason our intuition led us astray in the preceding examples is that we used a simple intuitive rule for adding two velocities that works well in the everyday low-velocity realm but fails when combining speeds if either speed is close to that of light. According to Albert Einstein's theory of relativity, there is a more complex rule for adding two velocities.[1] The more complex formula essentially reproduces the commonsense result for speeds in the everyday realm, when both velocities are a tiny fraction of the speed of light. But when either velocity is close to the speed of light, the results are quite different. In particular, when a spaceship moving at any speed shines a light beam, the relativistic formula yields the constant speed *c* for the speed of light from the moving ship. The reason for the failure of the commonsense formula at high speeds can be traced to "strange" effects on space and time that are especially pronounced near light speeds (see essays 24 and 126). These effects predicted by the theory of relativity (the slowing down of time and contraction of space) would seem perfectly commonplace if the speed of light happened to be 10 miles per hour, and we would then see them in everyday life. In that case we might well regard the constancy of the speed of light and the associated "strange" effects on space and time as simply common sense. It is largely a matter of semantics, incidentally,

FIGURE 30. *When asked if he knew the speed of a light beam according to an observer chasing after it at half the speed of light, young Alberto answered correctly, sí.*

1. The relativistic rule for combining two velocities is not the "commonsense" addition rule $u + v$, but instead the more complex formula $(u + v)/(1 + uv/c^2)$. Note that when u and v are much less than c, we find that the term uv/c^2 is much less than 1.0, and so the two expressions give virtually the same result, as you can easily verify using, say $u = v = .0001c$. But when $v = c$, the formula yields the result c for any value of u.

whether we say the speed of light is constant *because* of these strange effects, or the reverse.

• — • — • — • — •

24.   Are Faster-Than-Light Speeds Allowed?

THE IDEA THAT faster-than-light speeds are actually possible would seem to contradict the idea of the speed of light as a universal speed limit. But it is only the speed of light in vacuum, c, that is a limiting speed; in media such as water or glass, where light travels at slower speeds, it is quite possible for objects such as subatomic particles to travel at speeds in excess of light. One result of particles exceeding the speed of light in a medium is Cerenkov radiation—a kind of shock wave similar to the sonic boom that occurs when objects exceed the speed of sound. Cerenkov radiation can be produced by subatomic particles created in the core of a nuclear reactor, and it is responsible for the eerie bluish glow you would see if you looked down at the submerged reactor core.

Furthermore, even though the speed of light in *vacuum* is a universal speed limit, it is not quite the barrier it might seem to be. For example, consider a star 100 light-years away—meaning that it takes 100 years for the star's light to reach us. For you to reach that star in a rocket ship in less than 100 years would seemingly require that your ship's speed exceed the speed of light (which travels a distance of one light-year in a time of one year.) But in fact, if your ship travels close to (but below) the speed of light, the elapsed time for the journey (according to ship clocks) can be far less than 100 years, because, according to relativity theory, time slows down for the ship's crew relative to Earth time.[1]

But are there any actual cases involving speeds in excess of the speed of light in vacuum? The only exceptions to the ban on faster-than-light speeds involve cases where neither energy nor information is transferred.[2] One such example would be if you pointed a flashlight toward the night sky and swept it in a circular arc. You could easily sweep the light beam past the Moon in a tiny fraction of a second. If the light is powerful enough, the edge of the light spot will move across

1. For example, according to relativity, if you made a journey at 99.995 percent the speed of light, you could reach a star 100 light-years away in only 1 year according to ship clocks, even though nearly 100 years would elapse on Earth clocks. See essay 126 for more details.

2. But see essay 120 for a possible counterexample.

the Moon's surface in that same tiny fraction of a second, and the spot will travel in excess of the speed of light. But the spot on the Moon is not a physical entity. The only *things* that move within the light beam are the light waves heading toward the Moon, and they continue to travel at their usual speed, *C*.

Another example of an apparent violation of the speed-of-light limit involves the transmission of information.

Let us imagine a series of hills atop which sit Native American persons using smoke signals to pass along information. Each individual sees smoke signals from a neighboring hill and immediately generates a new signal to relay the message to the next hill. If each person takes no time at all to react to the signal and pass it along, the signal's overall transmission speed in traveling from the first hill to the last is the speed of light. But now suppose that the group *by prearrangement* all agree to transmit a particular signal *before* the signal from the previous hill reaches them. To a distant observer who didn't know about the prearrangement, it would appear that signals were being relayed at a faster-than-light speed, although in reality no information would be transmitted, since each person would already know the message to be relayed before the signal from the prior hill arrived.

FIGURE 31. *The tribe tried to mess with the white man's mind by making him think they had invented a faster-than-light signaling method.*

25. What Is the Quickest Trip between Two Points?

THE SHORTEST DISTANCE between two points is a straight line, but the quickest trip may not be, as anyone who has taken a bridge rather than swum directly across a river will quickly realize. An interesting problem in finding the quickest path between two points involves a lifeguard who wants to reach a drowning victim in the shortest time (see the diagram). Which path, A, B, C, or D, would you imagine takes the least time? The straight-line path may be the shortest, but it is the path of least time only in the highly unlikely event that the lifeguard runs at the same speed as he swims. If the lifeguard can run *much* faster than he can swim, path D would be the best route, since it shortens the swimming portion of his route to the smallest distance. Most likely, something like path C is the best path for the lifeguard to take, since he probably runs somewhat faster

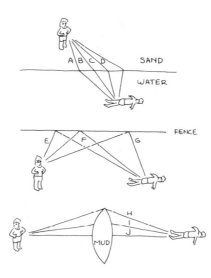

FIGURE 32. *Three path-of-least-time problems for lifeguards.*

than he swims, but obviously the exact path depends on the ratio of running and swimming speeds.

Let us consider another lifeguard problem. This time the lifeguard wants to rush to the aid of a heat prostration victim on the beach, but she first must pick up a first aid kit. These kits are positioned at numerous points along a fence at the back of the beach. Which path, E, F, or G, should the lifeguard take to reach the victim as soon as possible? In this case, since she runs at constant speed, the quickest path is also the shortest path, namely path F. Notice that for path F the angle between the path and the fence is the same when the lifeguard approaches the fence as when she leaves it.

For a final lifeguard problem, let's again assume she needs to reach a heat prostration victim. Between the lifeguard and the victim is a muddy area in the shape of a lens that slows her down to half her speed on sand. Which is the path of least time in this case, H, I, or J? The surprising answer is that

FIGURE 33. *Phyllis searches all possible paths so as to find the quickest one from point A to point B.*

45

for a certain shape of the muddy area, all three paths take exactly the same time. For example, the fact that H is a longer path than I is exactly offset by the fact that this path doesn't go through any mud. So if all three paths take exactly the same time, lifeguards who do not care about getting their feet muddy will take all three paths at one time or another.

Each of the three lifeguard problems is analogous to a situation involving light, which also takes the path of least time between two points in transparent media. For example, the bending angle of a light ray connecting two points in different media follows from the ratio of the light speeds in the two media, as in the first lifeguard example. Likewise, a light ray that hits a mirror must do so at a point that minimizes its travel time between two fixed points, which requires the ray to bounce off the mirror at the same angle it hits it, like path F in the second example. Finally, for a certain shape of lens, all light rays through the lens originating at a point on one side pass through a given point on the other (the focal point), since all paths take the same time.

You might wonder how light manages to "figure out" the quickest path between two points. Light manages this trick because in going from one point to another in a transparent medium, it essentially takes *all possible paths*. Through the phenomenon of interference (see essay 28), light waves taking most paths, all but those very close to the path of least time, cancel each other out.

26. How Slow Can Light Go?

STRANGE AS IT seems, light, which travels at the fastest possible speed in vacuum, literally travels at a snail's pace through certain materials. For all transparent media, the speed of light is less than its speed in vacuum, although the reduction may not be enormous. For example, in glass, light has ⅔ its speed in vacuum—though the exact value depends on the type of glass and the wavelength of light. Alternatively, we can say that the "index of refraction" of glass is ³⁄₂ (the index of refraction is the ratio of the speed of light in vacuum to that in the medium). Light traveling through diamond is slowed even more than in glass; its speed is 41 percent its value in vacuum. But the dense interior of the Sun is where *really* slow light can be found. Astronomers calculate that it takes light about 100,000 years to go from the core of the Sun to the surface. Apparently, the Sun could have stopped burning that long ago, and we would just be finding out about it![1]

1. If our Sun suddenly stopped burning fuel at its core, it would promptly collapse in the absence of some means of countering the inward force of gravity. For us not to notice that

The key to understanding why light takes so long to get out of the Sun is the sun's *opaqueness*—meaning that light travels only a short distance before being absorbed and reemitted. In transparent materials, light is also absorbed but then reemitted along the original direction—much like someone taking a series of steps in a straight line. In contrast, in opaque materials, the light is equally likely to be emitted in any direction after each absorption. The resulting sequence of absorptions and reemissions is much like the random walk of a drunk starting from a lamppost. After a random walk of N steps of distance 1 foot each, he could be anywhere between zero and N feet from the starting point at the end of the walk, but he would be N feet away from the lamppost only in the highly unlikely event that all steps were in the same direction.

To see what the average distance from a starting point would be, let us start with a random walk of only two equal-length steps. Picture a large clock with a grasshopper perched on the numeral 3. Suppose the grasshopper takes a hop to the center of the clock, a distance 1 foot to the left. If its next foot-long hop is in a random direction, the grasshopper is equally likely to land on any of the twelve numerals after its second hop. An "average" second hop would put the grasshop-per on the 12 (or the 6), which is $\sqrt{2}$ feet from its starting point, ac-cording to the Pythagorean theo-rem. We consider a hop to 12 (or 6) to be "average" because for every hop to a number on the right side of the clock that lies closer to the start-ing point than 12, there is a num-ber on the left side that is farther from the starting point than 12. We may therefore conclude that the average length of a two-step random walk is $\sqrt{2}$ feet. An exten-sion of this reasoning shows that a random walk of N steps would, on average, leave the walker (or hop-per) $\sqrt{N}$ feet from the starting point.

FIGURE 34. *All his life Sid was con-sidered "slow," when it was really only a matter of his optometrist's pre-scribing glasses with an* extremely *high index of refraction.*

Now, light starting at the Sun's core is absorbed after traveling less than 1 millimeter, based on the es-timated density of matter and tem-perature inside the Sun (see essays 75 and 109). Let us therefore assume the light path is a random walk with 1-millimeter steps. After a trillion trillion (10^{24}) such steps, the light will travel on average $\sqrt{10^{24}} = 10^{12}$ millimeters (or 10^6

---

the Sun had gone out, something would have to supply the outward pressure normally cre-ated by the heat generated in the core.

kilometers), which, in round numbers, is the radius of the Sun. But in order to travel a distance of 10^{24} 1-millimeter steps, light travels a total distance of 100,000 light-years, and requires a time of 100,000 years. We can therefore imagine the long time for light to escape from the Sun as being due to "drunken" light staggering out from the center.

27.   How Far Do Electromagnetic Waves Travel in One Second?

To CREATE A wave, all you need to do is to shake something. For example, sound waves can be created by vibrating vocal cords, and water waves can be created by a floating cork bobbing up and down in the water. In principle, it is easy to create an electromagnetic wave just by shaking a magnet up and down, but such a wave would be a very weak one. In practice, man-made electromagnetic waves such as radio waves are usually created by causing an electric current to flow up and down a transmitting antenna. In either case the frequency of the wave created is just the number of times per second you shake the magnet, or make the current flow up and down the antenna. The electromagnetic waves so created travel outward in all directions from the transmitter, and in the time of one shake of a magnet (or one oscillation of the electrons in the antenna), the waves reach a distance known as the wavelength. The wavelength can also be defined as the distance between successive wave crests (or troughs). Clearly, the frequency and wavelength must be inversely proportional: if you shake the magnet more times per second (higher frequency), the wave travels less distance in the time of one shake (shorter wavelength).

Light is just one form of electromagnetic radiation, other forms of

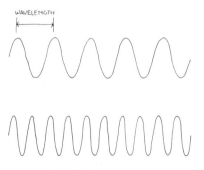

FIGURE 35. *The bottom wave has half the wavelength and twice the frequency, assuming the waves travel at the same speed.*

which include radio, microwaves (including radar), infrared, ultraviolet, X rays, and gamma rays, but *not* sound. All forms of electromagnetic radiation travel at the same speed in vacuum, *c*, and they differ only in regard to their frequency or wavelength. The various types of electromagnetic waves are listed here in order of increasing frequency, or decreasing wavelength. For the relatively narrow range of frequencies we call visible light, lying between the infrared and ultraviolet, the sequence from low to high frequencies (long to short wavelengths) is red, orange, yellow, green, blue, indigo, and violet—affectionately remembered as ROY G. BIV.

Devices that receive electromagnetic waves, such as radios, may need to be tuned in order to pick up a particular frequency being transmitted by a radio station out of a broad range of frequencies that may be present. In contrast, the retinas of our eyes are sensitive to a range of wavelengths without any "tuning," although we could, of course, wear colored glasses that would filter out everything but a narrow range of wavelengths corresponding to a particular color. Nowadays, it is even possible to extend our vision beyond the range of visible wavelengths using night vision goggles, which allow you to see in total darkness. These goggles, developed by the army, are sensitive to the infrared radiation emitted by any warm object, which they convert to visible wavelengths. Infrared radiation is also produced by TV remote controls. You can investigate for yourself whether various materials such as glass, paper, or your hand are transparent or opaque to infrared radiation by trying to change channels while the beam from the remote is blocked by these materials.

One of the most important developments in astronomy has been our ability to build instruments that "see" the universe in wavelengths much longer than visible light, such as infrared and radio waves, and those much shorter than visible light, such as ultraviolet, X rays, and gamma rays. The long-wavelength window on the universe is important because many regions of the universe, like the center of our galaxy, are obscured by dust, which is transparent to radio waves. The ability to "see" X rays and gamma rays is im-

FIGURE 36. *Psychologists are concerned about the violence young astronomers are exposed to now that they can see the universe in all parts of the electromagnetic spectrum.*

portant because these very short wavelengths are produced in extremely high-energy processes, and they provide a window on certain kinds of violent events and objects we could not otherwise study, such as matter falling into black holes. In order to observe the universe in X-ray and gamma-ray wavelengths, satellite-borne instruments are necessary, because the Earth's atmosphere is not transparent to these forms of electromagnetic radiation.[1]

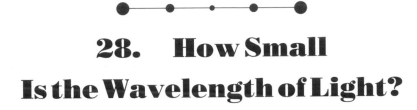

28. How Small
Is the Wavelength of Light?

SOMETIMES, when your neighbor's stereo is too loud, you may be tempted to turn yours up even louder so as to drown his out. But don't you wish you could instead turn on a device that would essentially cancel out the noise? Such "antinoise" technology, currently in use in some airplane cockpits and car mufflers, relies on a property possessed by all types of waves, including sound, namely their ability to interfere. The idea is that when two waves combine, the resultant wave may be either larger or smaller than the original two waves, depending on just how they overlap. When two equal-size waves overlap so that their crests are aligned, they are said to interfere *constructively*, and the resultant wave is twice the size of either one. In contrast, when the crests of one wave align with troughs of the other, the waves are said to interfere *destructively*, and the size of the resultant wave is zero. Thus, two water waves can produce still water, two sound waves can produce silence, and two light waves

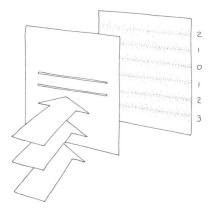

FIGURE 37. *Two-Slit Interference Experiment*
Light illuminates a screen with two horizontal slits in it. Light passing through the slits causes interference stripes on a screen to the right. The numbers next to each stripe indicate the number of extra wavelengths the waves from one slit travel to reach that point, compared with the waves from the other. The drawing is not to scale.

1. Thus, the cartoon should not be taken literally, because (a) astronomers looking through Earth-based telescopes cannot detect these short wavelengths, (b) an ordinary optical telescope of the kind depicted would not be used for these wavelengths, and (c) images do not appear on telescope lenses.

can produce darkness, at whatever places or times the interference is destructive. Interference of light waves accounts for the beautiful colors you see when looking at reflections off a compact disc—essentially a mirrored surface with many concentric grooves.[1] The color you see when looking at light reflected off a given point on the disc depends on whether the overlapping light from adjacent grooves interferes constructively or destructively for various wavelengths along that direction of sight. The concept of interference of waves has little connection to the everyday usage of the word. For example, when people interfere in one another's business, we usually regard the effects as being only negative. Also, the effect of such interference remains after the people separate, unlike the case of waves, which are completely unaffected after leaving the region of overlap.

One common method of observing interference of light uses two narrow, closely spaced slits illuminated by a distant light source (such as a laser) having a specific wavelength. When light from the source passes through each slit, it spreads out a bit, allowing the light waves that exit the two slits to overlap and interfere. When the two sets of waves reach a screen placed behind the slits, at certain points on the screen the interference is constructive, and at other points it is destructive—it all depends on how much farther the waves from one slit travel to reach a given point on the screen compared with the waves from the other slit. Clearly, the horizontal line on the screen that is equidistant from the two slits will be a place of constructive interference, because the waves from each slit travel the same distance to reach this line, and hence they arrive in step, with wave crests aligned. A bright line will be seen at this central line as a result of the constructive interference.

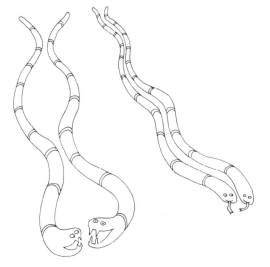

If we inspect the screen a short distance above or below this central line, the interference becomes *destructive*, because the waves from one slit travel a half wavelength less distance than the waves

FIGURE 38. *Snakes get along much better when their interference is constructive.*

from the other. In this case, the two waves cancel each other out, producing a dark line. Still farther above or below the central line, the waves from the two slits again constructively interfere when their path difference is one full wavelength, so the wave crests are again aligned. The alternating pattern of constructive and

1. Actually, compact discs and records have only one very long groove that spirals outward, but we can pretend that it is made up of many closely spaced concentric grooves.

destructive interference continues, resulting in a series of bright and dark horizontal bands or stripes centered on the midline.

You can observe the interference of light yourself using some simple items: a sharp needle, some aluminum foil, and an unfrosted light bulb. Using the needle, make pairs of holes at various places on the aluminum foil. Make the holes of each pair as small and close together as possible. You want many pairs of holes, since some pairs will turn out better than others. Put the lit bulb 10 or more feet away in a darkened room, and view it through the holes in the foil held very close to one eye. For some pairs of holes, you should see bright and dark interference stripes centered on the filament. In principle, if you can estimate the angular separation between these stripes and also the separation between the holes, you can find the average wavelength of visible light. For example, for a pair of holes ½ millimeter apart (a thousand times the average wavelength of light), you should see a stripe separation of $\frac{1}{1,000}$ of a radian (a mere millimeter width seen at arm's length).

29.   How Dark Can Light Get?

THE NEXT TIME you hear the pitter-patter of a downpour, think of light. Like rain, light has an intrinsic granularity that becomes particularly evident when dealing with low-intensity light sources. The light from a very weak source registers on a sensitive detector as though the light consists of a stream of particles or "packets" of energy, which we call photons. Individual photons received by the detector can be made to register as clicks, much like the clicks of a Geiger counter. Photons are, of course, also present in beams of light from intense sources, but they are so numerous that the granularity of the light is less evident. The human eye, unlike those of some animals, is not sensitive enough to register individual photons. The weakest signal your eye can register, when dark-adapted, is about twenty photons at a time. But the "darkest" that light can get is a single photon.

A strange fact about photons is that their energy is strictly proportional to the frequency of the light. Thus, X rays and gamma rays, which have a much higher frequency than visible light, also have a much higher energy per photon, accounting for their much greater power to penetrate most materials. When we say that a light source is bright or intense, we are referring to the high *number* of photons per second that it emits, not to the energy of each photon, which depends only on the light frequency. Thus, a high-intensity beam of low-energy visible light can be compared to a beam consisting of many Ping-Pong balls, while a low-intensity beam of high-energy gamma rays can be compared to a beam consisting of a few rifle bullets. It might seem that the gamma-ray beam will always have the greater potential for harm, compared with a beam of visible light. But visible light is not always benign: you probably would not want to get in the way of a high-power laser beam, for example. Even though the individual photons (Ping-Pong balls) in visible light have little energy, collectively they might have enough energy to melt a hole through you!

Perhaps the strangest aspect of photons is revealed in interference experiments, such as the double-slit experiment discussed in the previous essay. Suppose a pair of narrow slits is illuminated by a light source so faint that only one photon per second leaves the light source. If, using a very sensitive detector, you observe the places where individual photons strike a screen behind the slits, you will find that over time the photon "hits" (shown as dots in the figure in the previous essay) accumulate to produce the pattern of bright and dark stripes associated with the interference of light *waves*. The preceding observation shows that interference can occur even when only a single photon is present at a time. But if only one photon leaves the source per second, and it passes through either one slit or the other, it seems impossible that light from the two slits could interfere.

The explanation of this paradoxical situation is that every individual photon in effect must pass through *both* slits, and interfere with itself! So if photons may be thought of as particles, they certainly don't behave like particles in the everyday world of billiard balls and baseballs. No sober person has ever observed billiard balls going into two pockets at the same time, for example. But unlike the familiar world where a clear distinction can be made between entities that

FIGURE 39. *Photon surfers are more numerous on larger waves.*

are particles or waves, light manages to have properties of both, making it impossible to say whether light is "really" a particle or a wave.

30. How Far Apart Are the Earth's Two North Poles?

UNLESS YOU ARE a navigator, you might be unaware that the geographic and magnetic north poles of the Earth do not coincide. The magnetic north pole, the point toward which compasses point, is currently 11.5 degrees in latitude away form the geographic north pole, or the point on the Earth's surface through which the planet's spin axis passes. In fact, from the pattern of the Earth's magnetism, it looks almost as though there were a giant bar magnet inside the Earth tilted by 11.5 degrees from its axis of rotation. Rather than ask why the "bar magnet" is not exactly along the spin axis, a better question might be why should it be?

Let's consider how we know exactly where the magnetic and geographic poles are. Right at the magnetic north pole, a horizontally held compass needle wouldn't "know" which way to point, but if the plane of the compass were vertical, the needle would point straight down. In order to locate the geographic north pole, you can use the fact that due to the Earth's rotation the night sky appears to rotate around a point in the heavens close to the star Polaris—the North Star. In other words, the stars all appear to move in circular arcs nearly concentric with the North Star. This rotation can be captured on film using a time exposure of several hours, provided you have a clear moonless night, no outdoor lights nearby, a steady tripod, and sensitive photographic film. An exposure of several hours is needed if you want the stars to trace out appreciable arcs, because for each hour the Earth rotates $\frac{1}{24}$ of a revolution, or 15 degrees.

You could tell when you were located right at the north geographic pole because the north point in the heavens—the North Star—would be directly overhead. At any other point in the Northern Hemisphere, the North Star lies at an

FIGURE 40. *Being unsure which is the official North Pole, Peary plants two flags just to be on the safe side.*

angle above the horizon that is roughly equal to your latitude—which is what makes the North Star such a useful navigational guide. The assumption here is that the Earth's axis of rotation points toward a fixed point in the heavens, but actually the direction in the sky toward which the axis of the Earth points changes over very long time scales. In fact, you can think of the Earth as a spinning top that wobbles, or precesses, due to the tug of the Sun's gravity. As a result of this wobble, the north point in the heavens completes a large circle every 26,000 years. As time progresses, stars other than Polaris will have the honor of becoming the North Star.

During the Earth's 26,000-year wobble, its axis maintains a fixed 23.5-degree tilt to a line perpendicular to the plane of its orbit about the Sun. It is this tilt that causes the Sun to appear higher in the sky in summer than winter. When the Sun is higher in the sky, its rays create more warmth on the surface, because each square meter of surface intercepts a greater light intensity—in the same way that more raindrops land in a tray if the rain falls vertically than at an oblique angle. Incidentally, the Earth's annual variation in distance to the Sun (because the orbit is not perfectly round) has little effect on the seasons. In fact, in the Northern Hemisphere the Earth is *closest* to the sun in winter. Likewise, the annual variation in the number of daylight hours is also not responsible for the seasons, as you can appreciate by the lack of warmth at the poles where the sun is above the horizon for six months at a time.[1]

31. How Big Is the Earth's Diameter?

IMAGINE YOU LIVE on a tiny planet, perhaps 50 meters in radius. At some point on the planet, its sun will be directly overhead, and the length of your shadow will be zero. As you leave that spot, the sun will no

1. Only at the time of the spring and fall equinoxes does the Earth's north-south axis make a 90-degree angle with the line joining Earth and Sun, and we then have equal-length days and nights everywhere on Earth as a result. Given the 26,000-year precession of the Earth's axis, the time of the equinoxes must change by $\frac{1}{26,000}$ of a year, or about 20 minutes, for each revolution about the Sun. You might think that this precession would cause the seasons to shift slowly over the years. But the length of the year is *defined* by the time from one vernal equinox to the next rather than the time Earth takes to make one 360-degree revolution around the Sun. As explained in essay 125, a gradual shift in the seasons does occur, but it is connected to the incommensurability between the length of the day and the year.

longer be directly overhead, and the length of your shadow will gradually grow. For example, if you walk 5 meters away (10 percent of the planet's radius), your shadow's length will be 10 percent of your height. Exactly the same idea would apply if the planet were larger in size, except that you would need to walk a greater distance to travel 10 percent of a radius. But you could still find the radius of your planet by seeing how far you needed to travel for the length of your shadow, initially zero, to become 10 percent of your height.

Using a method very similar to this, Eratosthenes, who lived in Greece around 200 B.C., first estimated the size of the Earth by measuring the lengths of the shadows of two vertical poles that were hundreds of miles apart along a north-south line. Let us assume that one vertical pole was at the equator, and the comparison of shadow lengths was made at noon on the date of an equinox. In that case, the Sun would be directly overhead at the equator, and the length of one pole's shadow would be zero. From the distance to the second pole, and the length of its shadow at noon, Eratosthenes could find the radius of the Earth. For example, if a 1-meter vertical pole located 640 kilometers north of the equator casts a $\frac{1}{10}$-meter shadow at noon, the Earth's radius would be 10 $\times$ 640, or 6,400 kilometers (4,000 miles).

One tricky point that Eratosthenes faced in making his observation was that he and his assistant could not be sure they were measuring the shadow lengths at the same time—remember that no mechanical clocks existed until many centuries later. Basically, the two observers made their measurements at local noon, when the Sun was most nearly overhead. Essentially, each person measured the length of the *shortest* pole shadow found at his location. Eratosthenes's method for measuring the Earth's radius does not require the two observers be on a north-south line, or even that the measurements be simultaneous—just so long as each one measures the length of the shortest pole shadow during the day.

Nowadays, in the era of space travel, when we can see the Earth whole from space, we can easily measure its diameter from a photograph. For example, suppose we had a photograph of the Earth with a 1-meter ruler in the foreground the same size as the Earth's diameter. In that case the diameter of the Earth in meters would just equal the distance to the Earth divided by the distance to the meter stick at the time the photograph was taken. You can get the idea using a

FIGURE 41. *In the days before pi was known, scientists had to find the Earth's diameter the hard way.*

corresponding earthly example: measuring the height of a light pole with a ruler. Walk a distance away from the light pole, so that it appears as tall as a 1-foot ruler held at arm's length. The height of the light pole (in feet) will, by similar triangles, have to equal its distance from you divided by the length of your arm. For example, if the pole matched the length of a 1-foot ruler when you were 10 arm lengths from the pole, it would have to be 10 feet high.

Still another way to get the diameter of the Earth relies on a few simple facts about geography. Each time zone is roughly 1,000 miles wide at the equator (which you can easily remember, since the east and west coasts of the United States are roughly 3,000 miles and three time zones apart). Knowing that there must be 24 time zones around the Earth—one for each hour of the 24-hour rotation—we see that the Earth's circumference must be in the neighborhood of 24,000 miles. Dividing this number by π gives a rough figure of 7,600 miles for the Earth's diameter, which is close enough for our purposes to the correct figure of 7,926 miles, or 8,000 miles in round numbers. This last method for finding the diameter of the Earth could be considered a measurement only if you were actually to find the average width of a time zone at the equator by observation. Basically, you would have to see how far you needed to travel east or west for there to be a 1-hour time difference between sunrises. If you didn't feel like making the trip, you could just phone a good friend as the Sun was rising at your location. If your friend were to live a distance corresponding to 15 degrees east of you in longitude, she should find that at her location the Sun had already risen 1 hour earlier. (Don't try this with someone west of you unless that person enjoys pre-dawn phone calls.)

32. How Far Is the Moon?

NOWADAYS, finding the distance to the Moon is as easy as bouncing a radar pulse off it and measuring the round-trip travel time (about 2.7 seconds), which gives a distance of about 400,000 kilometers.[1] But this method has been available only during the last few decades. Before then, the lunar distance had to be found using the same method still relied on for other celestial bodies: the parallax method. Parallax refers to the apparent shift of an object's position relative to more distant objects as you change your viewing position. It is because of parallax that you get more depth information when viewing a scene with two eyes than with one eye closed.

1. Radar, which travels at the speed of light (300,000 kilometers per second), travels roughly 400,000 kilometers in the 1.35-second one-way Earth-Moon travel time.

To see how parallax can give you an object's distance, close one eye and view your thumb held at arm's length against a background of distant objects. Now close your other eye instead, without moving your thumb, and notice that the thumb's position relative to the distant objects will appear to have shifted by an angle of 5 degrees, or about 2.5 thumb widths. Five degrees is therefore said to be the parallax angle of your thumb at arm's length, and it in effect is a measure of the distance to your thumb. For example, if you repeat the observation with your thumb held twice as far away—better make that half as far away!—you will find a parallax shift twice what you found before, namely about ten degrees. In general, as this example illustrates, the shift in position or parallax angle of an object is *inversely* proportional to its distance from you. But the parallax angle also depends on the distance between your eyes, or more generally the distance between any two viewing points. In general, the parallax angle in radians equals the distance between viewing points divided by the object's distance—one radian being about 57.3 degrees.

The small distance between your two eyes results in very tiny parallax angles for all but nearby objects, so to gauge the distance of faraway objects you need a much larger distance between viewing points. For example, you cannot tell visually, based on the parallax provided by your two eyes, that the Moon is much nearer than the stars.[2] On the other hand, if two people were to view the position of the Moon against the background sky simultaneously from opposite sides of the Earth and somehow compare the views, they would observe a parallax shift relative to the background stars of about 2 degrees, or ¹/₃₀ of a radian. With a parallax shift of ¹/₃₀ of a radian, the Moon's distance must be about 30 times the distance between viewing positions, that is, 30 times the Earth's diameter.

FIGURE 42. *Darlene's strange mutation made shopping for sunglasses difficult, but it gave her great parallax.*

It is easy to find the size of the Moon once you know its distance, merely by looking at its apparent diameter. The apparent diameter of the Moon is about ½ degree (it seems to fill that much of the sky, or about the width of your pinkie seen at arm's length). If you express the distance to the Moon as a number of arm

2. Nor can you infer that the Moon must be closer than the stars, simply because it looks bigger. After all, the Sun and Moon look just about the same size, yet the Sun is actually about four hundred times bigger (and farther).

lengths (about 1 meter), the Moon's diameter is simply the distance to the Moon times the width of your pinkie.

You may have observed the well-known illusion that the Moon appears much larger when near the horizon. You can easily verify that this is due merely to psychological factors by seeing that the Moon is about a pinkie-width wide whether it is near the horizon or not. The Moon-on-the-horizon illusion is probably due to your unconsciously imagining the Moon to be a nearby object (and therefore small) when viewing it all alone high in the sky. In contrast, when the Moon is seen on the horizon together with distant objects such as buildings and trees, it is seen as being more distant, and therefore greater in size.

33. How Far Does the Moon Fall Each Second?

IN CASE YOU ever wondered why the Moon doesn't fall down, the truth is that it does, by about $1/16$ inch every second. By this we do *not* mean that the Moon gets closer to the Earth each second. Rather, due to its orbit it deviates from a straight-line path by about $1/16$ inch in one second. In other words, if gravity were suddenly turned off and the Moon did fly off on a tangent, it would be $1/16$ inch farther away from the Earth at the end of one second (see the diagram). The situation with the Moon is much the same as that of a ball at the end of a string that you can twirl around in a circle. The tension in the string keeps the ball "in orbit" around you, just as the Earth's gravitational pull keeps the Moon in its orbit. If you let go of the string while the ball revolves, it will fly off on a tangent, just as the Moon would if gravity could be suddenly turned off.

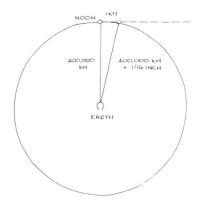

FIGURE 43. *By following its circular orbit, the Moon is $1/16$ inch closer to Earth than if it were to fly off on a tangent for 1 kilometer.*

Let's see how we know the distance the Moon "falls" is $1/16$ inch each second.

Given the distance to the Moon (about 400,000 kilometers), we can easily find the circumference of its nearly circular orbit to be about 2.5 million kilometers. The time for one orbit, 28 days, represents about 2.5 million seconds, so the Moon travels 1 kilometer of its orbit each second. If the Moon went off on a tangent for 1 kilometer, we could find its distance to Earth from the Pythagorean theorem as the square root of $400,000^2$ plus 1^2, or $400,000.0000015$ kilometers.[1] This means that if the Moon were to fly off on a tangent, it would be a mere .0000015 kilometers, or 1/16 inch, farther from the Earth than if it remained in its orbit. This calculation illustrates why we say the Moon falls toward Earth 1/16 inch in one second. (Actually, the more precise figure is 0.053 inches, which is a bit under 1/16 inch.)

Isaac Newton was the first person to explain the "fall" of the Moon toward Earth in terms of Earth's gravity. Near the Earth's surface, objects fall 16 feet in one second, so evidently Earth's gravity must be only 1/3,600 times as strong at the Moon's location, this being the ratio of 1/16 inch to 16 feet. Newton realized that a very simple rule could explain this factor of 1/3,600. He knew that the distance to the Moon is 60 times the radius of the Earth. The inverse of the square of 60 is 1/3,600. So Newton concluded that the strength of Earth's gravity must decrease as the *inverse square of the distance* from the center of the Earth.

THE MOON IS FALLING! THE MOON IS FALLING!

FIGURE 44. *Newton discovered his law of gravity based on an important observation made by Chicken Little.*

Newton, being the great scientist that he was, didn't stop by explaining the motion of the Moon. He went on to claim that every object in the universe attracts every other object with a force inversely proportional to the two objects' separation distance. This law of universal gravitation also took into account the two objects' masses. Specifically, Newton claimed that the force of attraction had to be proportional to the mass of each object as well as the inverse square of their separation distance— which is why the pull of the Earth on you is much greater than the pull of a friend only one meter away. But even though the gravitational pull of nearby objects is small, it can actually be measured using sufficiently sensitive instruments.

1. If you try to check this result on your calculator, you will be disappointed, since calculators do not keep enough digits. You can find the correct answer, however, using this approximation, which holds for x much greater than 1: $\sqrt{x^2+1} = x + (1/2x)$.

Using Newton's law of universal gravitation, we can easily debunk certain claims of astrologers, for example, the claim that the position of the planets at the moment of your birth has influenced your personality. If this influence is based on gravitational forces, the claim is highly dubious, because the pull of gravity due to the nearby attending physician is comparable to the pull of some of the planets—since the physician's closer distance (squared) compensates for the faraway planet's greater mass. Mars, for example, has a mass around 10 billion times that of a 70-kilogram physician, and the square of its nearest distance to Earth is also about 10 billion times the distance to a physician 1 meter away. During your birth, the attending physician therefore probably exerted a greater gravitational force on you than Mars did, unless Mars happened to be at its closest point to Earth, in which case the two forces would have been just about the same.

34.   How Far Are "Stationary" Satellites?

DO YOU HAVE the feeling someone may be watching you at this moment? In these days of spy satellites, which allegedly can read license plates, your paranoia may be justified. A particularly effective orbit for a spy satellite is one that allows it to hover over a fixed point on Earth.[1] Such satellites are also very useful for electronic communication, and they were originally proposed for this purpose by the science fiction writer Arthur C. Clarke. Such geosynchronous or "stationary" satellites orbit the Earth synchronously with its 24-hour rotation, and so they appear stationary as seen from a point on the rotating Earth. To see why, visualize a satellite orbiting above the equator while the Earth rotates beneath it at the same rate.

As it happens, satellites can appear stationary only if they are at a particular distance, namely 26,500 miles or 6.6 Earth radii, *and* they orbit the Earth at the equator. Nonequatorial orbits of 6.6 Earth radii also have 24-hour periods, but they do not lead to a satellite's appearing stationary above a fixed point on the surface, as you can easily see by visualizing an orbit passing over the poles while the Earth rotates. The calculation of the distance to a geosynchronous satellite is exactly like the one we did for the "fall" of the Moon. It can easily be shown that by traveling in its 24-hour orbit rather than along the tangent line, a satellite at a

1. Actually, the great distance of synchronous satellites make them unsuitable for taking high-resolution pictures of the Earth's surface. Their primary spying mission is to watch for any launches of nuclear missiles.

distance of 6.6 Earth radii "falls" toward Earth 0.37 feet in one second. Comparing 0.37 feet with the 16 feet that an object on the Earth's surface falls in one second, we see that gravity at the satellite's location must be weaker by a factor of $\frac{1}{44}$ than on the Earth's surface. But that is exactly what gravity should be for a satellite located at 6.6 Earth radii, because $6.6^2 = 44$.

For any other distance from the Earth, the orbit period of a satellite could not be 24 hours. To see why, let's suppose a satellite closer to the Earth could complete an orbit in the same 24 hours. In view of its closer distance, the satellite would complete a smaller circle in the same time, and it would evidently fall toward Earth *less* than 0.37 feet in one second by following its orbit rather than the tangent line. A smaller distance fallen in one second would imply weaker gravity than for the original distance, but this is impossible since the satellite is closer to the Earth than before, so gravity should be stronger by the inverse square law. We also find a similar contradiction if we assume that a satellite can have a 24-hour period when the orbit radius is greater than 6.6 Earth radii. Thus, it is only for this radius that synchronous orbits can exist.

One flaw in the argument about there being a unique distance for 24-hour synchronous satellites is that we assume the satellites are unpowered and acted on only by the force of gravity. It would be possible to have a 24-hour satellite in a different-radius circular orbit if its engines were continuously firing so as to either supplement or counteract the force of gravity—but this is a highly unrealistic choice for actual satellites, which generally have only a small amount of fuel, used primarily for making small orbital corrections.

For this very same reason, synchronous satellites cannot be used as skyhooks to haul up supplies. If you tried it, the weight of the supplies being hauled up would pull the satellite down into a lower orbit having a period of less than 24 hours, so the satellite would not be able to hover above a fixed point on Earth. On the other hand, if the satellite fired thrusters downward to counteract the weight being hauled up, the idea might work conceptually. But of course in practice, the 26,500-mile distance to the satellite would make satellite skyhooks unfeasible. For one thing, even a cable made of the strongest steel would break under its own weight if hung vertically for a length much in excess of 25 miles.

FIGURE 45. *Clara, with trepidation, lets down a skyhook from the geostationary satellite to haul up some supplies. Will they pull her out of orbit?*

35.   At What Point Would the Earth and the Moon Balance on a Seesaw?

FROM YOUR experience with seesaws, you are probably aware that the heavier person must always be closer to the center to achieve balance. The center of mass of two objects can be defined as that point at which a stick would balance like a seesaw if the objects were placed on its opposite ends.[1] In general, if one mass is x times greater than the other, the center of mass lies between them, at a point x times farther from the smaller mass than the larger one. In the case of the Earth-Moon system, since the Earth is 81 times heavier than the Moon, the center of mass is located 81 times closer to the center of the Earth than to the center of the Moon. The center of mass must therefore be located $1/82$ the distance to the Moon measured from the Earth's center, in order that its distances from Earth and Moon have the required 1 to 81 ratio. The distance to the Moon happens to be 60 Earth radii, so the center of mass of the Earth-Moon system is less than an Earth radius from the Earth's center, or *inside* the Earth. It is of course somewhat misleading to speak of the Earth and Moon balancing on a seesaw, unless we imagine the Earth, Moon, and seesaw all acted on by the gravity of some other body—in the giant "playground" of the Sun, perhaps. Rather than speak of seesaws, the concept of the center of mass can also be related to the mutual revolution of bodies.

You may have thought that the Moon revolves around the Earth, but in fact both Moon and Earth revolve around their common center of mass, so as to keep the position of that point unaffected by the two bodies' revolutions. In order to get the idea, you can make a model of the Earth and Moon using two unequal-size clay balls placed at the ends of a soda straw to form a dumbbell. Locate the center of mass of the balls by finding the point on the straw where you can tie a string and have the dumbbell balance like a mobile. You can then weigh the two balls and see if the weight ratio equals the ratio of their distances to the string, measured from their centers. To simulate the Earth-Moon system, give the hanging dumbbell a spin and observe how it rotates about the string. The large ball goes in a small circle, and the small one in a large circle, so as to keep the center of mass fixed.

---

1. The mass of the stick would need to be much less than that of the objects; otherwise you would obtain an incorrect result.

You can extend the clay ball model to represent the motion of the Earth-Moon system as it revolves around the Sun by slowly moving your hand that holds the string in a large horizontal circle while the two clay balls rotate about their center of mass. Notice that it is only the center of mass of the balls that follows that large circle. Each ball, by itself, follows a complicated path known as an epicycle, which is exactly what the Earth and Moon do as they move around the Sun.

Actually, the Earth (or Earth-Moon system) does not quite revolve around the Sun, but rather the Earth and Sun revolve around *their* common center of mass, which is 333,000 times closer to the Sun than the Earth—since the Sun is 330,000 times more massive than the Earth. What happens when you add more planets to the system? As you might expect by now, the overall center of mass of the Earth, Moon, Sun, and all the other planets has a location that is unaffected by the planetary motions.

FIGURE 46. *Young God came up with his idea for creating the universe while playing with mobiles.*

36.   At What Point Do Earth and Moon's Gravity Cancel?

IMAGINE YOU are located at some point between the Earth and the Moon. Toward which body will you fall? Whether Earth or lunar gravity exerts the stronger attraction depends on your relative distance from each body. Obviously there is some point at which the strength of gravity due to each body is the same, and an object located at that point wouldn't "know" which way to fall. This "zero gravity point" is clearly closer to the Moon than the Earth, because the Earth has 81 times the Moon's mass. In order to find the point where the gravity due to Earth and Moon are of equal strengths, just remember that the strength of gravity varies as the inverse square of the distance from a body. So you would need to be 9 times closer to the Moon than the Earth in order to compensate for the Earth being 81 times more massive.

The zero gravity point must therefore be located nine-tenths of the way to the Moon, as measured from the center of the Earth, since at this point the distances to the centers of the Moon and Earth have the required one to nine ratio. This conclusion neglects the important effect of orbital motions of Earth and Moon. In the real-life situation, if we viewed the Earth and Moon in a rotating frame of reference in which the two bodies were (approximately) at rest, we would need to take into account centrifugal force as well as gravity, and this would change the location of the effective zero gravity point significantly.[1]

You might think that if you are initially at rest located at a zero gravity point between two massive bodies, you will remain at rest forever, but that is not the case. An object at rest at the zero gravity point is much like a ball placed atop a sphere. Even though the ball may have no "preference" to roll in any particular direction, it will before very long roll in some direction off the sphere. The same situation occurs for a pencil balanced on its point. In all three situations, the object is said to be in a state of "unstable equilibrium," which means that the tiniest movement away from its initial position causes the object to move farther and farther away.

The situation is in sharp contrast to that of stable equilibrium, in which an object that is disturbed slightly tends to move back toward its equilibrium position—just like a rocking chair, or a ball at the bottom of a bowl.

If you were at rest at the zero gravity point between Earth and Moon, you could not predict toward which body you would fall, any more than you can predict which way a pencil standing exactly on end will fall. Normally, the motion of celestial bodies or spacecraft is entirely predictable—otherwise NASA could hardly plan its missions. But as we have just seen, there are exceptions to this generalization. To take another example, if a spacecraft approaches a

FIGURE 47. *His ship's fuel was almost gone. If only he could reach the zero gravity point, he'd be home free.*

1. In this rotating frame of reference, there are actually a total of *five* points, known as "Lagrange points," labeled L1, L2, L3, L4, and L5, at which a body would experience zero net force and be in equilibrium. Only one of the Lagrange points (L1) lies between the Earth and Moon, and only two of the five points (L4 and L5) are points where the equilibrium is stable.

zero gravity point from a certain direction (perpendicular to the Earth-Moon connecting line), its motion is completely unpredictable after it passes that point. Even if the spacecraft doesn't pass exactly through the zero gravity point but only comes close to it, the tiniest variation in the spacecraft's direction as it nears the point causes extremely large changes in its subsequent motion.

You might think that NASA would always want to be sure that its spacecraft avoided such unstable points, but there are times when they can come in handy. If, for example, your spacecraft has a very limited amount of fuel left for a course correction, you would want to make the correction near an unstable point, where the tiniest bit of acceleration can have a big effect later on.

37. How High Can Mountains Get?

MOUNT EVEREST, whose height is 29,028 feet (about 5.5 miles), is arguably the tallest mountain on Earth. But do we really know (or care) that it is not 29,029 or 29,027 feet high? Nowadays, scientists can, in fact, measure the elevation of any point on the Earth's surface to a precision of 1 foot. Such high precision relies on clocking the round-trip time of a radar pulse from an orbiting satellite, in much the same way that you can measure distances using the reflected ultrasonic pulse from a digital tape measure. In fact, much of the Earth's surface has been measured using this technique. Such data can be expressed in terms of elevation contour maps that are useful for accurate navigation. Those cruise missiles that supposedly can fly down a chimney have just such contour maps of selected locations stored in their computers.

But, getting back to the tallest mountains found on Earth, is it just a matter of chance that Everest is 5.5 miles high, or could it just as well have been 10 or even 100 miles high? Actually, there is a limit to the maximum height of mountains, based on the strength of materials from which mountains are formed. The rock underneath a mountain is subject to tremendous pressure from the weight of the overlying rock, which would be enough to liquefy the base if the mountain were tall enough. So you couldn't very well have a 100-mile-high mountain if the bottom nine-tenths were under enough pressure to liquefy! The maximum height possible for mountains is probably not much greater than Mount Everest, as indicated by the fact that the Earth's near liquid mantle is as little as 5 miles below the surface.

The maximum height of mountains on Earth depends not only on the strength of materials but also on the strength of gravity. On the Moon, where gravity has one-sixth its value on Earth, mountains made from the same materials as those on Earth could be six times higher than on Earth. Of course, the Moon is believed to be geologically "dead" compared with the Earth, meaning that it lacks a mountain-building mechanism, so we wouldn't actually expect lunar mountains to be six times as high as those on Earth. The tallest mountain we know of in the solar system is Mars's 15-mile-high volcano Olympic Mons. The fact that Olympic Mons is 2.7 times as tall as Earth's Mount Everest correlates with martian gravity being weaker than Earth's by roughly this same factor.

For the opposite case of celestial bodies having stronger gravity than Earth, the maximum height of mountains must obviously be correspondingly less. An extreme case is that of a neutron star—an extremely compact object on which gravity is an astonishing 300 billion times stronger than on Earth.

FIGURE 48. *"If this is the tallest possible mountain, what happens if I plant this flag?"*

If we make the unrealistic assumption of a constant-density material, the height of mountains on a neutron star would be one 300-billionth of those on Earth—a mere 3 millionths of an inch high. Such mountains would be every bit as hard to climb as 5-mile-high mountains on Earth, given the enormously greater gravity. On the other hand, the difficulty of climbing a mountain on a neutron star would be the least of your problems, since your weight of 25 billion tons would squash you instantly.

38. What Is the Largest Possible Cubic Planet?

MOUNTAINS can be thought of as small pimples on an otherwise more or less spherical body. We can get a feeling of just how small these pimples are by noting that the height of Mount Everest (5.5 miles) is a mere 0.069 percent of the Earth's radius—smaller proportionally than the little bumps on a basketball. As we shall see, smaller planets have less gravity, and therefore the maximum possible size of the "pimples" grows as a planet's size decreases. For a small body, gravity is so weak that the height of mountains can be an appreciable fraction of the size of the planet, and the planet (or moon) can depart dramatically from sphericity—as is actually the case for Hyperion, one of the smaller moons of Saturn, which has a football-like shape. For another extreme departure from sphericity, consider a cube-shaped planet—home to several twentieth-century painters, perhaps?

Let's see how we can estimate the size of the biggest possible cubic planet. First, we need to understand how the planet's surface gravity depends on its size. It can be shown that the strength of gravity on the surface of a planet is proportional to its radius, assuming a fixed density (see essay 72). In other words, on a planet half the size of Earth, gravity is half as strong, and mountains can grow twice as tall. In another sense, however, the mountains on the half-size planet could be said to be *four* times as tall as earthly mountains, when their height is expressed as a percent of the planet's radius.

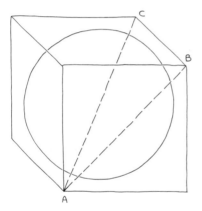

FIGURE 49. *The length of the main diagonal through the cube, AC, is found to be 173.2 percent of the diameter of the sphere enclosed by the cube. This result follows from the Pythagorean theorem: For a cube 2 units on a side, AB must equal* $\sqrt{2^2+2^2}$. The Pythagorean theorem can be used once more for right triangle ABC, *to find* AC = $\sqrt{2^2+2^2+2^2}$. This is 173.2 percent of the side of the square, 2.

How big would mountains have to be to form the corners of a cube? Imagine a sphere that just fits inside a cube—the sphere will define "sea level." Using some simple geometry, you can show that the distance from the sphere's center to one corner of the cube is 173.2 percent of the sphere's radius (see the diagram). This means that a corner of the cube, or the "peak" of the mountain, is 73.2 percent of a radius above sea level (the surface of the sphere). Let's compare this imaginary situation with Earth, where the tallest mountains are 0.069 percent of the Earth's radius. Clearly, earthly mountains are roughly 900 times smaller than those on the cubic planet, when their height is expressed as a percent of the radius.

We saw earlier that on a planet half the size of Earth, mountains could be four times as tall (as a percent of the radius). By extension, it would require a planet $\frac{1}{30}$ Earth's radius to produce mountains $30^2 = 900$ times taller, as a fraction of its radius. So the maximum size of a cubic planet is *roughly* $\frac{1}{30}$ of Earth, or about 420 kilometers on a side.

FIGURE 50. *Skiers enjoy skiing down flat slopes on cubic planets.*

It seems hard to imagine any natural process that could form a cubic planet, but it is conceivable that such a structure could be built if there were some reason to do so. The direction of "down" on such a body would everywhere point approximately toward the center of the cube. If you were standing at the center of one face of the cube, you would be on level ground, but if you were standing near an edge you would be on a 45-degree hill. Thus, an object placed near one edge would roll or slide back and forth along the face, even though the surface would look perfectly flat. Also, if you went past an edge you would not fall off, but would begin to descend another 45-degree hill.

39.   How Big a "Bulging Waistline" Do Planets Develop?

THE PLANET Saturn is one of the most glorious sights you can see in the night sky with an inexpensive telescope. Saturn is interesting not only for its beautiful rings but also for its flattened appearance, arising from its rapid rotation. For a nonrotating large planet, the inward force of gravity acting equally in all directions, of course, requires that its equilibrium shape be a sphere. But rotation can cause noticeable departures from sphericity, since planets are not completely rigid bodies. You can study the effect of rotation on a nonrigid body using a roughly spherical water balloon. Give the balloon a spin and observe its deformation, which increases the faster it is spun.

For rotating objects, an inward force is needed to keep all parts of the object moving in circles about its axis. We sometimes refer to the tendency of a rotating object to fly apart in the absence of such an inward force as being due to an outward "centrifugal" force. The strength of this centrifugal force increases the more rapid the rotation, and the greater the distance from the rotation axis. You can observe the increase of centrifugal force with distance from the axis by placing a row of pennies along a radius on a turntable. When the turntable is spun, the pennies farthest from the axis will be the first ones to fly off, because for those pennies the centrifugal force exceeds that of friction. Also notice that when you spin the turntable faster, pennies need to be closer to the center not to fly off. If you want to see exactly how the spin rate influences the centrifugal force, you need to use an adjustable-speed turntable, such as a multispeed phonograph. You will find in this case that the centrifugal force is proportional to the *square* of the rotational speed, as well as being directly proportional to the distance from the rotation axis.[1]

One way to explain why rotating planets develop an equatorial bulge is to think of their parts as pennies on a hugh turntable. The parts of a planet closest to the equator are farthest from the rotation axis, and therefore those parts experience the greatest centrifugal force. The size of a planet's equatorial bulge obviously increases with a planet's rotation rate and its radius, which accounts for the no-

---

1. One way of checking this relationship is to see how far from the axis you can place a penny and not have it fly off when the turntable is rotating at 33 and then 45 rpm. You should find that the penny can stay on the turntable $(^{45}/_{33})^2 = 1.86$ times farther out at the slower speed.

ticeably flattened appearance of the rapidly rotating giant planets, Jupiter and Saturn. Jupiter's diameter is about 7 percent larger at the equator than the poles, and for Saturn the figure is about 11 percent.

There is one planet that cannot be seen through an Earth-based telescope, namely our own. In the days before the Earth could be observed from space directly, how could we tell the size of Earth's equatorial bulge? The shape of the Earth can be discovered by conventional Earth-based mapping techniques, or by analyzing anomalies in satellite orbits. Due to its rotation, the Earth's diameter is 43 kilometers larger at the equator than the poles—a mere 0.3 percent difference between polar and equatorial diameters.

Many physicists do not like to use the concept of centrifugal force in explaining the tendency of rotating objects to fly apart, and they use the adjective "fictitious" in referring to centrifugal or other forces that arise only in a rotating (or accelerating) reference frame.

FIGURE 51. *Jupiter had great difficulty in convincing his significant other that his equatorial bulge was due to a "fictitious" centrifugal force.*

But one of Albert Einstein's great contributions, the general theory of relativity, explains that the effects of accelerated reference frames are locally indistinguishable from the effects of gravitational forces, so in a sense centrifugal forces are no more fictitious than gravity.

40. How Much Farther Is the Moon Each Month?

SURPRISINGLY, each time the Moon completes an orbit, it is slightly farther away from Earth. Its gradual departure can be linked to the twice-daily tides, for which the Moon is primarily responsible. To explain why the Moon is receding, let's first see how the Moon causes the tides. The Moon's gravity distorts the shape of the Earth, because it pulls on different pieces of the Earth with a slightly different gravitational force, since each piece of the Earth is at a slightly different distance from the Moon. Note that lunar tides are more than twice as big as solar tides, even though the Sun exerts a far greater gravitational force on the Earth than the Moon does. The dominance of lunar over solar tides arises because the strength of the tidal force depends on the *difference* in the force of gravity on opposite sides of the Earth, and the Moon's "differential gravity" is much greater than the Sun's because the Moon is much closer to Earth.

The lunar tidal distortion occurs primarily in the Earth's water envelope,

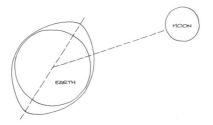

FIGURE 52. *The angle between the tidal bulges and the line joining Earth and Moon stays constant as the Earth rotates.*

which forms an ellipsoidal shape with bulges on opposite sides of the planet. (This tidal distortion is quite apart from the equatorial bulge due to the Earth's spin.) The line joining the two tidal bulges has a constant angle with the line joining Earth and Moon (see the diagram). So, as the solid Earth rotates underneath the oceans' tidal bulges, at any point on the seacoast, you see two high and two low tides each day. The tides occur about an hour later each day, because the positions of the Moon and the tidal bulges it causes advance an additional 1/28 of Earth's circumference each day as the Moon revolves about the Earth.

The rotation of the Earth underneath the tidal bulges creates friction, which has the effect of slowing the Earth's spin—a fact we can verify from the recorded times of eclipses made by observers over the last few thousand years.[1] In order to understand how the slowing down of the Earth causes the Moon to gradually depart, picture yourself on frictionless ice. Imagine that in front of you is a large truck tire lying on the ice and spinning rapidly. In the absence of friction, the tire, like the Earth itself, keeps spinning at a constant rate. Suppose you reach out and put your hands against the sides of the tire, causing it to slow down. We say that the force of friction here creates a "torque" that slows the tire's spin. At the same time you slow the tire's rotation, the force of the tire on your hands will start you spinning in the same direction the tire is spinning—some of the tire's rotational motion will be transferred to you.

---

1. Based on historical records, it appears that eclipses about 2,000 years ago actually occurred roughly 9 hours later than they should have, if we assume a constant 24 hours per rotation. A 9-hour loss over 2,000 years is equivalent to a loss of 0.04 seconds every day over those twenty centuries. Over a very long time, such a tiny rate of slowing down can have an appreciable effect. For example, a billion years ago the days would have been only 18 hours long.

Exactly the same transfer of rotational motion occurs when the Moon's gravitational "hands" slow the Earth's rotation due to tidal friction. As the Earth loses spin, its loss of rotational motion is the Moon's gain, and the moon revolves about the Earth faster. As a result, the Moon must move out to a larger orbit, since there is a definite relationship between size of orbit and orbital speed. The increase in distance to the Moon every time it completes one revolution (one lunar month) is 0.3 centimeters—a motion that can actually be measured by bouncing pulses from a laser off a reflector left on the Moon by astronauts.

Will the Moon eventually leave us for good? Fortunately for lovers and werewolves, the answer is no. At some time the Earth's spin will slow to such a point that it will always keep the same face toward the Moon—just as the Moon now keeps the same face toward the Earth (a result of *Earth* tides on the Moon). After that time, the Earth will no longer rotate underneath its tidal bulges, and so no friction will act to slow the Earth's rotation any further.

FIGURE 53. *Her constant tugging caused him to lose some of his old spin, and as a result she gradually withdrew.*

41.   How Close Can a Moon Get?

THE MOONS and planets of the solar system are believed to have formed out of a rotating disk of material surrounding the Sun during its infancy. According to this theory, the orbits of moons and planets are based on an accident of their birth. Moons and planets formed wherever the greatest concentrations of dust and debris happened to be, as the matter coalesced into larger and larger lumps during random collisions. On this basis, you might think that a moon could be located at any distance from its parent planet, but there is in fact a closest possible distance for any given planet, which we can understand based on the following scenario.

Imagine two nearby lumps of matter, Flotsam and Jetsam, which lie along a line to a planet and are in circular orbits about the planet. Whether or not the two lumps coalesce depends on their distance from the planet. The lump nearer the planet is pulled toward the planet with a greater force than the farther lump, and this differential attraction or tidal force on the two masses in effect pulls them apart. The tidal force does not have to be very large to prevent the lumps from coalescing—it need only exceed the small gravitational attraction between the two lumps. The force is called a tidal force because of its similarity to the way the Moon causes tidal bulges on the Earth. As explained in the previous essay, the tides can be thought of as a pulling apart of the planet due to differences in the strength of lunar attraction for different parts of the Earth.

The reason there is a closest distance to the planet where lumps of matter can coalesce is that the tendency of the two lumps of rocklike material to pull apart (the size of the tidal force) increases the closer they are to the planet, but the attraction between the lumps depends only on the separation between them, not how close they are to the planet. Thus, for everything within some distance from the planet, repulsion wins over attraction. To take an analogy from everyday life, suppose you and a friend are competing for the same job. The bigger the job, and the closer it seems, the greater is the tendency to break the bonds of your friendship.

The closest distance to the planet that two lumps can no longer get together to form larger lumps is known as the Roche limit. For distances closer to a planet than the Roche limit, it is not possible for a collection of small masses to coalesce and form a moon. Does that mean an existing moon wandering inside the Roche limit would get torn apart? Actually, the Roche limit exists only for objects held together by gravity alone. Since rocks and other solid objects are held together by interatomic forces, an already-formed small moon could survive inside the Roche limit. But a large moon probably would be torn apart, because of the greater difference in the pull of the planet's gravity on the large moon's two halves.

As you might guess, our Moon is

FIGURE 54. *If two lunar fragments drift apart due to tidal forces, the Moon is within the Roche limit.*

safely outside the Earth's Roche limit (16,000 kilometers), and it is in no danger of disintegration. Larger planets like Jupiter and Saturn have larger Roche limits than Earth, by virtue of their stronger gravity. In fact, the bulk of the rings of Saturn lie inside the planet's Roche limit. Are Saturn's rings the remnant of a moon that got too close to the planet and disintegrated, or are the rings debris from a moon that never was—and never will be—since the matter is too close to Saturn to coalesce? We may never know the answer.

42. How Far Is the Sun?

FINDING THE distance to the Sun is harder than finding the distance to the Moon because the Sun's greater distance means its parallax is much less, and hence much harder to measure. (For the parallax method, see essay 32.) Also, seeing the Sun against the background of stars, so as to observe its parallax shift, is a bit difficult, although it can actually be done during a solar eclipse. But seeing the Sun and stars at the same time is not the main problem. To get a big parallax effect, you need to make observations from two different places as far apart as possible. Yet even as seen from opposite sides of the Earth, the parallax shift of the Sun (0.005 degrees) would have been beyond the ability of ancient astronomers to observe. The ancients might have observed a solar parallax shift from opposite sides of Earth's *orbit*, but they did not know that the Earth orbits the Sun.

Actually, it was primarily the absence of *stellar* parallax that seemed to imply to the ancients that the Earth was at rest. Not realizing just how far the stars are, the ancients reasoned that if the Earth orbits the Sun, it should be noticeably closer to certain stars on one side of its orbit and to other stars on the other side of its orbit. Failing to detect any stellar parallax, some ancient peoples imagined that the stars were simply dots on a "crystal sphere" that rotated about the stationary Earth, and that the Sun and planets also rotated about the Earth on their own crystal spheres. Although this model of the universe now seems bizarre, it was consistent with ancient observations, which showed no stellar parallax. The lesson here is that you need to be very careful when you measure something to be zero, because you cannot tell if it really is zero or simply too small to be detected, given the limitations of your measuring instruments.

Nowadays, astronomers' instruments are sensitive enough to show that the Earth actually does orbit the Sun, based on stellar parallax. The apparent change in the stars' positions during the year is known as "stellar aberration." If you view stars along a direction perpendicular to the Earth's orbit at the same instant each night, the stars will be found to travel in tiny circles during the course of the year because of the Earth's orbital motion. In order to understand the reason for these apparent stellar motions, think of light from the stars as vertically descending raindrops that you are trying to catch in a tube (the telescope) as you run around in a circle (orbiting the Sun). If you want the raindrops not to hit the tube walls as they descend vertically, you need to tilt the tube forward in the direction you are moving. For example, if you were to move to the right at $\frac{1}{1,100}$ the speed of light, it would need to be tilted at $\frac{1}{1,100}$ radians from the vertical. During one orbit around the Sun you would need to tilt the tube around a cone of directions (see the cartoon for essay 116).

In the actual case of starlight rather than raindrops, no attempt is made to vary the tilt of the telescope during the Earth's orbit, and the stars overhead are found to travel in small circles during the year. The size of these circles can reveal the Earth's orbital speed: given observed stellar motions of $\frac{1}{1,100}$ radians, we conclude that our orbital speed is $\frac{1}{1,100}$ the speed of light. In other words, in the one year it takes the Earth to complete an orbit, Earth must travel $\frac{1}{1,100}$ light-years, or 50 light-minutes. This value for the circumference of Earth's orbit implies that the orbit radius, or its distance from the Sun, must be 8 light-minutes (150 million kilometers). (To say the Sun is a distance of 8 light-minutes means, in effect, that we see the Sun as it was 8 minutes ago.)

FIGURE 55. *Vladimir was unclear how much time he had for a quick bite. The Sun was just beginning to rise, but that meant it actually rose eight minutes ago.*

An alternative way to find the distance to the Sun—one of the first methods used—is based on the rare crossings of Venus across the disk of the Sun, as seen from two widely separated points on Earth. The different times at which Venus just begins to cross the Sun's disk at the two locations can be used to calculate the difference between the orbital speeds of Earth and Venus, and hence the distance to the Sun, assuming that the distance to Venus has been found by parallax. Then, once the distance to the Sun is known, you can easily find its size based on the apparent visual size of its disk. (You should NOT try to observe the Sun by eye or through any ordinary optical device, including dark glasses—it could be the last thing you ever see!)

43. How Large Are Planetary Orbits?

Twinkle, twinkle little planet.
How I wonder why you cannot.

THE NEXT TIME you spot what appears to be a bright star that doesn't twinkle, the chances are that you are looking at a planet. Stars twinkle because the light from them takes slightly different paths through the Earth's distorting atmosphere to reach our eyes. Sometimes the light taking different paths interferes constructively and sometimes destructively, as atmospheric conditions momentarily change. Hence the stars appear to change brightness at random, or twinkle. But planets, being much nearer than stars, appear as tiny disks rather than points. Consequently, the nature of the interference (constructive or destructive) differs, depending on what point on the disk the light originates from. The net result is to average out the interference pattern over the disk. Although a sharp distinction exists between stars, which are self-luminous bodies powered by nuclear reactions, and planets, which shine only by reflected light, this distinction produces few obvious differences to the naked eye. Aside from a lack of twinkle, the primary observable difference is that the planets change their positions relative to the stars from night to night as they orbit the Sun, which accounts for the term *planet*, from the Greek for "wanderer." Since the ancients thought all celestial bodies orbited the Earth, the motion of the wanderers among the stars was highly perplexing to them.

The primary method for determining the distances to the planets is the parallax technique. One difficulty in applying the parallax method is that the distance to any given planet changes continuously as the planet and Earth both orbit the Sun at different speeds. What you would measure in mapping out a planetary orbit is actually the orbit's size *relative* to the size of the Earth's orbit. The absolute size of planetary orbits can then be found, provided the Earth-Sun distance is known.

Observing planetary distances using parallax is beyond the ability of most casual observers, but there is one simple naked-eye observation that demonstrates changing planetary distances from Earth, namely their *brightness*. In particular, Venus—the brightest starlike object in the night sky—changes its brightness noticeably as its distance from us varies. Unfortunately, you cannot use the simple inverse square distance rule of brightness (given in the next essay) to account for Venus's variation in brightness, because, like the Moon, Venus goes through phases, which also affect its apparent brightness.[1] Venus's brightness may account for its being mistaken for a UFO more often than any other object. Most (terrestrial?) astronomers, incidentally, take a dim view of the idea that UFOs are associated with extraterrestrial beings, despite acknowledging the possibility of other intelligent civilizations in the universe.

FIGURE 56. *"That's no UFO, you snorkhead—that's just Venus."*

Another method for finding planetary orbit sizes was originally discovered by Johannes Kepler. By examining the data recorded on planetary orbits, Kepler found that the *square* of a planet's period (the time for one orbit) is proportional to the *cube* of its average orbit radius. This law must also apply to undiscovered planets—if there are any. For example, suppose Professor Gluesniffer were to report that he observed a new planet X with a period of 10 years and a distance from the Sun that is 4 times that of Earth. We could immediately infer that Gluesniffer was a crackpot based on Kepler's law, since 4 cubed (64) does not equal 10 squared (100). Kepler's law, which is a direct consequence of the inverse square nature of gravity, can be used to find the orbit sizes of distant planets from their periods much more accurately than when the orbits are measured from parallax. The law also applies to any set of bodies in orbit about another central body to which they are all bound by gravitation.

1. Venus's phases and brightness variations during its orbit offer clear evidence that Venus orbits the Sun. But they do not show that the Earth also orbits the Sun, because the same phases would be seen if Venus (and other planets) orbited the Sun which in turn orbited a stationary Earth. It is the observation of stellar aberration (see essays 42 and 116) that definitively refutes the geocentric theory.

44. How Far Is That Candle?

LET'S CONSIDER an illuminating experiment. Suppose you observe a distant candle outdoors on a dark night. Now suppose you place four lit candles held together by a rubber band still farther away. How far do you think you need to place the "candle quartet" so that it appears just as bright as the lone candle? The candle quartet should be placed *twice* as far away as the lone candle to appear equally bright. This prediction is a direct consequence of the inverse square law for illumination. According to this law, if you double the distance to a candle, it will appear one-quarter as bright, so you will need four candles at the greater distance to have the same apparent brightness as one candle at the closer distance. If you feel inclined to carry out this experiment, just be sure that the candle quartet is far enough away so that the four candles appear as one. An alternative way of doing the experiment is to use photography. Take a picture of a distant candle on a dark night, and then take a picture of the candle when its distance is doubled. You should find that you need to quadruple the exposure time in the latter case for the two images to appear the same.

The reason the inverse square law applies to illumination is easy to understand. Light from a candle spreads out in all directions. At any particular distance, it illuminates an imaginary sphere centered on the candle. The area of this imaginary sphere is proportional to the square of its radius—your distance from the candle. So the fraction of that area occupied by the pupil of your eye, through which light from the candle enters, is *inversely* proportional to the square of the distance. For example, if at a distance of 10 meters from a candle, one-millionth of the light going in all directions happens to enter the pupil of your eye, then at 20 meters only one-quarter as much light will enter your eye.

You probably wouldn't actually want to use the inverse square law to find the distance to a candle,

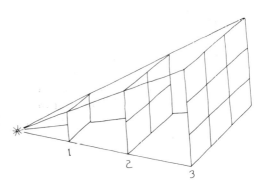

FIGURE 57. *Inverse Square Law for Illumination*
As the distance to a point source increases, light from the source spreads out over an area proportional to the square of the distance. The amount of light reaching one of the small squares at the distances labeled 2 and 3 is, therefore, ¹/₄ and ¹/₉ the amount of light passing through the area located at 1.

79

since much better methods are available—like tape measures! But the same method outlined here works just as well when applied to situations for which better methods don't exist, such as when you want to measure the distance to a galaxy. One pitfall in using the inverse square law to judge distances (for either

candles or galaxies) is that you will be in error if absorption of the light occurs. For example, if you try to measure the distance to a candle based on its apparent brightness, on a smoggy night your estimates of its distance will be systematically too large if you assume the candle's faintness is due to its great distance rather than light absorption. Obviously, in order to use the inverse square law to measure distances of celestial objects, such as stars or galaxies, you need to know the actual brightness of the object—which is a lot easier to know for candles than for stars and galaxies.

FIGURE 58. *The moth, off by a factor of 4 in its estimate of the candle's brightness, was off by a factor of 2 in estimating distance—with fatal consequences.*

One final point to keep in mind when using the inverse square law to judge distances is that the relationship applies to sources whose size is small compared with their distance. Actually, the inverse square law can be applied to large luminous spheres as well, provided that you measure your distance from the center of the sphere. Thus, the inverse square law applies to both distant candles and stars, as well as nearby spherical light fixtures. But it would not apply to a nonspherical lamp shade or a large fluorescent fixture unless you were very far away compared with the size of the lamp.

45.   How Far Are the Stars?

ARE THE brightest stars in the sky intrinsically brighter than others, or are they just closer? For example, our Sun, the nearest star, appears much brighter than any other star simply because it is much closer.

At typical stellar distances, the Sun would appear to be a fairly dim star. If we were to observe a star known to have an intrinsic brightness equal to the Sun, we could easily tell its distance by using the inverse square law: just calculate how far we would have to be from the Sun for it to look as faint as the star. Clearly, we cannot use this simple technique to judge the distances of stars, unless we have a way to know their intrinsic brightness. And unfortunately, stars do have very different intrinsic brightnesses, so if you see one star that appears brighter than another, you may have no idea whether it is intrinsically brighter or merely closer.

The most reliable method for finding the distance to the nearer stars is—you guessed it—parallax. Basically, you measure the star's shift in position relative to more distant stars during the Earth's orbit about the Sun. Parallax shifts are, in fact, used as a direct measure of distance: the parsec is a unit of distance at which an object has a parallax of 2 seconds of arc ($\frac{1}{1,800}$ of a degree) when viewed from Earth at opposite sides of its orbit. One parsec is equivalent to 30.9 trillion kilometers or 3.26 light-years—a light-year being the distance light travels in one year. Present-day Earth-based telescopes are capable of measuring parallax shifts as small as 0.1 seconds of arc, which is equivalent to the width of a human hair seen at a distance of a quarter of a mile! Stars that exhibit parallax shifts greater than 0.1 seconds of arc must be closer than 20 parsecs, since the amount of parallax shift is *inversely* proportional to a star's distance.

Of the approximately 2,000 stars closer than 20 parsecs, the nearest is Alpha Centauri, whose 4.2 light-year distance makes it roughly 300,000 times farther away than the Sun. One way of envisioning the enormous distances between stars (compared with their size) is through a scale model. If stars were represented by grains of sand, their average separation would be 50 kilometers! On this basis, it is easy to see why stars virtually never collide in our region of the galaxy. In fact, even when two

FIGURE 59. *When his ship crashed through the crystal sphere with dots painted on it surrounding Earth, Captain Jones knew something was terribly wrong.*

galaxies "collide," they pass through each other. Even with billions of stars in each galaxy, collisions are extremely rare. If the spacing between atoms in solid matter were proportionally the same as for stars in a galaxy, "solid" matter would likewise be interpenetrable, and you could fit quite a few cars in the same parking space.

Given that the parallax method can be used only to find the distances of stars closer than 20 parsecs, you might wonder how the distances of stars beyond 20 parsecs are found. One method makes use of the inverse square law, which as noted can be used provided we know the star's intrinsic brightness.[1] In the case, for example, of two stars having the same intrinsic brightness, if one star *appears* a hundred times brighter than another, it must be ten times closer.[2] As it turns out, astronomers have found that the brightest stars in the sky are usually intrinsically bright, rather than merely close.

46.   How Far Do Stars Move in One Second?

DO YOU HAVE trouble connecting the dots in the night sky to see all the hunters, bears, lions, and scales that some ancients apparently saw? You are certainly not alone. But the fact that these constellations, familiar to *some* people, have not changed their shape over centuries tells us something about the distances to the stars. Astronomers have found that nearby stars move at a brisk speed of typically 30 kilometers per second in random directions. The stars appear to have fixed relative positions only because of their enormous distances. If the stars did not appear to maintain their relative positions, mankind would not have distinguished the stars from the planets, and we would not recognize familiar constellations. Actually though, the shapes of the constellations *do* change over many thousands of years due to the stars' motions. The motion of a star is usually described in terms of its speed along our line of sight (the *radial* velocity), and its speed at right angles to our line of sight (the *tangential* velocity). These two components of a star's motion are found by completely different methods. To find a star's tangential velocity, you need to know the star's distance and observe its angular motion over some period of time, which may be many years if you want to see an appreciable movement for distant stars.[1] The tangential velocity will be directly proportional to the distance of a star, in the same way that the speed of the tip of the minute hand of a clock is proportional to

1. One method for finding a star's intrinsic brightness is to make use of an empirical regularity between the star's intrinsic brightness and the relative intensity and shape of various lines in the stars' spectrum. This regularity is established based on observations of those stars whose intrinsic brightness can be inferred from their distance determined by parallax.

2. But this estimate will be in error if an appreciable amount of interstellar dust is present (see essay 47).

---

1. In practice, we can measure a star's tangential velocity only relative to other objects, which normally means relative to the "fixed" background of more distant stars.

the length of the hand. Thus, if two stars are seen to move through the same angle in a given time, and one is twice as far away, it must have twice the tangential velocity.

The radial velocity of stars is found using the so-called Doppler shift, which is the observed shift in the frequency of waves occurring as a result of motion.[2] The change in pitch of a police siren as it goes past you is a result of the Doppler shift in sound waves. For light waves, a shift in frequency means a shift in color, the direction of the shift being directly linked to the direction of motion. For example, the observed frequency of light waves from a star moving toward us at 10 percent the speed of light is increased ("blueshifted") by 10 percent, while light from a star moving away at this speed would be "redshifted" by 10 percent. A 10 percent increase in frequency would make a red star appear green. (The same Doppler shift is used by police radar guns to measure the speed of approaching cars by bouncing radar waves off them. Obviously, since cars travel at a tiny fraction of the speed of light, the frequency shift is exceedingly small for police radar.)

The reason the Doppler shift occurs is easy to understand. When you approach a source of waves, more waves reach you in one second, so the wave frequency is higher. But if you go away from the source, fewer waves reach you in one second, and the frequency is lower. In the case of light or radar waves, the shift in frequency is exactly the same whether you approach the source of waves or it approaches you. Of course, in order to measure any shift in frequency at all, we need to know what the frequency of light was in the absence of motion. How can that be known? It appears that stars are made of the same elements found on Earth, although in different abundances. We know this because, when the light from a heated gas of any element is separated into its constituent frequencies (by passing through a prism,

FIGURE 60. *Based on her successful Doppler effect defense, Carla was found not guilty of running a red light and instead was found guilty of speeding and fined eight trillion dollars!*

for example), you see a characteristic spectrum of lines that serves as a "fingerprint" of the element. When we observe stars, we see the same spectral patterns as on Earth, but often with all spectral lines slightly shifted in frequency. We can deduce the star's radial velocity from the size of the shift. You can observe the

2. Remember that the velocity of light is not affected by any motion of the source; only the frequency is shifted.

frequency spectrum of a single element yourself by looking at a mercury-, neon-, or sodium-vapor streetlight through a prism, or even better by looking at the streetlight's reflection off a compact disc. But you shouldn't expect to see any shift in color while approaching the light, unless you are a *really* fast walker![3]

47.　How Empty Is Space?

AT ONE TIME, astronomers mistakenly believed the space between the stars to be completely empty. Clearly, there cannot be much gas or dust in space, because we are able to see many stars unobscured. On the other hand, very distant stars *are* obscured by gas and dust. In fact, it was precisely due to that obscuration that astronomers originally falsely concluded that we were at the center of the galaxy, because they mistook the portion of the galaxy we can see in each direction to be all there is. How can we tell just how much matter (gas and dust) exists in the space between us and the stars we see?

One way to measure interstellar dust and gas is based on the amount of light received from a star of known intrinsic brightness at a known distance. From details of a star's spectrum, we can find its intrinsic brightness, and then based on the inverse square law, we can find out what its apparent brightness would be if there were no obscuring dust between the star and us. If the star, for example, appears only half as bright as it should be at that distance, we can easily estimate how much dust would cause a reduction of its brightness by half.

FIGURE 61. *The incredible emptiness of space beckoned to the pioneers of the solid waste disposal industry.*

In addition to being dimmed by absorption, the light from distant stars is also reddened. This apparent reddening is due to the fact that shorter wavelengths

---

3. That's a joke of course. To see any shift in color, you would have to approach the source at an appreciable fraction of the speed of light.

are absorbed or scattered by interstellar gases and dust more than longer wavelengths, just as occurs in the Earth's atmosphere. For the same reason, the setting Sun appears redder than the Sun overhead, since in the latter case the light travels through much less atmospheric gas and dust.

Another method for finding out the amount of gas in interstellar space is to look for telltale emissions of light which occur when the gas is heated by nearby hot stars. This heating causes the gas to glow and emit light at radio wavelengths in a narrow range of wavelengths, called bright spectral lines. For example, the 21-centimeter wavelength line emitted by heated hydrogen gas is particularly useful for mapping concentrations of hydrogen, since this wavelength is not obscured by dust. Based on observations of the brightness of the 21-centimeter spectral line, astronomers have concluded that the space between the stars contains an average of only one hydrogen atom per 3 cubic meters in the central plane of the galaxy. To get a feeling for what such an incredibly dilute concentration means, consider that the air you breath has 2,000 trillion trillion (2×10^{27}) times more molecules per unit volume. Nevertheless, given the vastness of space, even the extremely dilute concentrations of gas and dust in the galaxy contain enormous numbers of atoms. In fact, all the stars that continue to form in our galaxy and other galaxies pull in their hydrogen from vast interstellar "clouds" of hydrogen gas.

48. How Big Are Stars?

UNLIKE THE much nearer planets, stars appear merely as points of light through ordinary telescopes. Surprisingly, even without seeing a circular disk, it is possible to figure out the radius of a star using a method that is analogous to a simple technique for finding the area of a lawn you cannot see. Suppose you weigh the grass clippings gathered by someone who has just mowed the lawn, and also the clippings from 1 square meter of the lawn chosen at random. The area of the lawn in square meters must obviously just equal the ratio of the weights of these two sets of clippings. For example, if the clippings from the entire lawn weigh 100 times the clippings from 1 square meter, the lawn area has to be 100 square meters.

Applying a similar technique to a star, we first find its total light output (from its apparent brightness and measured distance), and then find its light output per square meter (from its temperature, which can be inferred from its color). The ratio of these two numbers tells us the area of the star, and hence its radius. In case you are wondering how a star's temperature is used to find its light output per square meter, just think of the burner on an electric stove. The hotter the burner gets, the more light emitted per square inch (or meter) of burner. In fact, it can be shown that glowing objects such as electric burners or stars emit an amount of light per unit area that is proportional to the fourth power of the absolute temperature. According to this "fourth-power law," if the temperature of a star were doubled, for example, it would emit $2^4 = 16$ times as much light from each square meter of surface. Thus, using the "lawn clipping" method, it is possible to find the size of any star.[1]

The preceding method for finding the radius of a star from its temperature and intrinsic brightness is rather indirect, because we perceive the star only as a point using a conventional telescope. A new type of telescope that relies on a technique known as "aperture synthesis" gives a more direct method for finding the size of stars. The idea is to combine the light waves reaching many pairs of separated detectors, and electronically create a collection of interference patterns from each such combination. If the distances between detectors are known very accurately, to a fraction of the wavelength of light, the exact nature of the interference for all pairs of detectors can be related to the size and shape of the object emitting the light, allowing a computer to produce an artificial image of the star. One surprising result from the aperture synthesis method is that not all stars are spherical. Mira, a star in its red giant stage (which our Sun should reach in another 5 billion years) is distinctly oblong in shape, one dimension being 10 percent longer than the other. You can find Mira in the constellation Cetus, but don't expect to see an oblong! In fact you will be lucky even to locate the star, because Mira (from the Latin for "wonderful") undergoes drastic changes in

FIGURE 62. *Omar, the first astronomer actually to observe the shape of a star through a telescope, was reluctant to tell the emir what he had seen.*

1. For example, suppose we deduce that a star has an intrinsic brightness 16 times that of the Sun, based on its measured distance and its apparent brightness. Also, suppose we judge the star's temperature to be half that of the Sun, based on its color. How could we find the star's radius from these two facts? Using the fourth-power law, we know that if the star's temperature is half that of the Sun, then the light *per unit area* emitted by the star must be only $\frac{1}{2}^4 = \frac{1}{16}$ that of the Sun. But if each square meter is emitting only $\frac{1}{16}$ as much light as the Sun, the star must have 256 times as much area for its total light output to be 16 times that of the Sun. A star whose area is 256 times that of the Sun has a radius 16 times the Sun's radius, since a sphere's area is proportional to the square of its radius.

brightness over the course of a six-week period, and is not visible to the naked eye for much of that time.

49. How Large Is Our Galaxy?

A MAJOR REASON it is difficult to find the size and shape of our galaxy is that we see it from the inside, and we cannot see very far, at least in visible light, in those directions lying in the galactic plane. Just imagine trying to tell the size and shape of a forest from inside it, with trees blocking your vision in all directions. Before this century, in attempting to map out the universe, astronomers incorrectly put us at the center, because the farthest stars that could be seen in the plane of the Milky Way—which they took to be a starry structure surrouding the Earth—were roughly equally distant in all directions. Moreover, nineteenth-century astronomers had no conclusive evidence for the existence of any other galaxies. Of course, what we now know to be other galaxies had been observed through telescopes as small fuzzy patches, but who could be sure that they weren't simply nearby clouds ("nebulae") of glowing gas, rather than the distant "island universes" of billions of stars that we now know them to be?

A major clue to the existence and shape of our galaxy is that faint band of light known as the Milky Way, which can be seen stretching across the sky on moonless nights in those parts of the country lacking smog or light pollution. Although the Milky Way may appear to the naked eye as a band of glowing dust, telescopes can easily resolve it into numerous stars. The Milky Way completely encircles us, because it is an edge view of our disk-shaped galaxy as seen from inside. The stars we see in other directions are much less numerous, because the thickness of the galactic disk is much less than its diameter. If the galaxy were a solid object, it would resemble a fried egg sunny-side(!) up—better make that a fried egg "over easy" for the sake of symmetry.

Given the important clue that the Milky Way consists of a vast number of distant stars apparently concentrated into some kind of structure, you would think that someone might have figured out earlier that we live in a disk-shaped galaxy. But one major problem was that nothing resembling a galactic center (the "egg yolk") had been seen, due to the obscuring dust in the plane of the galaxy. The breakthrough came in 1915 when Harlow Shapley studied the distribution of huge spherical-shaped aggregations of stars known as globular clusters. These clusters, each containing a few hundred thousand stars, were found to be distributed in three dimensions, centered on a point lying far away from us in the plane of the Milky Way. In other words, the globular clusters formed a spherical halo about a point that was then correctly identified as the galactic center.

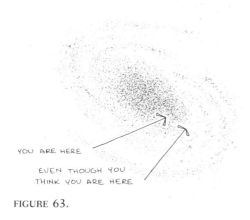

YOU ARE HERE

EVEN THOUGH YOU
THINK YOU ARE HERE

FIGURE 63.

Since the discovery of our galaxy, now referred to as the Milky Way galaxy, much has been learned about its structure. Much of this knowledge has been gleaned by observing the galaxy in wavelengths such as infrared that are not obscured by dust. By mapping out the galaxy to distances much greater than before, we know that we are in the outskirts, about a third of the way in from the edge in one of the many spiral arms making up the disk. These spiral arms represent regions of the disk where star formation appears to be concentrated. The dimensions of the galaxy are about 1 million light-years in diameter by about 100,000 light-years thick, and it contains an estimated 100 billion stars.

50. How Far Are Other Galaxies?

ON A CLEAR moonless night, you may be able to spot a small fuzzy patch in the constellation Andromeda. What you would be looking at is the Andromeda galaxy—the most distant object that can be seen with the naked eye. Light reaching us from Andromeda started its journey 2.3 million years ago, when our apelike ancestors roamed the Earth. But it was not until the twentieth century that powerful enough telescopes existed to make out individual stars in other galaxies, and reveal their true nature. Before making this crucial observation, astronomers were unable to distinguish galaxies from nebulae—much nearer clouds of glowing gas and dust in our own galaxy. Unfortunately, the distances to other galaxies are much too great to measure using parallax. The primary method for finding galactic distances is to identify some object whose intrinsic or true brightness is known—in effect a "standard candle"—and find the distance from the object's apparent brightness, using the inverse square law.

Several types of so-called variable stars, which change their brightness over time, are useful as "standard candles." One relatively rare type of star known as Cepheids changes brightness at a regular rate. Cepheids, named for the constellation in which the first one was seen, pulsate in brightness over a period of days or weeks, so you wouldn't see one literally blinking on and off if you looked at it. By observing the apparent brightness of Cepheids in our own galaxy at measured distances (from parallax), we can determine their intrinsic brightness using the inverse square law. It has been found that the intrinsic brightness of Cepheids is directly correlated with their period—the time for one pulsation. In other words, the brighter a Cepheid, the longer the pulsation period. Astronomers can use Cepheids as "standard candles" because of this relationship between brightness and period. For example, suppose you observe a Cepheid whose period implies an intrinsic brightness one hundred times that of the Sun. If the star in fact appears to be a trillionth the sun's brightness, it would have to be ten million times farther away than the Sun, based on the inverse square law. The Cepheid technique for measuring galactic distances works only for the nearer galaxies, beyond which a brighter "standard candle" is needed. Another type of variable star, which can be used out to much greater distances, is the supernova—the final cataclysmic explosion of a massive star. When a star becomes a supernova, it

briefly shines as bright as all the 100 billion stars in its galaxy. In theory, the brightest of these outbursts can be seen as far away as 8 billion light-years.

Supernovas that can be seen by the naked eye are extremely rare events that typically occur centuries apart. A particularly impressive one occurred in 1054 A.D. The star was so bright that it could be seen for months during the daytime. Interestingly, it was only the Chinese astronomers who recorded the appearance of this "guest star." Apparently, during the "Dark Ages," Europeans were more involved in earthly pursuits. We know that the Chinese astronomers were not deluded, because that supernova created a remnant

FIGURE 64. *Marvin knew how to get the distance to the next galaxy, if only he could convince someone there to light a standard candle.*

(the Crab nebula) that has been dated as originating in an explosion occurring in 1054 A.D.—a date based on the measured rate at which the nebula is expanding.

Astronomers have observed enough supernovas in nearby galaxies (at measured distances) to estimate their intrinsic brightness. When a supernova occurs in a distant galaxy, we can therefore measure its apparent brightness and use the inverse square law to estimate the galaxy's distance. For example, if a supernova in galaxy A appears one hundred times fainter than one in galaxy B at some known distance, galaxy A must be roughly ten times farther away than galaxy B, *assuming* both supernovas have equal intrinsic brightness. The uncertainty in this distance estimate can be considerable, however, because supernovas do vary from one another in their intrinsic brightness.

Some galaxies are so far away that we cannot even make out a supernova within them. If the galaxy is associated with a number of others in a cluster, we can still estimate its distance using the inverse square law. First, we assume that galaxies *apparently* in a distant cluster are in fact about the same distance from us. Then we must assume that galaxies of average apparent brightness in that faraway cluster are much like average nearby galaxies of known intrinsic brightness. In other words, we use nearby galaxies like Andromeda as the "standard candle" for the dimmest reaches of the universe—where our own local standards may not apply.

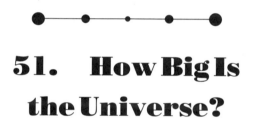

51.   How Big Is the Universe?

IF WE LIVED on a planet that was perpetually cloud-covered, we might conclude that the size of the "observable" universe was rather small. Even though we fortunately do not live on such a world, there is a built-in limit to what we can observe, based on the speeds of recession of distant galaxies. According to a discovery made by Edwin Hubble, the speed with which galaxies move away from us is roughly proportional to their distance. Such a proportionality between galactic distance and speed is just what you would expect if all the matter in the universe flew apart from some small region of space in a gigantic explosion—the *big bang*. In other words, by now—many years later—the galaxies originally moving fastest would have gotten farthest from us, in direct proportion to their original speed.

The size of the observable universe follows from Hubble's law, because at some distance, estimated to be between 13 and 20 billion light-years, galaxies would have to be moving away from us at the speed of light. Since the speed of light is believed to be the limiting speed in the universe, galaxies at that distance can be considered at the "edge" of the universe. One reason for the large uncertainty in the figure of 13 to 20 billion light-years is that it is based on observing the distances and speeds of faraway galaxies—both of which are highly uncertain.

In looking out a distance of 13 to 20 billion light-years, we are actually looking back in time 13 to 20 billion years, since it takes the light from those distant galaxies that many years to reach us. We don't see any galaxies beyond about 98 percent of that distance, probably because at that early age of the universe gravity had not yet caused the necessary collapse of matter to form the stars contained in galaxies. Actually, it is not completely certain that the most distant bright objects (the quasars) are in fact extremely distant. A few astronomers believe that the extreme Doppler shifts, or redshifts, of the quasars (from which we infer extreme velocity and hence extreme distance) are actually explainable in some other way. (See essay 46 for Dopler shifts.) The quasar with the greatest redshift seen to date has spectral lines whose wavelengths are five times longer than would be seen for a stationary source. If this extreme redshift is due to the universal expansion, the quasar would have to be receding from Earth at 98 percent the speed of light, which according to Hubble's law would put it at 98 percent of the way to the "edge" of the observable universe.

You may have noticed something strange about Hubble's law, which refers to the speed of galaxies *away* from us, when, in fact, many galaxies—at least some of the nearer ones—move toward us. The explanation is that the motion of galaxies is partly random, partly determined by their gravitational attractions, and partly associated with the overall expansion of the universe resulting from the big bang. It is only for relatively distant galaxies that the third component of their motion dominates, and among those distant galaxies the proportionality stated by Hubble can be clearly observed.

But Hubble's law has an even stranger aspect to it: why do distant galaxies all move away from *us*, as though we were at the center of the universe? Could the ancients (and some moderns) have been right all along about mankind occupying a privileged place in the cosmos? Well, not really. The fact is that an observer at any point in an expand-

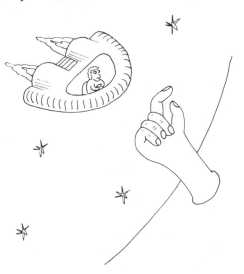

FIGURE 65. *Reaching the edge of the universe, Ted hesitated when he saw the arm beckon him farther.*

ing collection of points will see all the other points moving away. It is believed that even observers riding on galaxies at what we consider the "edge" of the universe would have much the same view of things as we do—that is, they would not perceive themselves at the "edge," and they would see equal numbers of galaxies in all directions. Astronomers account for this hard-to-visualize situation by saying that the big bang was not an expansion of matter into a preexisting space (in which case there would be a real center and edge), but that space itself was created during the big bang. For an analogy, just think of a balloon with many random painted dots on it. As the balloon inflates, a tiny observer residing on any one dot will see all surrounding dots moving away.

Everything in this essay, of course, relates to the size of the "observable" universe. Presumably, you can take the size of the unobservable universe (with all its other dot-covered expanding balloons) to be as big as you want.

52. How Big Are the Bubbles in the Cosmological Milk Shake?

ON A HUMAN scale of distances, the size of a galaxy like our Milky Way, comprising 100 billion suns, represents an unimaginably vast object. But on the scale that cosmologists analyze the universe, a galaxy is a mere speck of matter. Until recently, an article of faith among cosmologists was that on the largest distance scales, the universe was "homogeneous" and "isotropic." In other words, apart from small clusters of galaxies, the average spacing between galaxies was thought to be the same everywhere (homogeneous) and in all directions (isotropic)—much like the distribution of molecules in a glass of milk. But recent observations suggest that the universe is more like a milk shake—mostly empty space, with "point" galaxies making up the surfaces of numerous connected bubbles.

The observations leading to this conclusion are in the form of maps made of the distribution of galaxies. These maps, on which each galaxy appears as a point, were made by selecting a thin strip across the sky and looking at all galaxies in that strip out to distances of 490 million light-years. The distances of galaxies were judged based on their observed redshift (which gives their recession velocity), and then Hubble's law was used to relate velocity to distance. The other coordinate on the map was simply the galaxy's angular position within the thin strip across the sky (using a coordinate system fixed in the plane of our galaxy, rather than one moving with the Sun or Earth).

The astronomers who made the map found that galaxies, instead of appearing as a random collection of dots on their map, formed connected filaments extending over vast distances, with many dot-free regions between the filaments. In order to get more details on this unexpected distribution of galaxies, the researchers proceeded to map out a series of strips across the sky, and found that some of the same structures seen in the first map persisted in the others. One of these structures, nicknamed the Great Wall, shows up on each map as a string of galaxies 550 million light-years long. The Great Wall appears as a string or filament on each map because each map slices through the "wall" in a different plane. When the observed distribution of galaxies is displayed in three dimensions rather than as two-dimensional slices, it appears that the galaxies lie on the surfaces of vast "bubbles"—comprising our "cosmological milk shake." The size of these bubbles is measured in millions of light-years.

Results from other sky surveys reveal that the Great Wall may be only one of many such enormous structures in the universe. In fact, in one survey, it was found that such structures may occur at regular intervals with a spacing of 780 million light-years, a finding that, if confirmed, will be completely unexplainable based on any current cosmological theories. A second huge structure besides the Great Wall has been dubbed the Great Attractor; its center appears 140 million light-years away, in the direction of the Hydra-Centaurus supercluster of galaxies. The Great Attractor was discovered by observing the redshifts of galaxies to find their velocities along that line of sight and independently measuring galactic distances based on their luminosity and spectra. It was found that galaxies nearer to us than 140 million light-years recede faster

FIGURE 66. "Good Lord! There's something climbing over the Great Wall of galaxies! No, never mind, it's just a fly on the lens."

than Hubble's law predicts, and those beyond that point recede slower than predicted. This is exactly what would be found if, superimposed on the overall expansion of the universe, galaxies were falling into a region of space centered at a distance of 140 million light-years—the presumed location of the Great Attractor. Based on the observed departures from Hubble's law, the Great Attractor appears to have a mass of 300,000 times that of our galaxy, and a diameter of 260 million light-years.

The formation of such enormous structures as the Great Wall and the Great Attractor requires that the universe must have contained large-scale nonuniformities (earlier "structures") that gave rise to them, because a completely uniform universe could not evolve into such a lumpy one. In fact, recent observations of the "cosmic background radiation"—a faint glow filling all of space, a remnant of the big bang—shows just such nonuniformities on a distance scale that dwarfs even that of the Great Wall and the Great Attractor. These irregularities consist of slightly hotter and cooler regions. Apparently, not all parts of the cosmological milk shake started out at the same temperature.

53. How Big Is a Fog Droplet?

IF YOU HAVE ever looked at bright streetlights on a foggy night, you may have noticed pretty colored halos or blobs around the lights. These patterns are the result of the interference of light waves that scatter off the fog droplets at particular angles. For example, if light waves for some color interfere constructively when scattering off droplets at a 10-degree angle, you would observe a 10-degree halo of that color centered about the light, because in that case the light scattering off all droplets surrounding the light interferes constructively when you look 10 degrees away from the light. (Ten degrees is equivalent to a diameter twice the size of your fist seen at arm's length.)

The angular size of a halo is proportional to the ratio of the wavelength of light to the diameter of fog droplets, so you can find either the wavelength or the droplet diameters if you know one or the other quantity and observe the angular size of the halo. Notice, incidentally, that since red light has a longer wavelength than blue light, the red must scatter through a

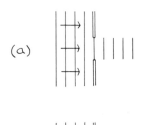

(a)

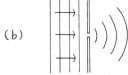

(b)

FIGURE 67. *When waves from a distant source reach an opening in a barrier, they will spread out very little if the size of the opening greatly exceeds the wavelength (a). But, if the opening size is smaller than the wavelength, the waves spread out appreciably (b).*

larger angle than the blue. As a result, the outer edge of halos around white streetlights tends to be red, and the inner edge blue.

You don't need to wait until the next foggy night to see these halos. If you wear glasses, just fog them with your breath, and view a bright streetlight through them in the few seconds before the mist on the glasses evaporates. You will probably see a colored circular halo around the light, and possibly an outer ring around this halo. If you don't wear glasses, you can use any sheet of glass or plastic. Here is how you can find the size of the fog droplets by observing the halo size. I hold a ruler at arm's length, and see what the diameter of the halo is, measured from edge to edge. You can find the average diameter of the fog droplets in nanometers (billionths of a meter) by simply dividing 750 by the halo radius (in meters) that you measure at arm's length. We have assumed here that the wavelength of red light is 750 nanometers, and that your arm length is about 1 meter. Note that because the fog droplet diameter is inversely proportional to the halo diameter, the smaller the droplet size, the larger the halo will be.

In order to understand the origin of the halos from fog droplets, let's consider the closely related problem of light waves that encounter a small circular hole in a barrier. For a hole that is large compared with the wavelength, light waves emerging from all different parts of the hole interfere destructively and cancel one another as they spread out at any particular angle. They interfere constructively only for waves traveling in the original (forward) direction. As a result, the light emerging from the hole does

FIGURE 68. *Perry began to suspect that the absence of the count's reflection in the mirror might not be due to destructive interference.*

not appreciably spread out from the forward direction. This is the situation we usually see in everyday life, which justifies the precept that light "rays" travel in straight lines.

On the other hand, for a small hole whose size is comparable to the wavelength of light, light waves emerging from all parts of the hole interfere constructively even for waves spreading out at angles from the forward direction.[1] As a result,

---

1. The reason that the interference is constructive for small angles is that light waves emerging from all parts of the *small* hole tend to be almost in step unless the angle is large, in which case some waves travel an appreciable fraction of a wavelength more than others, causing them to be out of step, so that they cancel for large enough angles.

the light spreads out after passing through the hole, which causes you to see a halo when looking at a light through the hole. You can observe these halos yourself by making a tiny hole in a piece of aluminum foil with a needle, placing the foil right next to your eye, and viewing a distant unfrosted light bulb through it in a darkened room. The angular size of the halo depends on the ratio of the wavelength of light to the size of the hole, just as in the case of the fog droplets. But the halos you see when looking through these holes will probably be much smaller than those seen for light scattered from og droplets, because the halo size varies inversely with the hole size, and it is difficult to make pinholes as tiny as fog droplets. Both patterns arise from the same basic phenomenon: interference of light waves. Even though in one case you are blocking out a central disk, and in the other you are blocking out everything but a central disk, the resulting halos have the same basic character.

54. What Is the Smallest Object That Can Be Seen?

WE GET MOST of the information about the size, shape, and texture of objects from the light our eyes receive. The outline of an object, its flatness or roundness, and its smoothness or roughness are perceived by the way light scatters off its surface. But owing to the wave nature of light, there is a smallest-size object whose surface features can be seen in this way—the size being about the wavelength of visible light, around a millionth of a meter. This seems perfectly reasonable because we are saying, in effect, that the smallest surface features you can detect are comparable to the size of your probe. For example, if you tried to figure out the detailed shape of an object in a dark room by throwing things at it and somehow detecting what angles they bounced off, you could probe much finer features if you threw marbles than basketballs.[1]

We saw in the previous essay that the degree of spreading out that occurs when light waves encounter an obstacle such as a fog droplet depends on the size of the object relative to the wavelength of light—smaller objects produce a greater degree of spreading out than large ones, and hence the angular size of their halo is

1. We are assuming that the object being probed has a hard, rigid surface whose shape affects the angles at which marbles or basketballs bounce off it.

larger. In other words, we can judge the size of the object based on the amount of light spreading, as we did for the case of fog droplets.

But when the object is much smaller than the wavelength of light (as in the case of, say, air molecules), the spreading out is complete, and all you see is a uniform haze, like the blue sky when sunlight scatters off air molecules in all directions. In this case we get no information about the size (or shape) of the scattering objects, except that they must be smaller than the wavelength of light. These results hold just as well for water waves as they do for light waves, as you can easily verify by the following simple experiment.

Make a wave tank using a large shallow container, such as a food tray, in which you can pour water to a depth of about ¼ inch. Put an object such as a ketchup bottle in the center of the water, and create waves at one end of the tank by moving a ruler back and forth. Observe the pattern of waves that scatter off the ketchup bottle, then

FIGURE 69. *Mark was not able to get much information about the shape of the chair by throwing pillows at it.*

replace it with other objects having a range of sizes and shapes. Based on the preceding discussion, you should find that for the objects with large cross sections, there is a noticeable difference in the appearance of the waves scattered from round and nonround shapes, but for the objects with small cross sections, the scattered wave pattern always looks the same, namely, expanding circular waves. In other words, for objects smaller than the size of the water wavelength, you get no information about the shape of the object from the pattern of scattered waves.

55. How Close Together Are Atoms in Solids?

MANY PEOPLE believe that it is not possible to take a picture of the individual atoms making up a solid. Certainly, no ordinary microscope could show an image of the atoms in a solid, because the wavelength of light is roughly ten thousand times larger than a single atom. But X rays do have a sufficiently small wavelength for this purpose, and the earliest methods for mapping the atomic structure of crystalline solids used this form of electromagnetic radiation. You can think of a three-dimensional crystal as being made up of planes of atoms stacked together. When a beam of X rays passes through a crystal, a fraction of the beam is reflected from the atoms in each plane.

Along certain directions, the X rays reflected from the various crystal planes constructively interfere, and along other directions they destructively interfere. Typically, X rays are recorded using photographic film, so along directions of constructive interference a spot will be produced on the film. The task facing the scientist is to figure out what atomic arrangement has produced the observed pattern of spots on the film. Essentially, she works backward by trying various possible atomic arrangements and spacings, and seeing which if any reproduces the observed spot pattern. The spacing between atoms found from such observations is around 0.1 nanometers, or 4 billionths of an inch.

While the X-ray method for probing the structure of solids is quite useful, it doesn't actually produce an image of individual atoms—something that was long considered impossible, until the discovery of the scanning tunneling microscope. The concept of tunneling refers to the bizarre ability of electrons and other subatomic particles to pass through barriers that they should not be able to penetrate, given their en-

FIGURE 70. *"What do you say we pretend we're electrons and call this tunnel done?"*

ergy. In classical physics, an object either has enough energy to make it through (or over) a barrier or it does not—as in the case of a marble rolling toward the crest of a hill. But in quantum physics we use *probabilities* to describe processes. Even if a marble doesn't have enough energy to make it over the top of a hill, there is still some probability of finding it on the other side—just as though it somehow tunneled through the hill. The probability may be vanishingly small for marbles, but not necessarily for electrons. In the scanning tunneling microscope, an extremely fine metal tip is positioned right on a metal surface and slowly dragged across it. As the tip moves up and down, following the contours of individual atoms, an electrical current between the tip and the surface is measured.

The size of this current depends very sensitively on the height of the tip above an atom, and this height is therefore deduced from the current using the theory of electron tunneling. From the measured current at each point on the surface, a computer can produce a contour map of the surface, which shows individual atoms looking like humps on a surface. More recent descendants of the scanning tuneling microscope have dispensed with the need for measuring tunneling currents. In one such device, the atomic force microscope, a very fine tip is slowly drawn across a surface, and its ups and downs are measured optically by reflecting a laser beam off a mirror attached to the tip.

56.   How Do We Know Atoms Have Nuclei?

DO YOU sometimes feel "all charged up?" Electrical charge is that property of matter responsible for the forces which can easily be observed in simple static electricity demonstrations, such as when you pick up bits of paper with a comb run through your hair, or when those little peanut-shaped pieces of styrofoam used for packing won't come off your fingers. Other examples of static electricity in action can literally make your hair stand on end—if you walk under some very high-voltage power lines, for example. We know there must be two kinds of electrical charge, referred to as positive and negative, in order to account for both repulsion and attraction, and also for the ability of one kind of charge to neutralize the other. On the microscopic level, charge is "quantized," meaning that it is found to exist only in integral multiples of some basic unit, the charge of one electron.[1] Electrons are bound in neutral atoms

1. It was an experiment by Robert Millikan that first demonstrated the quantization of charge. Millikan observed that small electrically charged oil droplets always seemed to

because of the electrical attraction between the negative electrons and the rest of the atom, which is positive. When charge is transferred from one body to another by rubbing, all we are doing is transferring electrons from the atoms of one body to those of the other. The electrons are transferred from the body whose atoms hold its electrons loosely to the body whose atoms hold its electrons more tightly.

The original technique for probing the internal structure of the atom, still in use today, is to shoot a beam of high-speed subatomic particles at a target, and see how the particles scatter. You cannot aim the beam of particles at a single atom, so the next best thing is to shoot the beam at a very thin sheet of material, so as to avoid complications when the incoming particles are scattered by more than one atom. The first experiment of this kind, performed by Ernest Rutherford in 1911, used a beam of positively charged alpha particles, emitted by a radioactive substance, and a target made from a very thin sheet of gold foil.[2]

FIGURE 71. *Ralph lucked out when he held up the piece of tissue paper to shield himself from the machine gun.*

Rutherford observed the directions of the scattered alpha particles passing through the gold foil by seeing tiny flashes of light when the alpha particles hit sheets of scintillating material placed all around the foil. At the time Rutherford performed his experiment, a prevailing view of the atom was that it resembled a raisin pudding, with negatively charged electrons (the raisins) embedded in a ball of positive charge (the pudding). It had been demonstrated earlier that the electrons contained only a tiny fraction of the atom's mass—about 0.05 percent—which fit in well with the pudding model. Based on this model, Rutherford expected that most of the incoming alpha particles would be scattered through very small angles, as a result of the electrical repulsion from the positively charged but insubstantial ball of "pudding." Instead, the shocking result of his experiment was that every so often an alpha particle was scattered nearly backward—a finding that seemed as crazy as a bullet bouncing backward off a sheet of tissue paper. Rutherford realized that the prevailing view of the atom was wrong: the positive charge had to be extremely

carry a multiple of some unit of charge, based on their motion in the vicinity of charged plates.

2. Alpha particles are the same as the nuclei of helium atoms. They are emitted by such radioactive nuclei as uranium and plutonium.

concentrated in a tiny massive nucleus (about a hundred thousandth the size of the atom).

It is easy to see why a tiny massive nucleus can exert a much greater repulsive force on an approaching alpha particle than a large sphere would. The situation is very similar to that of gravity, which like the electrostatic force obeys the inverse square law. If the mass of the Earth, for example, were compressed into a hundred-times-smaller sphere, the force of gravity on its surface would be increased a hundred squared, or ten thousandfold, according to the inverse square law. Likewise, if a nucleus of positive charge were compressed a hundredfold, it would repel an approaching alpha particle that had just made contact with ten thousand times greater force.

57. How Much of Your Body Is Empty Space?

A STRANGE FACT about "solid" matter is that it is mostly empty space. That is because 99.95 percent of the mass of all atoms is contained in their tiny nuclei. In order to estimate how much of your body is empty space, we first need to know the size of an atomic nucleus. The size of an atomic nucleus can be measured using a variation of the technique that led to its discovery, described in the previous essay. Let us suppose (incorrectly) that the tiny massive nucleus has no size at all and is a "point" particle like the electron is believed to be. In that case a positive electron (positron) moving directly toward a nucleus would *always* bounce backward, because no matter how much energy the positron had, it could not overcome the inverse square force of the electrostatic repulsion of the nucleus. That force would grow without limit the closer the positron approached the point-nucleus.

Now imagine a positron moving directly toward a *finite*-size nucleus. In this case a limit exists to the repulsive force between positron and nucleus, which is reached when the positron just makes contact with the spherical nucleus. For a finite-size nucleus, only positrons up to some maximum energy headed directly toward the nucleus will bounce backward. Above that maximum energy, positrons heading directly toward a nucleus will pass right through it and come out on the other side. Clearly, the value of the maximum energy for backward-scattered positrons is *inversely* proportional to the nuclear size, because the smaller the nucleus, the greater the positron energy must be to overcome the repulsion until the positron reaches the nuclear surface.

A possible experiment for finding the size of a nucleus involves counting the tiny fraction of positrons that scatter directly backward from a target. By raising the positron energy sufficiently, we could find some energy above which positrons passed through the nucleus, and the fraction scattered backward would be zero. The idea is similar to a blind man deducing the height of a hill by rolling balls up its slope faster and faster until he finds one that doesn't roll back down. Although the positron experiment just described could do the job, in practice a nuclear size is usually found using beams of electrons instead, and by counting the number of electrons that scatter through different angles.

Electron-scattering measurements rely on the fact that electrons and other elementary particles exhibit wave properties. For example, in an electron microscope, a beam of electrons can produce images having greater resolution than those obtained with a conventional optical microscope, because the electrons behave like waves that have a shorter wavelength than light. To probe the structure of a nucleus, extremely high-energy electrons need to be used for the electrons to have a wavelength comparable to the tiny size of an atomic nucleus.

FIGURE 72. *Phil's painful technique for finding the thickness of the walls of his cell was to see at what minimum speed he would no longer bounce backward.*

When beams of such short-wavelength electrons are incident on nuclei, it is found that constructive and destructive interference occurs at certain scattering angles, which depend on the nuclear size. By observing the number of particles scattering at each angle, we can estimate the nuclear size, just as in essay 53 we estimated the size of fog droplets from the angular size of the halo seen around a streetlight. Experiments show that nuclei have a range of sizes, with the smallest one (hydrogen) having a radius of about 1.4 femtometers (1.4 quadrillionths of a meter).

Experimental determinations of the sizes of various atomic nuclei show that the *volume* of any given nucleus is simply proportional to the number of particles that the nucleus contains. In other words, the density of all nuclei is found to be nearly constant (approximately 400 trillion times the density of water), which is *not* the case for the atoms that contain these nuclei. In atoms, unlike nuclei, most of the volume is simply empty space. If the empty space inside the atoms in your body could be removed, you would stand about 0.02 millimeters tall, a hundred thousandth your present height, and you would be as dense as nuclear matter. Actually, you couldn't "stand" at all, but as if in an Alice-in-Wonderland world, you would instantly fall through the Earth, and eventually come to rest at its center.

58. How Close Together Are Molecules in Air?

LET'S RELATE the topic of this essay to something personal, and ask how many molecules there are likely to be in your next breath of air. Surprisingly, the answer to this question does not depend on the particular mixture of gases that make up air. To understand why, we need to consider how gases chemically react. When hydrogen and oxygen combine to make water, for example, we find that volumes of hydrogen and oxygen vanish in an exact two-to-one ratio. Since two atoms of hydrogen are paired with one oxygen in H_2O, this implies that a cubic meter of either hydrogen or oxygen gas contains the same number of molecules. Similar observations with other gases show that equal volumes of *all* gases at a given temperature and pressure contain the same number of molecules.

As a result, the masses of various gases occupying a given volume will be directly proportional to the masses of the individual molecules. Hydrogen is the lightest gas, so let's suppose we have a volume of hydrogen gas whose mass is exactly 2 grams. We assume the mass to be 2 grams rather than 1, since the hydrogen molecule (H_2) consists of two atoms. In general, we will find that other gases occupying the same volume as 2 grams of hydrogen (22,400 cubic centimeters) will all have masses that are nearly integral numbers of grams: 4 for helium, 28 for nitrogen, 32 for oxygen, and so on. The integral numbers arise because the mass of the gas is the mass of an individual molecule times the same number of molecules for each gas, so the integers tell us the relative masses of different kinds of molecules. On the basis of this scheme, the eighteenth-century scientist Amedeo Avogadro defined the "mole" as the amount of a substance equal to the preceeding integral values—for example, a mole of hydrogen molecules has a mass of 2 grams, a mole of helium atoms 4 grams, and so on. While Avogadro understood that one mole of any gas contains the same number of molecules—a number now known as Avogadro's number, N_0—he had no idea what the value of "his" number was.[1] In fact, it was not until the early years of the twentieth century that a value for N_0 was found, and the reality of the atomic nature of matter firmly established.

One technique for finding N_0 is based on the observation, first made by the nineteenth-century botanist Robert Brown, that tiny particles such as pollen grains suspended in a liquid undergo a continual random motion. Although Brown didn't realize the source of this random "Brownian motion," it was later explained by Einstein as being due to random buffeting by unseen impacts from the molecules of the fluid. To understand the molecular explanation of Brownian motion, picture a large raft (the pollen grain) floating in perfectly still water being continually nudged by unseen fish (the molecules). These random impacts would, over the course of time, cause the raft to move from its original position and follow a pattern known as a random walk (see essay 26). The effect of this random motion is such that on average, the raft tends over time to move farther and farther from its original position (much as a staggering drunk starting at a lamppost, on average, moves farther and farther from the post). From careful measurements of many of these random walks of pollen grains, you can deduce the number of bombarding molecules per mole (18 grams) of water—that is, Avogadro's number.

One mole of a gas, by definition, contains the same number of atoms as one mole of a liquid, but its volume is much larger. As we mentioned earlier, under standard conditions of temperature and pressure (zero degrees centigrade and one atmosphere pressure), a mole of *any* gas occupies a volume of 22,400 cubic centimeters. Now, Avogadro's number has been found to be 600 billion trillion (6 with 23 zeros after it, or 6×10^{23}), so your next breath of about a twentieth this volume must have around 3×10^{22} air molecules. Finding the average distance between molecules is easy, once we know the number of molecules in a given volume of air. If 3×10^{22} molecules occupy the 1,000 cubic centimeters of your next breath, then on average, a volume of about 33×10^{-21} cubic centimeters contains one molecule. Think of each molecule of air sitting at the center of a cube of this volume. The side of the cube—about 3×10^{-7} centime-

FIGURE 73. *When called on in class, young Avogadro never did know his number.*

1. Because 2 grams of hydrogen contains N_0 molecules, each hydrogen molecule has a mass of $2/N_0$ grams, and each atom has half that mass.

ters, roughly a ten-millionth of an inch—is the average distance between molecules.

59.   On a Clear Day Could You See Forever?

IN TODAY'S urban society, visibility is often limited by smog or other pollutants. But would air be completely transparent if all such pollutants were absent? If air were absolutely transparent, light passing through it would have to be unaffected. However, the fact that the daytime sky is blue, not black as on the airless Moon, means that a fraction of sunlight is scattered by the molecules of the atmosphere, with blue light scattered the most. In other words, some fraction of the light from the Sun is removed when it is scattered in all directions by air molecules. Unlike clouds, however, which may completely obscure the Sun from view, the atmosphere is not thick enough to obscure celestial bodies, so the Earth's 10-kilometer-thick blanket of air is not enough to absorb the bulk of the light from the Sun. The thickness of air that would reduce a light beam to half its original intensity is called a "mean free path."

The British physicist Lord Rayleigh was the first to prove, using the laws of electromagnetism, that the mean free path for light in pure air at standard temperature and pressure is about 44 kilometers. Evidently, light passing through a distance equal to 2 mean free paths would have its intensity reduced by a factor of $\frac{1}{2} \times \frac{1}{2} = \frac{1}{4}$, and for N mean free paths it would be reduced by a factor of $\frac{1}{2}^N$. Rayleigh found a simple connection between the mean free path of light in air and the number of air molecules per unit volume: the two quantities are reciprocally related, because if you double the number of air molecules per unit volume, light needs to travel only half as far to encounter the same number of air molecules.

Actually, Rayleigh found that the mean free path is not the same for all kinds of light, but that it varies with the wavelength—44 kilometers being the mean free path for yellow light. Rayleigh proved that longer wavelengths have longer mean free paths. In other words, red light has a longer mean free path than yellow, and is absorbed less in passing through a given air thickness, with the opposite being true of blue light. As we shall see, these facts explain the apparent colors of the Sun and sky.

When the Sun is directly overhead, it appears yellow—its actual color—

because the 10-kilometer thickness of the Earth's atmosphere is much less than the mean free path for all wavelengths, and so all wavelengths are nearly undiminished in reaching us. However, the setting Sun is seen through a much greater thickness of the Earth's atmosphere. It therefore appears reddish, because more light is removed at short wavelengths than long ones. In other words, because blue light has the shortest mean free path, the blue wavelengths are preferentially removed from sunlight more than longer wavelengths. This blue light is scattered in all directions, which is why the clear sky appears blue. A very distant mountain also appears blue for the same reason, because some of the light that reaches you when you look toward the mountain is actually the blue component of sunlight being scattered from air molecules between you and the mountain. The fact that the size of air molecules is closer to the wavelength of blue light than red light is what accounts for the greater scattering of blue light (see essay 53). On very rare occasions, however, the air may contain many particles larger than air molecules whose size causes red light to be scattered more than blue light. At such times the Moon, for example, may appear blue, because blue light from it is more likely to reach our eyes. Now you know where the phrase "once in a blue moon" comes from.

FIGURE 74. *The budding urban scientist asks, "Daddy, why is the sky brown?"*

60. How Big Are Electron Orbits in Atoms?

THE IDEA OF the atom as a kind of miniature solar system, with electrons orbiting the nucleus much as planets orbit the Sun, has great intuitive appeal.[1] One major problem with this model is that according to classical physics, an orbiting electric charge should radiate energy, just as electric charges moving up and down an antenna do. Orbiting electrons, as a result of their energy loss, should then quickly spiral inward to the nucleus. According to classical physics, all atoms should be unstable!

Niels Bohr proposed a solution to the instability problem in 1913 by suggesting that perhaps electrons could exist inside atoms only in certain stable orbits, from which no energy would be radiated. One way of explaining these allowed orbits, although *not* the one Bohr proposed, uses the fact that electrons, like all other particles, are now known to have wave properties.

An interesting fact about waves is that, when confined, they reflect back and forth and tend to cancel themselves out except for certain patterns or "modes." For example, a guitar string fixed at both ends can vibrate only in certain modes, all of which must have some integer number of half-wavelengths just equal to the length of the string (see the diagram). In general, when you pluck the guitar string, harmonic frequencies corresponding to a number of these vibration modes are simultaneously heard, while nonharmonic frequencies cancel out at the waves ripple along the string. An electron in an atom is analogous to a "circular" guitar

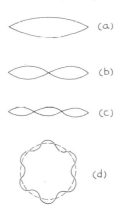

FIGURE 75. *Harmonic waves on a guitar string*
The length of the string equals one half-wavelength in (a), two half-wavelengths in (b), and three half-wavelengths in (c).
Harmonic waves in a circle
Twelve half-wavelengths fit around circumference in (d).

1. As a boy, I thought the atomic solar systems might be inhabited with miniature people made from even tinier atoms, leading to an infinite regress.

string. In this case, the allowed wave patterns correspond to some integer number of electron wavelengths exactly fitting around a circle—a condition that basically reproduces Bohr's allowed orbits, the smallest of which has a radius of 0.05 nanometers, or 0.05 billionths of a meter.

Bohr's model of electron "orbits" is no longer the way we picture atoms. Clearly, if electrons are to be understood as waves, the patterns cannot be one-dimensional, like waves on a guitar string, but rather they need to be represented three-dimensionally, like sound waves. The allowed wave patterns in an atom are therefore more analogous to the sound waves inside a musical instrument, or perhaps the microwaves inside your microwave oven. In such containers, the microwave (or sound) intensity varies in some well-defined way from point to point throughout the space of the enclosure. The wave patterns in a microwave oven account for the fact that at some points in the oven food does not cook very well, because the pattern has a "node" there—a point where waves reflecting from various directions cancel each other out, and the microwave intensity is zero.

But what exactly is the meaning of the wave patterns associated with an electron in an atom? According to quantum theory, the strength of the wave (actually its absolute value squared) gives the relative probability of finding the electron at various places in the atom. In this view, we no longer can consider an electron as following distinct orbits, but rather as being distributed throughout a region of space like a cloud, whose density gives the probability of the electron being found at different points. Using quantum mechanics, we can determine not only what electron wave patterns are allowed, but the probability of an atom jumping from one wave pattern to another. Such jumps accompany the emission or absorption of a photon—an elementary "particle" of light—by the atom. Absorption of a photon causes the atom to go from a lower energy pattern to a higher one, and emission causes the reverse process.

FIGURE 76. *Before repairing your car, quantum mechanics only quote you probability estimates.*

A strange aspect of quantum mechanics is that the precise time of a particular atomic transition is completely unpredictable. In other words, even though the theory predicts the probability or likelihood of a photon being emitted or absorbed, it cannot predict *when* it will occur.

61. How Far Could an Object Coast?

IF YOU HAVE ever driven a car on ice or skidded on an oil slick, you may be acquainted with the laws of low-friction physics. From such everyday experiences, you are probably aware that the smoother a surface is, the farther objects can slide before coming to rest. On a perfectly smooth surface, objects would slide forever given an initial push. Normally, we think of ice as being an especially low-friction surface, but you can find examples of much smoother surfaces by floating an object on a cushion of air, for example, which is done with certain toys. Generally, rolling objects tend to slow down much less than sliding ones, but objects require a certain amount of friction in order to roll, as you may have learned while trying to get a car moving on a sheet of ice.

As explained by Isaac Newton, all matter at rest tends to stay at rest, and matter in motion tends to maintain its motion at constant speed in a straight line, unless some outside force acts on it. We call this property of matter *inertia* or mass. Inertia is not an explanation of the tendency of matter to maintain its motion, but merely a name for the property. The greater an object's inertia, the more it resists having its velocity changed, or more specifically, the greater the force required to change its velocity in a given time interval.

One of the most common misunderstandings people have about motion is the false belief that a force is required to maintain motion at constant velocity. That misconception is probably based on the fact that in everyday life we often find situations where a force *is* necessary to keep an object—a row boat, say—moving at constant

FIGURE 77. *The crew was surprised that their U.S.-made space ship got 100 trillion miles per gallon.*

speed, but that is only because friction is present. In such situations the force you apply is equal and opposite to the force of friction, so that the *net* force on the object is zero—assuming the object is moving at constant speed in a straight line.

Nonzero net forces are present only when either the speed or the direction of an object is changing during its motion—that is, when the object *accelerates*.

The ultimate illustration of matter's tendency to maintain its motion is in the frictionless environment of outer space. If you have seen movies of astronauts in their space capsules or on space walks, you probably have noticed that once astronauts are in motion, they maintain that motion without expenditure of effort. As another example, the engines on a spacecraft need to be fired only during lift-off or during course corrections. Once the Earth and solar system have been left behind, the ship simply coasts through space all by itself. The ship could literally travel trillions of miles without consuming a drop of fuel.

HOW
HEAVY
OR
MASSIVE
IS IT?

62.   How Much Do
You Weigh Wet and Dry?

IF YOU ARE concerned about your weight, be sure to step on the scale *after* drying yourself following a bath, because about a pound of water clings to your body when you are soaking wet—as you can easily verify by weighing yourself before and after drying off. You can also find the weight of water on your body by weighing your bath towel before and after you use it. Surprisingly, if you weigh the towel when it is *soaking* wet, you will find that a large bath towel can hold about four times as much water as it removes from your body. But before you conclude that you could make do with quarter-size bath towels, think about what it would feel like to use a towel that was three-fourths the way to saturation—say, after three other people had used it.

Suppose we assume that the pound of water (0.00045 cubic meters) on your soaking wet naked body is spread out in a film of constant thickness over your body's approximate 2 square meters of surface area. We can easily find that the average thickness of that film of water must be around 0.2 millimeters in order to have the required volume. Even though the

FIGURE 78. *"Sorry, ma'am, the divers have been dragging the water droplet but haven't yet recovered the body."*

amount of water on you when soaking wet is small (about 1 percent of your weight), that is not the case for much smaller creatures.

113

For example, the water on a soaking wet mouse is about equal to its weight. Aside from the fact that fur absorbs water well, a more important reason for the hundredfold greater water retention of mice is that smaller objects have a greater ratio of surface area to volume. The thickness of the water film can be assumed to be the same for a shaved mouse and human. So, for example, if your dimensions were all reduced by a hundred to mouse size, your surface area (and hence the weight of water on your body) would be reduced by 100^2, but your volume or weight would be reduced by 100^3—a hundred times more. You would then have a hundred times as much water on your body, expressed as a fraction of your weight—the actual situation for mice.

Becoming wet may be a minor nuisance for people, or a major nuisance for mice, but it can be fatal for insects, who can drown in a single drop of water. An insect's body is so tiny that a "film" of water only 0.2 mm thick is many times its own weight, and the insect cannot break free once it gets wet. The exceptions are those insects that walk on water. They can touch it without getting wet, in part because the molecules of water-walkers' feet do not attract but instead repel water molecules—much as the surface of a freshly waxed car repels water droplets, causing them to bead up. Other insects for whom water contact can be fatal have solved the problem of how to drink through the evolution of a long thin proboscis, which can enter the water without fatal consequences.

●　　●　　·　　●　　●

63.　What Is the Heaviest Creature That Could Walk on Water?

CREATURES LIKE ourselves that are much larger than water droplets are often unaware of the fact that water surfaces act like stretched membranes. Because of this so-called surface tension, a water surface can support a modest amount of weight without the "membrane" tearing. Water bugs can walk on water because of both surface tension and their possession of feet made from hydrophobic (literally "water fearing") material.[1] Most

1. Hydrophobic materials are those which attract water molecules less than the water molecules attract each other. As a result, they do not become wet when in ontact with water.

bugs, however, lack hydrophobic feet. They become wet and drown if they land on water, since they cannot break free from the surface.

Surface tension also accounts for the ability of some metal objects to float, even though they are denser than water. For example, if you gently place needles and razor blades on a water surface, you will find they float if they don't break the surface. By experiment, it has been found that pure water has a surface tension that can support a weight of up to 0.073 newtons (about ¼ ounce) for every 1-meter perimeter length of the object resting on it.

Unlike water bugs, most people weigh far too much to walk on water. For example, someone whose weight is 730 newtons (160 pounds) would need feet having a perimeter of 10,000 meters in order to stay under the limit of 0.073 newtons per meter. A typical perimeter for someone's foot is roughly 1 meter, which means that neglecting the effect of buoyancy, your feet would need to be about ten thousand times bigger than normal in order to walk on water.[2] Anyone for canal boat shoes?

Instead of enlarging your feet, we can instead imagine keeping your body proportions constant, and ask how small you would need to be shrunk to walk on water. Your weight is proportional to the cube of your height, while the perimeter of your feet is proportional to your height. Thus, the ratio of your weight to your foot's perimeter is proportional to the square of your height. We saw earlier that this ratio is ten thousand times too large for your weight to be supported by surface tension. Thus, to enable you to walk on water, we would need to shrink the square of your height by a factor of ten thousand, which means shrinking your height by a factor of one hundred—thereby reducing your height to a bit less than 1 inch. On the other hand, you would need to be shrunk well below 1 inch in height to walk on warm soapy water,

FIGURE 79. *With his size 94 million EEEEEE shoes, staying afloat was the least of Ralph's troubles.*

which has appreciably less surface tension—a fact you can verify by observing that needles or razor blades are less likely to float in water after you have added a few drops of liquid detergent.

Liquid surfaces act like stretched membranes because molecules on the liquid surface are attracted to fewer neighbors than those in the interior. One

2. Actually, if buoyancy is taken into account, you could walk on water with shoes (or feet) no larger than surfboards.

consequence of surface tension is that bubbles and liquid droplets tend to form spherical surfaces, in order to minimize their surface area. A sphere has the smallest surface area for any shape having a given volume, and therefore it is the equilibrium shape. To get the idea, picture the molecules as a bunch of "magnetic" people who are free to slide past each other but who all attract their nearest neighbors. No matter what shape a densely packed crowd initially had, it would evolve toward a circular shape.

We can speak of surface tension in any situation where the constituent particles of a material, such as the protons and neutrons inside an atomic nucleus, are held together by short-range attractive forces. Thus, the "liquid drop model" has been very successfully applied to the nuclei of atoms, even though nuclei are not liquids in the usual sense.

64. What Is the Difference between Mass and Weight?

THE UNIT OF mass in the metric system is the kilogram, identified as the mass of a particular hunk of platinum kept in a vault in Paris, with many copies throughout the world. In the English system, with which people in the United States are more familiar, the unit of weight is the pound, and the unit of mass is the aptly named "slug." Many people mistakenly use the terms mass and weight interchangeably, but they are fundamentally different quantities.

Mass, or inertia, measures the resistance a body offers to having its velocity changed in a given time interval. Massive objects are hard to start moving, and hard to stop once they are moving. Weight, on the other hand, is a measure of the pull of gravity on an object. Weight, unlike mass, can vary depending on what planet an object is on, or even vary slightly from place to place on a given planet. But for any given location, it is found that the ratio of mass to weight for different objects is exactly the same.

For example, if one object is twice as massive as another, it must weigh twice as much as the other at a given location. It follows that if two objects are dropped from rest simultaneously from the same height, they will hit the ground at the same moment—assuming air resistance is negligible. Both objects must fall with the same acceleration, because the greater pull of gravity on the heavier object is exactly offset by its greater inertia.

The only known exception to the rule that all objects at a given location fall with the same acceleration is when air resistance is important, such as if you drop a piece of tissue paper side by side with a book. However, you can easily show that if it were not for air resistance, the tissue and the book would fall with precisely the same acceleration. Simply place the tissue on top of the book, and drop the book. The tissue will remain on top of the book as it falls, since the book clears a path through the air for the tissue, which experiences no air resistance. Birds and cyclists are well aware of this trick, which is why they often travel in formation, with the lead one helping to clear a path through the air for the others.

What causes the pull of gravity? All masses in the universe are found to attract one another, and we simply call that attractive force gravity, which is not the same as understanding its cause. Albert Einstein did attempt to explain gravity in more fundamental terms involving the warping or curvature of space and time. In Einstein's theory of general relativity, an empty universe corresponds to a "flat" space and time, which obeys the usual laws of Euclidean geometry.[1] According to Einstein, the presence of matter warps space and time (or "space-time") in proportion to the amount of matter. In this view, gravity is not due to a force at all; it is simply what happens when matter moves through a space-time that has been distorted by the presence of other matter. It is impossible to visualize what a distorted or warped three-dimensional space looks like without getting outside the space and looking at it from a higher dimension—a feat that we three-dimensional creatures are not capable of. The best we can do is to make analogies with two-dimensional space, which we *can* see from outside.

FIGURE 80. *Judy stole the standard kilogram in her feeble attempt to prevent the United States from converting to the metric system.*

One useful experiment to visualize curved space uses some plastic wrap stretched onto a 12-inch embroidery hoop, whose rim is supported above a table by a few blocks. Because the stretched plastic wrap is flat, a steel BB can be rolled straight across. Now, place a spherical or cylindrical weight in the center of the plastic wrap, causing a distortion in the two-dimensional space. A rolled BB no longer follows a straight-line path. If it is launched with just the right speed, it can actually be made to orbit the central weight, simulating the Sun. In the actual case of a planet orbiting the

1. For example, in a flat space, parallel lines never meet, the angles of a triangle add up to 180 degrees, and so on.

Sun, Einstein would say that the orbit is due not to a "force" of gravity, but rather a distortion of space (and time) created by the presence of matter.

65.   What Is Your Mass?

WOULD YOU stub your toe if you kicked a massive boulder on a low-gravity planet or moon? Remember, mass or inertia is a measure of an object's resistance to having its velocity changed. Massive objects are hard to start moving, and hard to stop once they are in motion. An object's mass is related to its weight through the acceleration of gravity at its particular location. For example, on a small asteroid, where objects fall with a small acceleration, a massive boulder would *weigh* very little, and you would have no difficulty lifting it very slowly. On the other hand, because of the boulder's large *mass*, you would have a lot of difficulty lifting it suddenly, and you certainly would not want to give it a hard kick. A massive boulder resists being suddenly accelerated, and it is not going to get out of the way of your swinging foot.

You can find the mass of any object by directly comparing it with some standard mass, such as the standard kilogram kept in a vault in Paris, or more likely one of the millions of copies. There are two different ways to make the comparison between masses, only one of which is really practical. The practical method is to use a balance, and see how many standard masses need to be placed on the opposite side from the unknown mass for balance to be achieved. The method is a bit of a cheat, because you are actually comparing two weights rather than two masses. The method works because the strength of gravity is the same on both sides of the balance, so equality of weight implies equality of mass. There is an alternative method for comparing masses directly, but it is impractical, in that it requires that the measurement be done on a frictionless surface (or in space).

If you were sitting on a frictionless ice pond (standing would be nearly impossible), you could find your mass by seeing how many 1-kilogram masses you had to load into a sack, so that when you heaved the sack, your recoil speed matched that of the sack. You could also find your mass by throwing only a single 1-kilogram mass, and comparing your recoil speed with that of the mass. If, for example, the speed of the 1-kilogram mass were forty times the speed of your recoil, your mass would have to be 40 kilograms.

The same type of observation could allow you to find the speed of a known mass. For example, if you fired a gun on frictionless ice, and you found that you recoiled at 1 meter per second when firing a bullet whose mass was one thousandth your own mass, the bullet's horizontal speed would have to be 1,000 meters per second. We can say that the momentum (mass times velocity) of the bullet in one direction equals your recoil momentum in the opposite direction, or the *net* momentum of you plus the bullet is zero, counting momentum in one direction as positive and the other negative. The preceding examples illustrates the law of conservation of momentum, which requires that the momentum of a system not change, as long as no outside forces act on it.

There are several ways you can make the same kinds of observations without going into space or finding nonexistent frictionless ice. A simple experiment uses rolling objects instead of sliding ones, so as to reduce greatly the effects of friction. For example, place two light balls of unequal mass on a level desk or table with a weak spring or a folded index card between them. Press the balls together and then release them,

FIGURE 81. *The astronaut found out the hard way that low weight does not mean low mass.*

allowing the uncoiling spring or unfolding card to gently drive the balls apart. Momentum conservation requires that if the heavier ball has x times the lighter ball's mass, it must move $1/x$ times as fast when the balls fly apart. One easy way to test this prediction is to find the ratio of the balls' speeds, by seeing where on a perfectly level table you need to place the balls originally in order for them to reach the table edges simultaneously when they fly apart. For example, if one of the balls is twice as heavy as the other, the balls will need to be placed at a point where the lighter ball has twice as far to roll to reach the edge of the table as the heavier one.

66. What Is the Heaviest Mass You Could Push?

ONE OF THE most remarkable short films I ever saw, called *A Million to One*, was about a real flea pulling an object a million times its own weight. Believe it or not, you could probably duplicate that feat under the right conditions. In fact, how heavy a mass you can pull or push on a level surface depends entirely on the amount of friction present. For example, if you are trying to push a crate considerably heavier than you are, most likely you will slide backward without the crate budging an inch. Of course, if the crate bottom is on wheels or grease, you can push a crate much heavier than you are. A single person can, for example, push a car on level ground. What about the situation in which *both* you and the crate are on an extremely slippery surface? In the absence of friction, there would be no limit to the mass of crate you could push or pull. But, when pushing an object on a frictionless surface, you would instantly lose contact with it due to your recoil.

FIGURE 82. *The thought that the Earth really did move excited Gail's passion to even greater heights.*

One way you could arrange to push an immense mass on Earth would be to float the mass on a cushion of air or in water. A trick performed by some strongmen is to tow a heavy boat with a rope. You could probably duplicate this feat, as long as you did not expect to produce any sizable acceleration. A sustained pull over an extended period of time will set the boat in motion. Once the boat is in motion, you will not be able to stop it in a short distance unless you exert a very large force. That is why it is extremely dangerous to leave an arm dangling in the space between a big boat and the dock. Even though the boat may be moving very slowly, it could still crush your arm, because a large force is required to stop the boat in a short distance.

The ratio of your recoil speed to that of the object you push depends on the ratio of your two masses, so pushing off against an object having a million times your mass results in the object acquiring a millionth your speed. A situation of exactly this kind occurs every time you push off against the Earth and jump into the air. The ratio of your speed to the recoil speed of the Earth equals the ratio of the Earth's mass to yours—roughly a hundred billion trillion (10^{23}). In jumping, after you lose contact with the Earth, its gravity pulls you back, and *your* gravity pulls the Earth back.

Of course, no one has actually observed the Earth move in situations like this, since its recoil speed and the distance moved are so tiny—but the movement must occur. What about those situations where there is apparently no recoil—such as your pushing a crate or a car? Actually, you and the Earth must recoil backward in these situations also. It is impossible to push something in one direction without having it push you in the opposite direction, so that the net momentum remains unchanged. (I remember once reading a comic book in which a superhero pushed the Earth out of the path of an approaching asteroid. Unfortunately, even a superhero could not push the Earth without instantly recoiling in the opposite direction!)

67.   What Does Air Weigh?

DO YOU KNOW why steel ships can float? The ancient Greek philosopher Archimedes first discovered an explanation for the buoyant force felt by floating (and submerged) objects. Buoyancy occurs because the pressure of the water on the underside of a submerged object exceeds that on the topside. Everything in water is pushed upward by this buoyant force. (But not everything floats, because the force of gravity pulling down is sometimes stronger.) The upward buoyant force on an object must depend only on its shape, and not its composition. To understand how this can be so, imagine a water-filled balloon the same shape and size as the original object—the steel ship. The water-filled balloon barely floats. Clearly, the buoyant force on the balloon must exactly equal the weight of the water it contains, in order to allow the balloon to just barely float when completely submerged. The buoyant force on any submerged object must, therefore, equal the weight of the fluid that the object displaces.[1] Steel ships can float because, given all the hollow compartments they contain, they displace their own weight in water with a portion of the ship above the water surface. In fact, if a ship, or other lighter-than-water floating object, is pushed below the water, it pops right up when the pushing stops, since it is displacing more water than before, and hence has a greater buoyant force.

According to legend, Archimedes discovered his buoyancy principle while sitting in the bathtub. Supposedly, he excitedly exclaimed "Eureka!" (I have found it!) as he raced through the town. Archimedes's principle applies to objects in any fluid, including air. For example, because of buoyancy, lighter-than-air objects, such as helium balloons, rise when released. An object the same density as air would neither rise nor fall in air, and it would be weightless. This fact makes weighing air itself a very tricky business. If, for example, you place two balloons, one filled and one empty, on opposite sides of a sensitive balance, you will not find any significant difference in their weight, because the buoyant force on the air-filled balloon will nearly cancel the weight of the air it contains—assuming the air pressures outside and inside the balloon are not too different.

One way you could weigh air would be to pump all the air out of a container and weigh it filled and empty, but that would be a lot of trouble unless you had a

1. The displaced fluid has the same volume as the object in the case of a submerged object. For a floating object, the displaced fluid has a volume equal to the volume of that fraction of the object which is submerged.

vacuum pump and a sealable container strong enough not to collapse when the air was pumped out. One easy way to get an approximate value for the weight of a fixed volume of air is to measure the buoyant force on a large helium-filled balloon, by seeing how much weight you need to tie on the balloon for it to neither rise nor sink.[2] If helium weighed nothing at all, you would need to add an amount of weight to the balloon equal to the weight of the air it displaced, according to Archimedes' principle. But helium, of course, is not weightless. In fact, it weighs only 17 percent as much as air. Therefore, the weight of air occupying the same volume as a helium-filled balloon is 20 percent more than the weight you need to hang on the balloon to just keep it from rising (including the weight of the empty balloon itself). Once you find the weight of air the balloon displaces, you can then find its volume, by first measuring the balloon's circumference with a string, and then calculating its diameter and volume. Finally, by dividing the weight of displaced air by the balloon's volume, you can find out how much air weighs per unit volume. You should find a mass per unit volume of about 1.2 kilograms per cubic meter.

FIGURE 83. *"Poor Archimedes; I think he's really lost it this time."*

● — ● — ● — ● — ●

68. What Would You Weigh in a Falling Elevator?

ANYONE WHO has ever ridden on a roller coaster or a high-speed elevator should be familiar with the "g-forces" that occur during periods of acceleration and deceleration. These g-forces change your apparent weight, as you can easily verify by bringing a bathroom scale with you the next time you ride a high-speed elevator. You should find that the scale reads your

2. You may have seen those delightful helium balloons with long paper legs. The balloon rises to the exact height for which the weight of the suspended paper lifted off the ground plus the weight of the balloon itself just equals the upward buoyant force.

normal weight when the elevator is either at rest or moving with constant speed. But if the elevator accelerates upward, your apparent weight will increase, because the scale must press harder than usual on your feet in order to accelerate you upward.

Your weight will also increase if the elevator is moving downward and decelerating. In this case, the scale must again press upward on your feet with more than the usual force in order to slow your descent. If the deceleration is large enough, you may feel your knees buckle. The two situations for which your apparent weight will be less than usual will be when you are accelerating in the downward direction, and when you are moving upward but decelerating. In these cases, you will likely feel the sudden decrease in your apparent weight in your stomach, rather than your knees.

Thus, on a trip from the ground floor to some higher floor consisting of an initial acceleration, a constant-speed portion, and a final deceleration, you will first weigh more, then the same, and finally less than your usual weight. Just how much heavier or lighter you feel will depend entirely on the ac-

FIGURE 84. *Nick spent the rest of his short life trying unsuccessfully to tell if he was in a freely falling elevator or the gravity-free environment of outer space.*

celeration and deceleration of the particular elevator. For example, in the case of a really high-speed elevator whose accelerations and decelerations were half the acceleration due to gravity, the scale readings during the accelerations and decelerations would be 50 percent more or less than your usual weight.

As far as you would be concerned, the sensation would be just as though someone were turning a knob to strengthen or weaken gravity by 50 percent, since the effects of g-forces are completely indistinguishable from those of gravity. Albert Einstein, in his so-called equivalence principle, enshrined this indistinguishability between gravity and g-forces as a central element of the theory of general relativity.

One consequence of this principle is that being inside a freely falling elevator is equivalent to being in a gravity-free environment. In fact NASA uses freely falling elevators (among other methods) to simulate weightlessness for brief times. Here is a way for you to observe the effects of weightlessness without the nasty consequences of taking a freely falling elevator. Make a hole in the bottom of a water-filled styrofoam cup, and cover the hole with your finger to keep the water from flowing out. Now drop the cup and carefully observe it during its brief descent. You will find that no water flows out of the hole while the cup falls, because the water is weightless during that time.

69. How Much Does Your Weight Vary on Earth?

GOT A WEIGHT problem? Here are three things you could do about it: go on a diet, move to the Moon, or ride in an elevator with the cable cut. These weight-reducing methods illustrate the three factors on which your weight depends: your mass, the strength of gravity, and the acceleration of your reference frame. If you want to reduce your weight by less drastic methods, you can rely on the variation of gravity with altitude and latitude, as described below.

If you climb a mountain, for example, you are farther from the center of the Earth, and the pull of Earth's gravity is a bit less due to the inverse square law. If you climbed Mount Everest, your weight reduction due to its altitude would be about 0.32 percent.[1] You probably would not consider it worth the trouble to climb Mount Everest to achieve such a modest weight reduction, but then again the calories you would burn getting there could lead to a greater weight reduction than you would get from the weakened gravity, assuming you didn't eat more calories than you burned.

How about taking a trip to the equator instead? A point at the Earth's equator traces out a circle every 24 hours equal to the circumference of the Earth. Due to this circular motion, the point "falls" off the straight-line tangent by 0.054 feet in one second, making its acceleration 0.35 percent that due to gravity. As a result of this acceleration, a scale at the equator reads 0.35 percent less than it would if the Earth didn't rotate. The scale reads less because it is, in a sense, falling out from under your feet, much like a scale in an elevator that is accelerating downward. Your weight at the equator would be further reduced by a comparable amount due to the Earth's equatorial bulge, which would increase your distance

1. Atop 5.5-mile-high Mount Everest, you would be about 1.0016 Earth radii from the Earth's center. According to the inverse square law, the strength of gravity atop Everest should be $1/1.0016^2$, or 0.9968 times its surface value—a 0.32 percent reduction. Of course, we get only an approximate answer using the inverse square law, since it basically assumes you are suspended in space 5.5 miles above a spherical Earth. A more realistic estimate would take into account the gravitational pull of the mountain itself, which might reduce your weight loss to perhaps 0.25 percent, depending on the shape of the mountain.

from the Earth's center, but again the amount of weight loss would probably not be worth the trip.

On the other hand, if the Earth completed a rotation every 1.4 hours (seventeen times faster than it does now), your weight at the equator would be zero! Your weightlessness would be due to the fact that at this rotation rate, a scale you were standing on would be falling out from under you by 16 feet in one second, just like the scale in a freely falling elevator.[2] By no accident, 1.4 hours is the orbital period for a low-Earth-orbit satellite. If you were standing weightless on the equator while the Earth rotated once every 1.4 hours, you would in effect be in orbit if you pushed off a few inches. If you were located at the north pole, on the other hand, you would experience your normal weight. The

FIGURE 85. *Marty wanted to take a vacation to lose some weight, but he couldn't decide whether to go to a health spa, the equator, or Mount Everest.*

amount of centrifugal force is proportional to your distance from the Earth's axis of rotation, and at the poles your distance from the axis is zero.

70. What Would You Weigh in a Space Station?

YOU PROBABLY have seen film clips of astronauts floating around their space capsule in a state of weightlessness. A space station or satellite in orbit about a planet is essentially in free-fall. Like occu-

2. Incidentally, the reason that the Earth needs to rotate only seventeen times faster for you to be weightless at the equator is that centrifugal force is proportional to the *square* of the rotation rate, and 17^2 times 0.35 percent gives 100 percent weight loss.

pants of a freely falling elevator, people inside a space station experience weightlessness because they are following exactly the same orbit as the space station, and therefore fall neither up nor down relative to it.[1] Although it might seem like fun to float around a space station in complete weightlessness, if subject to prolonged periods of weightlessness, humans can suffer serious health problems, especially loss of bone mass and muscle strength. It is quite possible that someone living in a weightless environment for a very extended time would at some point not be able to return to the one-g environment of Earth.

Large space stations shown in science fiction movies are often in the shape of a doughnut, and rotate about their central axis—a line through the center of the doughnut hole. Occupants of the space station would feel "artificial gravity" due to the rotation. How fast would a doughnut-shaped space station need to rotate in order to simulate the strength of Earth's gravity? Clearly, the necessary rotation speed depends on the size of the space station.

FIGURE 86. *What is the question most frequently asked of astronauts?*

As we saw in the last essay, people at the equator would be weightless if Earth rotated seventeen times faster—the centrifugal force would just cancel gravity. Consequently, in the *absence* of gravity, an Earth-size space station rotating at 17 revolutions per day would achieve one g of artificial gravity. In this case, your weight would feel completely normal, and you would experience no dizziness. How about a less ridiculous-size space station, say one that is 640 meters in radius, or one ten-thousandth the size of the Earth? This space station would have to rotate one hundred times faster than the Earth-size station, or one rotation every 51 seconds.[2]

People in a rotating space station would experience artificial gravity in a direction pointing outward from the center of the station, so they would walk with their feet facing outward inside the (hollow) doughnut, and their heads pointing toward the center of the doughnut. Space station occupants would experience a slight difference in the strength of artificial gravity between their heads and their

1. As explained in essay 76, the orbit of a body does not depend on its mass, so there is no reason for your body to move relative to the space station if you are initially at rest relative to it—ignoring the very small gravitational attraction between you and the station.

2. A factor of one hundred in the rotation rate just compensates for a factor of ten thousand decrease in radius, because centrifugal force is proportional to the square of the rotation rate, but is directly proportional to the radius (see essay 39).

126

feet, because their heads would be closer to the center of rotation. This varying gravity would not be a serious problem for a large space station, in which the difference in gravity from your head to your feet would be quite small, but it could be a problem for a space station with a small radius. The effect of this difference would be experienced only if you were standing rather than lying down. Your head would quite literally be lighter in the former case—giving new meaning to "light-headedness."

The orbit of a large space station would have to be planned with care to ensure that it was stable over a long time. One proposed location is L5—one of the five "Lagrange points" of the Earth-Moon system mentioned in essay 36. A group of would-be space colonists has formed the L5 Society to promote the idea of building a gigantic space station at L5, complete with rain forests, rivers, and cities— in effect, a self-sustaining artificial world.

71.   What Would You Weigh inside the Earth?

IMAGINE THAT it is possible to dig a tunnel clear through the center of the Earth to the other side. How can we figure out what your weight would be at various points in the tunnel? At the entrance to the tunnel your weight would, of course, have its normal value. At the center of the tunnel your weight would have to be zero. If gravity were not zero at the center, it would have to be pulling you along some direction we could call down, which is impossible, since at the Earth's center all directions are up—just as at the north pole all directions are south.

A reasonable guess for the strength of gravity at points in between the entrance to the tunnel and the center might be that its strength varies in proportion to your distance from the center of the tunnel. In order to see if this guess is correct, we first need to consider the science fiction problem of a hollow planet. How would gravity on the surface of a hollow planet compare with gravity inside?

If the planet had Earth's mass and radius, on its surface you would have your normal weight, and there would be no indication that the planet was hollow. But inside the planet the situation would be quite different—there gravity would be zero everywhere! In order to understand this surprising result, let us imagine that you are inside the planet.

You can think of the spherical shell making up the hollow planet as consisting of a very large number of equal-size small masses. Each of these masses is pulling you toward it by an amount given by the inverse square law. Since you are surrounded by these masses, you are pulled in every direction, and the sum of all these pulls can be shown to give a net result of zero no matter where you are inside the sphere. If you were standing on the hollow planet's surface, where you would have your normal weight, you could open a hatch to climb inside, push off against its inner surface, and then coast clear across the planet in a zero-gravity environment.

FIGURE 87. *A guide attempts to show tourists to the center of the Earth the direction "up."*

Let us return to our original problem of gravity inside a tunnel through the Earth. Imagine yourself at a point halfway between the Earth's center and its surface. You are, in effect, inside a large collection of onionlike concentric shells of radii between one half and one times the radius of the Earth, and as we have just seen, the net gravity due to all those spherical shells must be zero (since you are inside them). So the only gravity you feel is that due to the layers of the inner "onion"—the part between you and the Earth's center. This part of the onion has half the radius of the whole Earth and an eighth its volume and mass, assuming a constant density of material throughout.

Compared with the strength of gravity on the Earth's surface, gravity at your location, halfway to the center, is decreased by a factor of 8 due to the reduced mass, and increased by a factor of $2^2 = 4$ due to the inverse square law (you are twice as close to this inner mass). Taken together these two factors require that the strength of gravity at a point half the way from the center to the surface is just half the value on the surface, exactly as we had originally guessed. Actually, for the real Earth, the strength of gravity at a point halfway to the center would be considerably greater, because the assumption of constant density with depth is a poor one.[1]

Assuming it were possible actually to dig such a tunnel through the Earth, what would happen to you if you fell in? Clearly, if there were no air resistance, you would accelerate due to gravity all the way to the center, but the *rate* of in-

1. Given estimates for the variation of density with depth, it is believed that the strength of gravity at a point halfway to the center of the Earth is roughly the same as its value on the surface. The reason for this is that the average density of material composing the inner half of the Earth is roughly twice its overall density.

128

crease in your speed would slow as you neared the center and gravity steadily weakened. As you passed the center with maximum speed, gravity would slow you down, bringing you to rest just as you reached the other side of the Earth. If someone didn't grab you at this point, you would find yourself oscillating back and forth through the tunnel until friction brought you to rest at the center.

72. How Much Would You Weigh on Different Heavenly Bodies?

THERE ARE ANY number of ways to find the strength of gravity on the surface of another planet, if you can get there. You could, for example, time the period of a pendulum, or else time the fall of an object dropped from rest through a known distance. But how can we earthbound types deduce the strength of a planet's gravity relative to Earth? If we have a way to find the mass and radius of the planet, deducing its gravity is easy. The strength of gravity on the surface of a moon or planet is directly proportional to its mass and inversely proportional to the square of its radius. On this basis it is easy to show, for example, that the Moon, whose radius and mass are 27 percent and 1.2 percent of those of Earth, respectively, must have about one-sixth of Earth's gravity.[1] But suppose you know only the radius of a planet, and don't know its mass. You can still get a rough estimate for the strength of its surface gravity if you assume the planet to be made of Earthlike material. It can easily be shown that, under this assumption, the strength of gravity on the planet's surface is simply proportional to its radius.[2] In other words, on a planet twice the radius of Earth, you would weigh twice as much.

Even though the planets in our solar system do vary in their density, the larger

1. Gravity on the Moon's surface relative to that on Earth is given by $0.012/0.27^2$, which is about $\frac{1}{6}$.

2. For example, suppose a planet's radius is twice that of Earth. In that case its volume and mass are eight times that of Earth. This alone would increase gravity eightfold, but gravity on the planet's surface is also reduced to one-fourth that of Earth due to the inverse square law. Taking both factors into account, we find a surface gravity that is twice that of Earth. Now, if a planet twice the radius of Earth has twice Earth's gravity, then planets generally must have a surface gravity in direct proportion to their size, assuming a constant density.

ones tend to have larger gravity, and the smaller ones lower gravity. For example, on Jupiter you would weigh 253 times your weight on Earth, and on Pluto, the smallest planet, you would weigh only 6 percent of your Earth weight. In addition to the nine planets of the solar system, there are thousands of smaller objects—asteroids or "minor planets"—most of which orbit the Sun in the region between Mars's and Jupiter's orbits. The largest of these minor planets, Ceres, has a diameter of 1,000 kilometers, which is 44 percent the size of Pluto. But most of the asteroids are much smaller in size than Ceres. In fact, because their small size makes them hard to spot, astronomers have been able to track the orbits of only about a third of the asteroids. If you should be lucky enough to be the first to determine an asteroid's orbit, you would have the privilege of naming it!

FIGURE 88. *"Sure, it's only a minor planet, but it's* my *minor planet,"* *thought Penelope.*

Life on a small asteroid would be quite amusing, due to its low gravity. For example, on an 8-mile diameter asteroid (one-thousandth that of Earth) with the same density as Earth, you would weigh only a thousandth your Earth weight, so you could jump thousands of feet high, and you could easily throw objects into orbit. The rule that gravity is less on small celestial bodies than on large ones has an important exception in the case of very dense bodies. In the case of a neutron star, for example, for which most of a star's mass has been compacted by gravity into a very small object, gravity would be enormously strong. On the surface of a neutron star the average person might weigh around 25 billion tons, and would instantly be crushed by his own weight.

73. On How Big a Planet Could You Hit a Baseball into Orbit?

CLEARLY, gravity on Earth is far too strong for anyone to throw or hit a baseball into orbit. To do so would require that you launch the ball with the speed of a satellite in low-Earth-orbit, namely about 7.9 kilometers per second. A satellite in a circular orbit travels horizontally by 7.9 kilometers in one second, and simultaneously "falls" off a straight-line tangent by 16 feet, causing its path to match exactly the curvature of the Earth. Now suppose that you lived on a planet half the size of the Earth. Surface gravity would be half its strength on Earth, and objects would fall only 8 feet in the first second. For a half-size Earth, the velocity of an orbiting satellite would need to be only half as great in order that it fall 8 feet in one second, so as to match the curvature of a planet. We can see from this example that a direct proportionality exists between the speed of an orbiting satellite (or baseball) in low orbit and the radius of a planet.

Professional pitchers can pitch balls at 100 miles per hour, or 44 meters per second, which represents only 0.56 percent of the

FIGURE 89. *The inhabitants of the small planet Orbpit came up with its unusual name by putting "p" into "orbit" as a reminder to dog walkers not to do the same.*

speed of a satellite in Earth orbit. But it would be just the right orbital speed for a planet 0.56 percent of Earth's radius, or 36 kilometers. On planets this size or smaller, professional pitchers could throw balls into orbit. Of course, if the planet were spinning, pitchers or batters could use that to their advantage by throwing or hitting the ball in the direction of the spin and achieving orbit more easily. The orientation of baseball parks on such small planets would have to be planned with care.

We have assumed that a satellite or baseball could be launched into orbit very close to ground level, which would certainly be possible on a very small planet or moon that could not have an atmosphere due to its weak gravity. But achieving a circular orbit near ground level would be a difficult undertaking, even apart from the problem associated with craters or hills that might get in the way. You would need to throw a ball at exactly the right speed in the horizontal direction. Otherwise, either the ball would hit the ground (if the speed were too low), or else the orbit would be elliptical rather than circular (if the speed were too high).

If you threw the baseball straight up with the same speed required to achieve orbit, the ball would reach some highest point and come back down. There is a speed known as the "escape velocity" for which a ball thrown straight up does not return. This speed turns out to be 41 percent higher than the velocity needed to achieve orbit on a nonspinning planet, and it is 11.2 kilometers per second for the Earth. If, like the "Little Prince," you lived on a small asteroid, you would need to watch your step, since you could easily jump off the asteroid faster than the escape velocity.

74. How Massive Is the Earth?

IN 1615 Isaac Newton made his great discovery that gravity is a force acting between any pair of objects anywhere in the universe. This magnificent discovery made it clear that heavenly bodies are acted on by the same fundamental force of gravity as objects on the surface of the Earth, including, for example, the apocryphal apple that fell on Newton's head. Because of his pioneering work, we now call the unit of force or weight in the metric system the "newton," one newton being about 0.22 pounds.

According to Newton, the force between any two objects (F) is proportional to their masses (m_1 and m_2) and is inversely proportional to the square of the distance (r) between them, assuming the dimensions of each object are small compared with this distance: $F = G \times m_1 m_2 / r^2$. Newton also proved that his law applies to two uniform spherical masses, provided the distance between them is measured center to center.[1] G, the constant of proportionality in Newton's law,

1. For example, the force of gravitational attraction between two people is not given by the inverse square law until they were much farther apart than their heights. However, you can get a rough estimate for the force of attraction between them using the inverse square law, even if they are only a meter apart. The inverse square law also applies to a non-

132

can be found only by experiment: take two known masses, place them a known distance apart, and measure the force of gravitational attraction between them. Clearly, the gravitational constant must be a very small number, because you don't feel any noticeable attraction for someone sitting next to you, or if you do it is certainly not due to gravity. Given the small size of the gravitational constant, its measurement required a rather delicate experiment (first performed by Henry Cavendish).

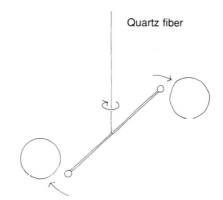

Quartz fiber

FIGURE 90. *The Cavendish Experiment to Find the Gravitational Constant The amount of twist in the thin quartz fiber measures the force of gravity on the small dumbbell masses due to the two large masses.*

In 1798 Cavendish made a dumbbell by placing two spherical masses at the ends of a horizontal rod, which was hung from its center by a thin quartz fiber. He then placed two large masses on the ground next to each of the dumbbell masses. The tiny gravitational attraction between each pair of adjacent masses could be found from the amount of time it took for the dumbbell to twist the fiber through a particular angle. The use of a quartz fiber was important in getting enough sensitivity because quartz fibers are very strong, thus allowing large masses to be hung. Quartz fibers can also be made very thin, so that only a very tiny force is needed to twist them. Unfortunately, Cavendish's experiment is not one you can easily do yourself, because the size of the force being measured is so small that extraneous influences such as air currents can easily produce spurious results.

The smallness of the gravitational constant means that you find an appreciable gravitational

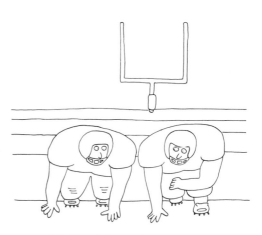

FIGURE 91. *The defensive linemen would not even consider the possibility that their mutual attraction was anything other than the usual inverse square Newtonian gravitation.*

---

spherical body (such as you) attracted to a spherical body (such as the Earth) whose center is a large distance away.

force only when at least one of the attracting masses is enormous, like the Earth. In that case the force of gravitational attraction between an object and the Earth, that is, the object's weight, is given by the formula: you just plug in the values of the gravitational constant and the masses of the object and the Earth, and divide by the square of the Earth's radius (which is their center-to-center separation). Based on the preceding relationship, Cavendish could find the mass of the Earth once he measured the gravitational constant from the force between two known masses. Let's see how.

Given the value of the gravitational constant, we can predict the force between any two known masses placed a known distance apart. Alternatively, we can predict the value of an unknown mass, provided we measure both its attraction for a known mass and the masses' separation. In this way, by measuring the attraction of the Earth (unknown mass) for a 1-kilogram mass, we can solve the formula for the mass of the Earth. Note that the attraction of the Earth for an object is simply the weight of the object—9.8 newtons in the case of a 1-kilogram mass. Cavendish, in his famous experiment, literally weighed (massed?) the Earth, finding the value 6×10^{24} kilograms (a 6 with 24 zeros after it).

75. How Massive Is the Sun?

FINDING THE mass of the Sun is easy once we have weighed the Earth (see previous essay). Basically, we first need to find out how far the Earth "falls" toward the Sun in one second, using the known distance between Earth and Sun and the time it takes the Earth to complete its orbit, just as we did earlier in the case of the Moon (see essay 33). It turns out that the Earth falls toward the Sun by about 1 inch in a second. This figure is a measure of the gravitational acceleration of the Earth toward the Sun. From Newton's law of gravitation (previous essay), we can now find that the Sun's mass is 2 million trillion trillion (2×10^{30}) kilograms, or 333,000 times the Earth's mass.[1] If the Sun were reduced to the size of a basketball, the Earth would be about the size of a grain of sand, only much lighter.

The mass of the Sun is not constant over time, because as the Sun emits en-

1. Given the known volume of the Sun, we find that, on the average, the mass of each cubic meter of the Sun is 1.4 times that of water. But the density of the Sun is believed to vary greatly from the center to its surface. Given the weight of the overlying layers, the Sun's central density has been estimated as 150 times that of water, because of the tremendous pressure due to gravity. Thus, while the Sun may be considered a ball of gas, it is an extremely dense gas by earthly standards. In fact, it wouldn't even float in water.

ergy, it must lose mass by the well-known formula from Einstein's theory of relativity: $E = mc^2$. The c^2 in this formula represents the square of the speed of light, which is here just a conversion factor that tells us how many joules of energy are emitted for each kilogram of mass that is entirely converted to energy. The numerical value of c^2 is 90 thousand trillion joules, which is the equivalent of the energy released in the largest H-bomb ever detonated, or three days worth of electrical energy consumption by the entire United States.

The enormity of the energy content of 1 kilogram of mass means that even the tiniest changes in mass correspond to sizable energy releases. This is why mass changes are not noticeable in ordinary chemical reactions, such as burning oil. Conversely, in the much more efficient or potent nuclear processes, which typically produce a million times more energy per kilogram of fuel, the changes in mass are noticeable, but still only a small fraction of the original fuel mass—so concentrated is the energy content of matter. In order to account for the observed output of the Sun's energy, the equation $E = mc^2$ predicts that the Sun must be losing 4.2 million metric tons every second.[2] By earthly standards that figure sounds alarmingly high, but it represents only the tiniest fraction of the Sun's mass. So you may be reassured to learn that the Sun could go on shedding 4.2 million tons every second and still continue burning for another 5 billion years.

In the days before scientists knew about nuclear reactions, they thought the Sun produced its energy in an ordinary fire through chemical reactions, or alternatively through heat generated by gravitational contraction. (The energy released in gravitational contraction is just like the energy released when the water in a waterfall descends—see essay 102.) Unfortunately, neither chemical reactions nor gravitational contraction could account for the age of the Sun, because both are so

FIGURE 92. "Sol, I'd be concerned about your weight loss if you weren't so heavy to begin with."

much less efficient than nuclear reactions. For example, given the Sun's prodigious rate of energy output, if this energy were due to chemical reactions, the Sun should have burned itself out in only 5,000 years—far short of the age of the Earth, according to geological estimates. Producing energy by gravitational contraction would have allowed the Sun to shine much longer than 5,000 years, but

2. A metric ton is 1,000 kilograms, or about 2,200 pounds.

still far less than the estimated 4.6-billion-year age of the Earth (see essay 131). Only the nuclear "fire" is potent enough to explain the Earth's (and solar system's) great age.

76. How Massive Is the Moon?

A SCIENCE fiction writer once proposed that our Moon was actually a hollow spaceship used by aliens to spy on Earth. The idea was that if the Moon were hollow (and very light), its orbit would be unaffected, and so we couldn't tell whether it was hollow or not. At first thought this may seem plausible (not the hollow spaceship part). For example, if the Moon were replaced by an object having a hundreth the mass, its attraction to the Earth would be a hundreth as great. But reducing both the force and mass a hundredfold produces exactly the same acceleration—for the same reason light and heavy objects on Earth fall with the same acceleration in the absence of air resistance. The flaw in the argument is that the Moon doesn't actually orbit the Earth, but rather both bodies orbit their common center of mass (see essay 35).

Therefore, we can find the ratio of the Moon's mass to that of the Earth based on the wobble in the Earth's position during each lunar orbit. The size of the Earth's wobble, and hence the mass of the Moon, can be found by observing the apparent circular motion of "fixed" stars during each lunar orbit. We can conclude that the Moon must have $\frac{1}{81}$ the mass of the Earth from the fact that during each lunar orbit the Earth travels in a small circle whose radius is $\frac{1}{82}$ the distance to the Moon—much

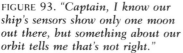

FIGURE 93. *"Captain, I know our ship's sensors show only one moon out there, but something about our orbit tells me that's not right."*

too large a value for the hollow-Moon theory. There are two other ways you could find the mass of the Moon, provided you could get there. One way would be to time the fall of objects on the Moon, so as to measure its surface gravity. You could then find the moon's Mass from its measured surface gravity, its radius, and the known value of the gravitational constant—in much the same way as Cavendish "weighed" the Earth (see essay 74).

Another way would be to observe the orbits of man-made satellites about the Moon. Clearly, the greater the Moon's mass, the stronger its gravity, and the more rapidly a satellite will complete a given-size orbit. To get the idea, you can use one of those toys consisting of a ball attached to a wooden paddle by a long rubber band. Cut the rubber band free from the paddle, and twirl the ball in a circle at the end of the rubber band. The faster you twirl the ball, the more the rubber band stretches, and the harder it must pull to keep the ball going in a circle.

In principle, the same three methods discussed here could be used to find the masses of moons around other planets. The first method, however, does have its problems when applied to a planet such as Jupiter, which has many small moons. The wobble in Jupiter's motion created by these small moons is very tiny, and does not give much information about their mass. A flyby of a spacecraft past the moons would give the most accurate measure of their mass. Notice that you don't need to land on a body or orbit it in order to measure its gravity; just observing the deflection of a spacecraft at a known distance and speed gives enough information to determine the body's mass. For example, from the figure-eight shape of its orbit, we can deduce that the (unpowered) spacecraft in the cartoon must be orbiting *two* equal-mass moons.

77. How Massive Are the Planets?

THE MASSES of the planets cover a vast range, from Jupiter, equivalent to 300 Earths, to tiny Pluto, whose mass is merely $\frac{1}{600}$ that of Earth. Jupiter alone, in fact, has more than twice the mass of all the other planets put together. Our principal means of figuring out the masses of the planets is by observing satellites that orbit them. Basically, the idea is to see what gravitational attraction is needed to keep the moons in their observed orbits, and then work backward to find what planetary mass would produce that gravitational attraction at the moon's distance. The masses of Mercury and Venus, the two planets that lack moons, can most easily be found by seeing how the paths of passing comets or spacecraft are affected by those planets' gravity.

Another approach is to see the effect planets have on one another's motions. The usual statement that the planets move in elliptical orbits about the Sun is approximately true only if we ignore the gravitational attraction of the planets for one another. These planet-planet attractions are much smaller than the attraction of the Sun for each planet, in view of the Sun's much greater mass, but they are sufficient to alter or "perturb" each planet's orbit, by an amount that depends on the planets' masses and the distances between them. By carefully observing each planet's orbit and looking for small departures from what is predicted, we can figure out how much mass a nearby planet must have in order to cause the observed perturbation.

Astronomers have even carried such calculations a step further, and discovered hitherto unknown planets (Neptune and Pluto), based on perturbations in the orbits of nearer planets that could not be accounted for by all the other known planets. Actually, even though the search for Pluto was motivated by anomalies in the orbits of other planets, these calculations were in error, and Pluto was discovered by pure luck. The relative recency of the discoveries of Neptune (1846) and Pluto (1930) may seem surprising. You might think that the "wandering" nature of planets would make them obviously stand out from the "fixed" stars. The observational problem is that distant planets appear faint compared with the five planets known since ancient times (Mercury, Venus, Mars, Jupiter, and Saturn). In fact, even through a powerful telescope a small distant planet is likely to be indistinguishable from the billions of faint stars in our galaxy. In principle, any one of these billions of pointlike objects could be a candidate for being a planet.

As noted in essay 43, stars can be distinguished from planets in that only the former twinkle. But this distinction would not be true for small distant planets, which, like stars, would have a pointlike appearance and would therefore twinkle. Of course, the planets orbiting our Sun do have a much larger parallax than the much more distant stars, and they could be distinguished on that basis. But astronomers are unlikely to launch a program to measure the parallax of billions of random starlike objects in the hope of finding a planet. Thus, we cannot rule out

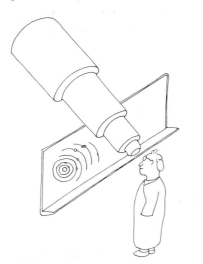

FIGURE 94. *Carl's discovery of Goofy, a tenth planet just beyond Pluto, has not yet won universal acceptance.*

the possibility of there still being undiscovered planets in our solar system, particularly if they are small and distant from the Sun (and Earth).

78. How Massive Are Stars?

DO OTHER stars have planets? Other stars may well have planets, but such bodies, which shine only by reflected light, would unfortunately be much too faint to be seen at stellar distances. Barring a message from their inhabitants, the only way we have at present for telling whether other stars have planets is through the small wobble the unseen planets cause in the stars' motions. At the time of this writing, only one neutron star has been found to have planets. Many other stars may have planetary systems that have not yet been observed, because we cannot track their wobble as well as we can for neutron stars.

While the fraction of stars with planetary systems remains speculative, numerous cases exist of a pair of stars in orbit about each other. In fact, astronomers believe that such so-called binary stars may actually be the norm rather than the exception. By naked eye, we usually see only single stars, be-

FIGURE 95. *The little wobble in the star's motion meant that it either had a companion or was drunk.*

cause the stars comprising a binary pair are usually quite close together compared with interstellar distances, and also because one member of the pair is often too faint to be seen by eye.[1] Some astronomers believe that even our Sun may have a companion star that has gone undetected because it is either too faint to be seen or is simply indistinguishable against the background of billions of other faint stars.

1. The ancient Romans used a binary star in the Big Dipper as a vision test for soldiers. See if you can make out which of the stars in the Dipper is actually a binary.

We can easily find the ratio of the masses of the stars making up a binary pair by observing each star's relative distance to their common center of mass as they orbit this point. For example, if one star's orbit radius is half that of the other, it must have twice the other's mass (recall the twirled dumbbell on a string in essay 35). In order to find the masses themselves, and not just their ratio, we need to measure the actual separation between the stars, as well as the period of their orbit. Obviously, for a given orbit size, the faster the stars circle each other, the greater must be their masses to provide the needed gravitational attraction.

How about stars that lack a companion—how are their masses determined? Unfortunately, we cannot apply the perturbation method used for planets lacking moons, because nonbinary stars are much too far apart to have a significant influence on one another's motion. One method that has been used to find the masses of lone stars is based on an empirical relationship between a star's mass and its brightness (see essay 48). According to this relationship, a star's intrinsic brightness has been found to be roughly proportional to the fourth power of its mass. For example, we can infer that a star whose intrinsic brightness is ten thousand times that of the Sun must have a mass roughly ten times that of the Sun, and one whose brightness is one ten-thousandth that of the Sun must have roughly a tenth of the Sun's mass.[2] Clearly, massive stars are *much* brighter than those of lower mass.

79. What Are the Lowest and Highest Masses a Star Can Have?

LIKE LIVING creatures, stars go through a life cycle from "birth" to "death." Here we take a look at how stars are born. Stars are formed out of clouds of dust and gas, primarily hydrogen and helium, that sometimes form in the space between the stars.[1] Astronomers believe that stars are born as a result of some initiating event, possibly a shock wave created by a super-

2. Actually, this relationship between a star's mass and brightness applies only to stars during their hydrogen-burning stage, which occupies the bulk of their lifetime.

---

1. According to some believers in the concept of creationism, this theory of the spontaneous formation of our world from a collapsing cloud of gas and dust makes no sense. How, they argue, could all the richness and complexity we see around us arise from some formless cloud? What are your thoughts on this difficult question?

nova—the final cataclysmic explosion of a massive star. The shock wave compresses the cloud to the point where it can collapse under its own gravity and form one or more stars.[2] Computer simulations show that if the cloud is very large, it will not collapse about a single center, but will form numerous stars at points where the density is initially greater than elsewhere. The largest mass for which an initial cloud collapses to a single center is found to be around a hundred times the mass of the Sun (100 solar masses), which is the astronomers' estimate of the most massive possible star.

The reason for the existence of a lowest-possible-mass star is also easy to understand. A star is born when the collapsing cloud of hydrogen creates a high enough pressure and temperature in its center, or core, to ignite the nuclear fusion reactions that power the star—the star literally turns on as a result of the collapse. Basically, if its mass is too low, the "wannabe star" doesn't have enough gravity to turn itself on. High temperatures in the tens of millions of degrees or more are needed to ignite fusion, because at lower temperatures the electrical repulsion between colliding hydrogen nuclei keeps them too far apart to fuse. In these fusion reactions, four hydrogen nuclei are "burned"—that is, converted into one helium nucleus plus a tremendous amount of energy.[3]

FIGURE 96. *The little cloud couldn't collapse enough to turn on, the big cloud collapsed too quickly to form a single star, but the middle cloud's collapse was just right.*

The enormous heat created by nuclear fusion is what stops gravity from making the star collapse any further during the bulk of the star's lifetime, while it proceeds to consume the hydrogen fuel at its core. But if the amount of mass present initially is insufficient, not enough pressure and heat are generated to ignite the fusion reaction at the core, and the end result may be a large planet rather than a star. The essential property that differentiates stars from planets is that stars are self-luminous bodies powered by nuclear fusion.

2. Astronomers sometimes speak of having "observed" stars formed from collapsing clouds. But while such collapses are rapid compared with a star's lifetime, they occur over many thousands of years and cannot be directly observed. In addition, newly formed stars remain embedded inside the cloud from which they formed, and so are not directly visible.

3. "Burning" is here used in the colloquial sense. We are speaking of hydrogen fusion, which occurs at tens of millions of degrees, not the ordinary chemical burning of hydrogen.

Based on calculations, it is believed that collapsing hydrogen clouds of mass less than about a hundredth of a solar mass do not create pressure and temperature high enough to ignite nuclear fusion, although such objects can still emit some heat and light during their gravitational collapse. The planet Jupiter, for example, while apparently a net emitter of radiation and hence self-luminous (though not at visible wavelengths), had a near-miss at "stardom."

The allowed range for the mass of stars is thus believed to be roughly $\frac{1}{100}$ to 100 solar masses. The brightest possible stars would therefore be about a 100 million times as bright as the Sun, based on the fourth power relationship between a star's mass and its luminosity discussed in the previous essay. The reason massive stars are so extremely bright is that, due to their stronger gravity, their cores are hotter and larger, and hence can generate much more energy.

Can we verify the estimated upper and lower mass limits of stars by direct observation? Astronomers have carried out censuses of stars according to their brightness, but such censuses are biased, because very bright stars can be seen at very great distances and so tend to be overcounted. In contrast, very dim stars shine so faintly that we might not be aware of their presence even if they were all around us. In fact, such so-called brown dwarfs, the subject of much speculation by astronomers, have not yet even been observed.

80. What Is the Lowest Mass of a Neutron Star?

SOME STARS go out with a whimper, and others with a bang—the cataclysmic explosion we call a supernova that occurs toward the end of a massive star's life. To understand the process, we need to trace the life history of a star once it begins to burn hydrogen. Through most of a star's life, an equilibrium exists between the outward pressure from the heat of nuclear fusion and the inward pressure due to its own gravity. But after most of the hydrogen fuel at the star's core is exhausted, the heat and pressure are insufficient to counter the inward force of gravity. This imbalance first results in a star entering the so-called red giant phase, in which its core collapses and separates from its expanding outer layer. Strangely, the star's outer portion expands at the same time its inner portion contracts. The core heats as it collapses, eventually getting hot enough to ignite helium, the "ash" left over from the hydrogen burning. Helium burning supplies the heat and pressure to prevent further gravitational collapse—but only temporarily.

After a star has burned most of the hydrogen and helium at its core, the internal collapse resumes, and the resulting pressure raises the core temperature still higher. If the star is massive and hot enough, the "ashes" from the helium burning (carbon and oxygen nuclei) are themselves ignited, and fuse to form still heavier elements. At some point in this process of successive collapses, each temporarily halted by new ignitions, it is no longer possible to generate energy by fusing light elements into heavier ones, and the star faces a "mid-life crisis." Like people, some stars handle their crisis much better than others. In a star's case the resolution depends solely on its mass.

The Indian astrophysicist Subrahmanyan Chandrasekhar first showed theoretically that only stars whose mass is less than 1.4 solar masses can have a peaceful end to the core-collapse crisis. Such low-mass stars can settle down to become "white dwarfs" (so called because they are much smaller than other stars of the same brightness). In white dwarfs further core collapse is prevented by the material of the star becoming, in effect, an extremely dense solid. On the other hand, in stars having a mass larger than 1.4 solar masses, the force of gravity is sufficient to squeeze electrons and protons together to form a solid ball of neutrons having a density equal to that of the atomic nucleus, namely 4 thousand trillion grams per cubic meter—or 150 million tons per teaspoonful! When the outer layers of a collapsing star fall onto this fantastically hot neutron core, a supernova explosion occurs—for a brief time, the star shines as brilliantly as all the 100 billion stars of its entire galaxy. After the star explodes, it leaves a tiny but incredibly massive remnant core: the neutron star. We know that neutron stars must be highly compact objects, based on the extreme narrowness of the light pulses they are observed to emit. The fact that these pulses are sometimes as little as .0001 seconds wide implies that the size of the emitting region must be no more than .0001 light-seconds (or 30 kilometers) wide, because otherwise the parts of the signal from the front and back of the object would reach us with a spread greater than .0001 seconds.

What is the source of the extremely narrow pulses we receive from (some) neutron stars? During the core collapse leading to the neutron star, the star's original leisurely rotation rate must increase tremendously. The principle at

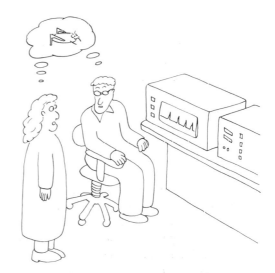

FIGURE 97. *Having detected the steady "chirp, chirp, chirp . . ." from the first pulsar, astronomers concluded that the first extraterrestrial civilization to make contact were crickets.*

work is known as conservation of angular momentum, and it is best illustrated in the speeding up of a figure skater's spin rate as she brings her arms in. Rotating with the rapidly spinning neutron star is an intense magnetic field. Electrons spiraling in the star's magnetic field produce beams of radiation that are, in effect, like searchlight beacons that sweep a narrow region of space and may happen to sweep past the Earth once per neutron star rotation, producing the effect of periodic pulses. These signals, dubbed "pulsars" when they were originally detected in 1968, are seen at optical and radio wavelengths. They were initially suspected of being signals from extraterrestrials—a possibility quickly rejected after a number of such pulsars were found, with no information content in their "message." But then again, what would extraterrestrials think of the "information content" of our radio and television broadcasts, which may eventually reach them?

81. How Massive Are Black Holes?

BLACK HOLES are even more extraordinary objects than neutron stars. For neutron stars, the relentless crush of gravity after a star has exhausted its fuel is eventually stopped by the repulsion of adjacent neutrons, a phenomenon known as neutron degeneracy pressure. But for stars larger than a critical value estimated at around 3 solar masses, gravity is too strong to be resisted by neutron degeneracy pressure or any other known force in the universe. The neutrons are literally squeezed into one another as the star collapses into a point "singularity," with a black hole as the outcome.

Consider imaginary spheres surrounding the black hole. The smaller the radius of the sphere, the greater the strength of gravity on its surface, and the larger the escape velocity is for an object at that point. For a sufficiently small-radius sphere, known as the "event horizon," the escape velocity equals the speed of light. The event horizon may be considered the "surface" of the black hole. Any matter or light inside the event horizon cannot escape, because to do so would require that its speed exceed that of light. Contrary to their popular image, black holes do not act as cosmic vacuum cleaners sucking up everything in sight. It is only matter that wanders inside the event horizon that is never seen again. Outside that point of no return, your spaceship could safely orbit the black hole without any danger of falling in, although tidal forces might well tear your ship apart at close distances.

The radius of the event horizon of a black hole is directly proportional to its mass. For the lightest black hole that can be formed from a star (3 solar masses), the radius is 18 kilometers. This number is obtained by seeing how small a sphere of three solar masses would have to be compressed so that the escape velocity from its surface would be the speed of light. Once the sphere contracted beyond this point, nothing could escape from it, since the speed of light is a universal speed limit. For an imaginary observer on the collapsing star, the collapse to within the event horizon would occur very rapidly. But another observer, watching the star collapse from a safe distance, would see the collapse occur much more slowly, because of the great distortion of space and time in the vicinity of a black hole. In fact, according to the distant observer, the final collapse of the star would be so prolonged that its surface would appear never to quite reach the event horizon. Such gravitational distortions of the rate of passage of time have actually been observed, although not in connection with collapsing black holes.

So how are black holes actually observed? Although black holes themselves emit no light or other radiation, they can reveal their presence to distant observers as outside matter nears the event horizon, where it is acted on by tremendous tidal forces. These tidal forces are great enough to heat the matter to the extraordinarily high temperatures at which X rays and gamma rays are emitted, before the matter passes beyond the event horizon of the black hole. It is primarily this X-ray and gamma radiation to which astronomers refer when they speak of "observing" a black hole. The situation is reminiscent of "observing" the Chesire Cat in Alice in Wonderland, while seeing only the smile it leaves behind.

Black holes have another observable characteristic, namely their gravitational pull on other matter. If astronomers find a star wobbling without a visible companion, and if the size of the wobble suggests the companion has a mass greater than 3 solar masses, there is an excellent chance its companion is a black

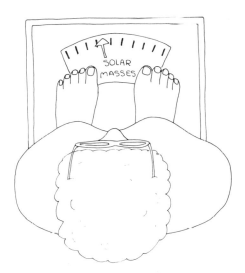

FIGURE 98. *Her fuel nearly gone, Stella tried desperately to shed some weight before the inexorable contraction of gravity began.*

hole—particularly if X rays and gamma rays are observed. But the 3-solar-mass limit does not mean that a star above the limit is preordained from its birth to become a black hole. Stars can change their mass throughout their lifetime by either accreting or shedding matter, as sometimes happens in violent outbursts known as novae. A high-mass star would need to shed enough matter to get below

145

the critical value of 3 solar masses, or else it presumably could not escape becoming a black hole, once the fuel at its core was exhausted and its gravitational collapse began.

82. What Are the Most Massive and Least Massive Black Holes?

THE THOUGHT of a black hole gobbling up all matter that comes too close can be a bit disconcerting. There is no upper limit in principle to the mass of black holes, which can grow indefinitely provided there is nearby matter to accrete. The centers of galaxies are just such a matter-rich environment, permitting any massive black holes there to grow steadily. In fact, astronomers now believe massive black holes exist at the center of our galaxy, as well as others. One such supermassive black hole observed at the heart of the galaxy M87 in the constellation Virgo is estimated to have a mass of 2.6 billion times that of the Sun, based on its gravitational attraction for orbiting stars.

Supermassive black holes are not observed directly; rather, astronomers see the high-energy radiation emitted by matter in the process of being heated as it falls into the black hole. In the case of the M87 black hole, in addition to the radiation, astronomers also found two huge jets of high-temperature gas squirting out to a distance of 4,000 light-years from the core of the galaxy. These jets of hot gas appear to be a general feature of all models of accretion of matter by black holes. According to theory, as matter spirals into the black hole in a rotating flattened disk, some matter is ejected in both directions along the axis of rotation perpendicular to the disk. Recent observations with the Hubble telescope have also revealed the disk around several supermassive black holes.

At the lower extreme of black hole masses, the smallest black hole that could result from a dying star is thought to be about 3 solar masses, as mentioned in the previous essay. Lower-mass stars just don't have enough gravity to compress matter beyond the nuclear density of a neutron star. But if it were possible to achieve such a compression by nongravitational means, an object of *any* size could be transformed into a black hole, provided it was compressed to the point where the escape velocity at its surface equaled the speed of light. For smallest stellar black hole (with a mass of 3 solar masses), the required size would be a sphere of radius 18 kilometers. Since the required size is proportional to the mass, the Earth, for example, with a mass a million times less than the smallest stellar black hole, would need to be compressed to golf ball size (1.8 centimeters in radius) to become a black hole! No known force in the present-day universe would be capable of compressing the Earth to golf ball size, but shortly after the big bang, when unimaginably high temperatures existed, such mini black holes might well have been created. No one knows if primordial mini black holes actually exist, but if they do, they could be observed because of a most remarkable property. In seeming contradiction to the very concept of a black hole, from which nothing can escape, mini black holes supposedly can emit great quantities of radiation and "evaporate."

How can a black hole evaporate, when not even light can escape from it? Actually, though a photon of light cannot permanently escape, it can leave the black hole for a short time before return-

ing, as explained in essay 86. While such "virtual" photons are outside the black hole, they can spontaneously dissociate into an electron and a positron. Normally, the electron-positron pair would have to recombine rapidly into a photon. But just outside a mini black hole, gravitational tidal forces are so strong that the evanescent pair can be ripped apart, with one member falling back into the hole and the other ejected from the vicinity. To picture the process, think of a yo-yo tethered at the end of a powerful rubber band representing gravity. No matter how fast you throw the yo-yo upward, the rubber band always pulls it back. But sometimes the rubber band, in pulling the yo-yo downward, breaks it apart, caus-

FIGURE 99. *The author tries in vain to come up with a nonracist, nonsexist, nonobscene, nonflaky, funny cartoon about black holes.*

ing only half to return. In the case of a mini black hole, the loss of an electron or positron causes it to lose a bit of mass and shrink slightly in size. The net result is that the tidal forces just outside the hole become *stronger*, and the "evaporation" process is slightly accelerated—eventually leading to a runaway explosion and the disappearance of the black hole. If there were any mini black holes formed shortly after the big bang, those with masses of about 200 million tons (the size of a very small asteroid) should be popping off just about now.

83. How Massive Are Galaxies?

ALL THE STARS you can see by naked eye on the clearest night are but the tiniest fraction of the stars making up our galaxy. The mass of our galaxy—between 100 billion and a trillion solar masses—can be deduced from the orbital motions of stars about the galactic center. The complexity of observing the rotation of the galaxy can be illustrated by picturing someone in total darkness on a slowly rotating merry-go-round who wants to find its rotational speed by observing the motion of lights held by people milling around at random on the merry-go-round as well as on the ground. But the galactic case is even more complicated, since the galaxy does not rotate as a rigid object like a merry-go-round. Instead, the orbital speed of stars varies with their distance from the galactic center. On the other hand, it is precisely because different parts of the galaxy rotate at different rates that we can deduce its rotation without reference to outside objects. (A bunch of flies sitting all along the second hand of a clock would all see the others at rest, which would not be the case if the flies orbited the center of the clock at different rates, like the stars in our galaxy.)

Once we have determined how the average rotational speed of stars in our galaxy varies with their distance from the galactic center, we can then figure out how strong the pull of gravity must be at each distance to keep the stars in their orbits. Finally, from the strength of gravity at each point, we can tell how much mass must be between that point and the galactic center. Applying this method to stars near the edge of the galaxy allows us to calculate the mass of the entire galaxy. A second method for finding the mass of the galaxy is to look at other nearby "satellite" galaxies, and see how their motions are affected by the

FIGURE 100. *Neutrinos, shuminos! I'll bet the dark matter really consists of all those missing socks that have been accumulating since the dawn of time.*

pull of gravity from our galaxy. In principle, the idea is just like finding the mass of a planet by observing the orbit of its moons, or finding the mass of binary stars by observing their mutual orbits. Still a third way to find the mass of the galaxy is to estimate the number of stars in it (about 100 billion) and multiply by the average mass of a star.[1] This last method gives a mass for the galaxy only about a tenth of that given by the first two methods. Basically, there does not seem to be enough *visible* matter (in the form of stars) for the galaxy to hold itself together as it rotates, and to keep satellite galaxies in their orbits about us.

The masses of other galaxies can usually be found more easily than that of our own, since we can see them from the outside. Using the same three methods for finding our own galaxy's mass, it appears that other galaxies (as well as the space between galaxies) do not seem to have enough visible matter to hold them together. These observations imply the existence of some kind of dark (non-luminous) matter, which accounts for perhaps over 90 percent of the mass of our galaxy and others. Astronomers are uncertain about the nature of the dark matter, but one possibility among many would be neutrinos, which are subatomic particles present throughout space in fantastic numbers. Unlike some scientific puzzles that lack a solution, the problem of the nature of the dark matter has too many possible answers—we just don't know which is (or which are) the right one(s)!

84. How Massive Is the Universe?

IN NORSE mythology, the Ygdrasil is the great ash tree whose roots and branches hold the universe together. In today's cosmology, we call the Ygdrasil "gravity." Whether or not there is enough gravity to hold the universe together depends on the amount of matter present, or more precisely its density. The mass of the observable universe can be found if we estimate the average mass of galaxies, and multiply by the estimated number of galaxies in the universe (found from a random sample for various regions of the sky). We also need to take into account the dark matter between galaxies that may, in some estimates, comprise ten to one hundred times the observed mass of the galaxies themselves (see the previous essay). If we divide the mass of the universe by its volume, we obtain a value for the average density of matter in the universe that is

1. Astronomers don't actually count the 100 billion or more stars in a galaxy. Rather, they rely on a sampling technique for various regions of the galaxy.

the equivalent of a mere three hydrogen atoms per cubic meter. That doesn't sound like much, but then again there are a lot of cubic meters out there—in the neighborhood of 10^{79} (a one followed by 79 zeros).

For cosmologists—those scientists who study the structure and evolution of the universe—the average density of matter in the universe is a crucial parameter, because it determines the ultimate fate of the universe. This mutual gravitational attraction of all matter for all other matter obviously has an effect on slowing the rate of expansion of the universe. For example, if the universe were nearly empty, the force of gravitational attraction on one piece of matter due to the rest of the universe would be very small. Therefore, for a nearly empty universe, the slowing down of the expansion would be negligible, and the expansion would continue forever.

FIGURE 101. *Make that universe lite.*

Cosmologists describe that possibility as an open universe. In contrast, if the density of matter in the universe exceeds some critical value, the force of gravity is sufficient to reverse the expansion at some point, and the primordial big bang will ultimately be followed by the "big crunch." For obvious reasons, this possibility is referred to as a closed universe. The intermediate case, when the density of matter in the universe just equals the critical density, would be a barely open universe, in which the parts of the universe just manage to escape one another's gravity, allowing the expansion to continue indefinitely at a slower and slower rate.

If we estimate the average density of matter found in the universe, we should, in principle, be able to discover whether we live in a closed, open, or barely open universe. The actual matter density appears to be fairly close to the critical density, which would imply a barely open universe, but uncertainties in the estimated density don't allow for a definite conclusion. One other test is to look at the speed of recession of the most distant galaxies. If the universe is closed (and the expansion slowing down), we might expect the most distant galaxies to be receding faster than predicted. The idea is that nearby galaxies (whose light reaches us from a later time in their history) have been slowed by gravity longer than more distant ones. Thus, by looking at whether the speed of distant galaxies is strictly proportional to their distance (as Hubble's law predicts), or whether it increases slightly faster, we can, in principle, decide whether the universe is closed or open. Unfortunately, the difficulty in measuring the speed and distance to the most distant galaxies again prevents a definitive judgment using this test.

One other possible test to resolve the question of whether the universe is closed or open involves the curvature of space. According to general relativity theory, the presence of matter is associated with a curvature or distortion of space-time—the more matter, the more curvature. In principle, we can observe the overall curvature of space by observing how the apparent number and size of distant galaxies varies with their distance. Not surprisingly, these measurements have not been able to settle the issue either. The closed/open universe question remains open (or is that closed?).

85. How Massive Are Atoms?

Atom—A WORD DERIVED from the ancient Greek—means "indivisible." Clearly, given our current knowledge of *subatomic* entities, that earlier concept is obsolete. Atoms today are defined as the smallest units of matter that preserve the *chemical identity* of the approximately one hundred elements of which our universe is composed. Chemical compounds made from these elements ultimately consist of individual molecules, so any molecule must consist of one or more atoms. The water (H_2O) molecule, for example, consists of two hydrogen and one oxygen atoms. Still more complex entities (like you) cannot be expressed in terms of a single formula, since they consist of many different kinds of molecules, and have a complex structure.

The mass or weight of atoms tend to have close to integer ratios. For example, if the element carbon is assumed to have a mass of exactly 12, then the masses of the three lightest elements are 1.01 for hydrogen, 4.00 for helium, and 6.94 for lithium. Chemists have figured out these atomic masses by forming chemical compounds, such as H_2O, and seeing exactly how much mass of one element combines with how much mass of the other. For example, the fact that the oxygen atom is approximately sixteen times heavier than the hydrogen atom is deduced from the observation that when hydrogen combines with oxygen to form water, 8 grams of oxygen are consumed for every gram of hydrogen.[1] (What a wonderful fuel hydrogen is: when burned, its only by-product is water!)

Atoms have nearly integral mass ratios because all atoms are made of the same basic constituents: a nucleus, which contains particles known as protons and neutrons (both have nearly the same mass), and comparatively light electrons in a "cloud" surrounding the nucleus, which contain a mere 0.05 percent of the atom's mass. Thus, the mass of an atom is primarily determined by the number of

1. It is 8 grams of oxygen rather than 16, because two hydrogen atoms are needed for each oxygen atom.

neutrons and protons contained in its nucleus, which explains why atoms tend to have masses that are nearly integral ratios. (People too would have masses that had integral ratios if everyone were made from varying numbers of identical blocks.)

There are, however, two main reasons why the mass ratios of atoms are only approximately integers. First, the mass of the nucleus of an atom depends not only on the number of neutrons and protons it contains but also on the particular arrangement of these particles, namely how loosely or tightly they are bound together.[2] Second, any given atom can exist in a variety of atomic species known as isotopes. Isotopes of an element are chemically almost identical, and are distinguished by the number of neutrons in the atomic nucleus and, therefore, by their weight. For example, most hydrogen atoms in nature have a nucleus consisting of a single proton, but one in six hundred will have an accompanying neutron, and comprise the hydrogen isotope known as deuterium. Thus, one in six hundred water molecules consists of "heavy water" in which one hydrogen atom is deuterium. (Pure heavy water would taste just like ordinary water, but would be about 5 percent heavier.) If no attempt is made to separate the isotopes of a given element, what is found in nature is some mixture whose atomic weight depends on the relative amount of each isotope. Isotope separation is a difficult and expensive business, because all the isotopes of an element have nearly the same chemical properties, which are determined by the number of protons in the nucleus and the number of surrounding electrons.

FIGURE 102. *"Waiter, I'm on a diet. Could I have a glass of water with the heavy water removed?"*

2. In general, the more tightly bound the nuclear particles, the lower the nuclear mass is, as explained in essay 88.

86. How Is the Pion's Mass Related to the Range of Nuclear Forces?

A SUBATOMIC PARTICLE like the electron, proton, or neutron deserves the adjective "elementary," only if it does not consist of still more fundamental entities. On this basis, of the three particles just mentioned, only the electron is truly elementary, being regarded as a point particle. In contrast, the proton and neutron are each composed of three pointlike constituents, the whimsically named quarks. The three quarks making up the neutron and proton are believed to occupy a sphere of diameter about equal to 1 femtometer (a trillionth of a millimeter), a value that can be found in experiments in which a very energetic proton is scattered off a neutron or another proton. The pointlike nature of the electron and the three quark constituents of the proton were found in similar experiments by scattering high-energy beams of electrons off electrons and protons. Someone once compared these kinds of experiments to finding out how pianos are made by repeatedly dropping them down a flight of stairs, and listening to the sounds they make while falling.

Even though electrons are theoretically described as point particles, they are envisioned as being surrounded by a cloud of photons that are continually being emitted and reabsorbed by the electron—analogous to a swarm of bees around a flower. You might think that no electron could emit another particle and remain an electron—a process that would seemingly violate the principle of energy conservation. (A woman obviously cannot "emit" a child, and still remain exactly the same mass after giving birth.) Yet according to the Heisenberg uncertainty principle, such "virtual" processes are allowed, at least for particles. The uncertainty principle requires that the product of the amount of energy nonconservation, E, and the time during which it is not conserved, t, must not exceed a certain tiny quantity known as Planck's constant. The term *virtual* refers precisely to the fact that if the process were to occur with real particles that could be observed in detectors, the process *would* violate energy conservation.[1]

The virtual photons emitted by an electron are not always emitted and absorbed by the same electron. In fact, the virtual photons exchanged between any

---

1. The "violations" of the energy conservation principle by virtual particles are violations only if we ignore the fact that the rest mass of virtual particles is not the same as that of real particles, that is, particles that can register in a detector.

pair of charged particles account for the force they exert on each other. To understand how the exchange of a particle leads to a force, think of a pair of people on frictionless ice tossing a heavy ball from one to the other. When one person throws the ball she recoils, and her partner recoils when he catches the ball. Effectively, the exchange of the heavy ball has the same effect on each person as if he or she exerted a repulsive force on the other. An exchanged object can also have the effect of an *attractive* force between the skaters if, for example, one skater snatches the object away from the other who tries to hold on to it.

When virtual photons are exchanged between charged particles, the range of the force between the particles is infinite, because the photon rest mass is zero (see essay 93). The idea is that a rest mass of zero makes it possible for exchanged photons to have arbitrarily small energy. Thus, according to the uncertainty principle, the arbitrarily small photon energy implies an arbitrarily large range of the force between a pair of charged particles, just like gravity. Putting it in colloquial terms, the length of time the photon can get away with "violating" the conservation of energy law depends inversely on the length of time it is violated—long violations require that the extent of violation be incredibly tiny.

FIGURE 103. *The more money Ralph "borrowed" from his bank, the faster he had to return it before its loss was noticed.*

In contrast to two charged particles, a pair of neutrons (or a neutron and a proton) exert only a *short-range* nuclear force on one another. The mediator of the strong nuclear force between protons and neutrons can also be described as a virtual exchanged particle—the pion, a particle of mass about three hundred times the mass of the electron. The nonzero mass of the pion implies a lower limit to the energy it can have, namely mc^2. According to Heisenberg's uncertainty principle, a minimum nonzero amount of energy nonconservation therefore implies a limited virtual particle lifetime, and hence a maximum range for the strong force of about 1 femtometer.

87. What Is the Heaviest Possible Stable Atom?

ATOMS, like people, can be stable or unstable. Atoms of the unstable variety, also known as radioactive atoms, fall apart (decay) without any outside provocation. Actually, as with people, the dividing line between stability and instabilitiy is somewhat blurred. If an atom (actually an atomic nucleus) were absolutely stable it would *never* disintegrate: it would have an infinite half-life, which is the time interval required for half of a given number of atoms to decay.[1] But all we can observe empirically is whether the half-life is longer than some particular value. Consequently, we may arbitrarily define nuclei with half-lives longer than, say, a million years to be stable, in which case certain long-lived radioactive nuclei are classified as stable, even though they are known to decay.

The chemical identity of any atom is determined by the number of protons in the nucleus (and the corresponding number of surrounding electrons). The weight of an atom is determined primarily by the number of nuclear neutrons and protons but not the surrounding electrons, which comprise a mere 0.05 percent of the atom's mass. In fact, the total number of neutrons and protons in the nucleus is actually called the atomic weight, which ranges from 1 for hydrogen, the lightest element, to 209 for bismuth, the heaviest stable element. In order to understand why atoms heavier than bismuth are unstable, we need to consider the three forces that act on the neutrons and protons in the nucleus. A fourth force, gravity, will be ignored, because it is so much weaker than the other three.

Picture yourself as a proton in a large room (the nucleus of an atom), with a number of other protons and neutrons. You are slightly repelled (electrically) by all the other protons, but strongly attracted to whichever proton or neutron is standing next to you. This strong short-range attractive force that acts between any adjacent pair of nuclear particles is called the "strong" force. It is the "glue" that holds the nucleus together. The degree of stability of nuclei is determined in large measure by the overall difference between the repulsive electrical and attractive strong forces on protons and neutrons. For atomic nuclei with more

1. Thus, if you started with 1,000 intact atoms with a half-life of a thousand seconds, you would be left with 500 after a thousand seconds, and around 250 after another thousand seconds, although the exact numbers may vary because of statistical fluctuations.

than about twenty-six protons, each added proton makes the nucleus less stable. The decrease in stability occurs because each added proton is repelled by the long-range electrical repulsion from all the other protons in the nucleus, but it is attracted only by the strong short-range attraction of its nearest neighbors, so the number of repulsions grows faster than the number of attractions. For a large enough nucleus, the many small repulsions win out over the few strong attractions, and at this point the overall force on each proton you attempt to add is one of repulsion rather than attraction. For this reason, there is a maximum number of protons that a nucleus can have and still be stable.

FIGURE 104. *Even though Betty was strongly attracted to Bob, her mild dislike of each of his friends made her reluctant to attend parties with him when more than twenty-five friends were there.*

Seemingly the increasing instability that arises when more and more protons are added to a nucleus should not apply to neutrons, which do not feel the long-range electrical repulsive force. The number of neutrons in a nucleus is, however, limited by the third fundamental force, weaker than the other two, called, of all things, the "weak" force. The weak force acts to transform neutrons into protons or protons into neutrons, depending on the relative numbers of each particle in the nucleus. For neutrons and protons *outside* the nucleus, this transformation works only in one direction: the more massive neutron can spontaneously shed an electron, and in the process transform itself into a proton with a half-life of about a thousand seconds.[2] Inside the nucleus, however, the different binding strengths for protons and neutrons (see the next essay) sometimes makes up for this mass difference and allows protons to be converted to neutrons—depending on whether there are too many of one kind or the other in the nucleus. Thus, if there is a maximum number of protons a nucleus can have and still be stable, there is also some maximum number of neutrons. These maximum numbers add to 209, the mass of the heaviest stable nucleus.

2. Another particle known as the antineutrino is also emitted when the neutron decays.

88. What Is the Most Stable Nucleus?

IN EVERYDAY life, mass appears to be a conserved quantity: if ten people 70 kilograms each step into an elevator, the combined mass of all the occupants is 700 kilograms. The closeness of elevator occupants has no measurable effect on their combined mass (or weight)—ignoring weight loss through perspiration! Such is not the case for the neutrons and protons comprising the nucleus of an atom. The total mass of a nucleus can be as much as 1 percent less than the sum of the masses of its constituents. By analogy, it would be as though the combined mass of the ten elevator occupants together was only 693 instead of 700 kilograms.

The loss of mass that occurs when neutrons and protons are bound together in the nucleus is a consequence of Einstein's relation between mass and energy, $E = mc^2$. To free the particles of a nucleus, you must supply energy—actually quite a lot of energy, since they are bound together rather tightly. For the most tightly bound nuclei, the energy to separate each neutron or proton is equivalent to about 1 percent of the particle's mass. This is the reason that particles bound together in the nucleus have an effective mass that is about 1 percent less than when they are separated or free. The mass difference between the nucleus and the sum of the masses of its constituent particles accounts for the huge energy release in a hydrogen bomb. When two light nuclei combine (fuse) to form a heavier nucleus, the combined nucleus has less mass than the two lighter ones before they combined. The loss in mass must be accounted for by a conversion of the energy associated with mass into some other form, namely the energy of motion of the products formed in the reaction. Most of this energy is eventually transformed into light and heat as the reaction products undergo random collisions with the surrounding material.

The same loss of mass described above occurs any time particles or atoms are bound together. For example, when two hydrogen atoms are bound together with one oxygen atom to form H_2O, the mass of the water molecule is ever so slightly less than the sum of the masses of the three individual atoms. The mass loss when atoms are bound together is much less than in nuclear binding, because the forces holding atoms together are typically a million times weaker than those holding nuclei together. So instead of there being a 1-percent drop in mass when the two hydrogen atoms join an oxygen atom, the drop is perhaps only a millionth of a percent. For this reason, chemists, who are practical fellows, often say (incorrectly) that mass is conserved in chemical reactions—the mass difference is simply too small to notice. But strictly speaking, any time objects are bound together (even blocks glued together), the mass of the bound system must, according to $E = mc^2$, be lighter than the sum of the individual masses. Even the ten elevator occupants would, in fact, have a combined mass ever so slightly less than 700 kilograms, because of their mutual gravitational attraction (binding).

In the case of atomic nuclei, the element that shows the greatest percent difference between the mass of the nucleus and the sum of its constituent masses is iron, with an atomic mass of 56 (the nucleus has fifty-six neutrons plus protons). This fact is a direct consequence of the maximum binding energy of particles in the iron nucleus. To see why nuclei heavier than iron are less tightly bound, consider the forces felt by each proton in the nucleus: both a strong short-range attraction to its nearest neighbors, as well as many weaker long-range repulsions to *all* the other protons in the nucleus (see previous essay). For nuclei heavier than iron, there are so many protons that the many long-range repulsions increasingly tend to overwhelm the few short-range attractions felt by each proton, and as a result, the nuclei become less and less stable the more protons and neutrons they have. In nuclei lighter than iron, a different reason accounts for their relative instability. A larger fraction of protons or neutrons in light nuclei are on the nuclear surface, and these particles, which are bound to fewer neighboring particles than those in the interior, are therefore bound less tightly.

FIGURE 105. *Fortunately, the mass of all the elevator occupants together was less than the sum of their individual masses.*

One consequence of the maximum binding energy of the iron nucleus is that only those nuclei lighter than iron will produce energy when they fuse to form heavier nuclei. So if you want energy from atoms, you need to build fusion reactors for light elements and fission reactors for heavy elements.

89. What Is the Largest Possible Mass of a Plutonium Sphere?

A LARGE nucleus, like uranium or plutonium, bears a certain similarity to a large drop of water (or mercury). If you give a large mercury droplet a poke, it quivers and oscillates—perhaps even fissions if the poke is hard enough. Certain isotopes of uranium and plutonium do not even require an outside poke, and can fission spontaneously. In this case the atomic nuclei split apart into two smaller nuclei and one or more neutrons. The energy liberated in fission comes from the loss in mass (the original nucleus has higher mass than the final products). The neutrons emitted during a spontaneous fission can be absorbed by other nuclei, where they create enough instability to cause those nuclei to fission, creating still more neutrons and a possible runaway chain reaction.

Whether or not a runaway chain reaction occurs for a particular piece of plutonium or uranium depends on whether the mass of the material exceeds some value known as the "critical mass."[1] A critical mass exists, because if there is less material present, too many neutrons escape through the surface of the material to induce the next "generation" of fissions, and the chain reaction stops. The idea of a chain reaction is similar to what happens in the case of a population "explosion," where if each generation produces more than two offspring who themselves have children, runaway population growth occurs.

One difference between nuclear and population explosions is that in the nuclear case you need only an average of more than *one* neutron to create the next generation of fissions, but for a population explosion two surviving children are needed per generation. The other major difference is that unlike the case with human populations, the nuclear chain reaction occurs so quickly that once underway, human intervention is powerless to stop it. (Each generation of fissions takes only millionths of a second.)

In order to create a nuclear explosion, all you need to do is bring together two subcritical pieces of fissionable material, such as plutonium, to make a single piece whose mass exceeds the critical mass. The nuclear explosion will start before the two pieces actually touch, since neutrons shooting out from one piece can initiate fissions in the other. The main trick in achieving a "successful"

---

1. Actually, the value of the critical mass depends on the shape, purity, and density of the material.

unclear explosion, rather than a fizzle, is to bring the two pieces together very quickly (using high explosives). Otherwise, the start of the nuclear detonation will drive them apart before a sizable fraction of the atoms have fissioned.

In nature, the uranium isotope useful for nuclear weapons is mixed with other isotopes, from which it must be separated. The difficult process of isotope separation, or "enrichment," is needed to concentrate fissionable uranium or plutonium. How much enriched plutonium or uranium will you need if you want to create your own personal nuclear deterrent? The amount is somewhere in the vicinity of 7 kilograms, or 16 pounds, for plutonium—not a great deal, considering the amounts produced in nuclear reactors around the world.

FIGURE 106. *Unaware of the dire consequences, the cleaning lady unwittingly rearranged Professor Jones's plutonium bookends.*

Incidentally, in nuclear reactors, even though the fuel is not usually highly enriched, care must be taken not to let enough uranium or plutonium concentrate in one place lest this cause a runaway chain reaction. Even if a chain reaction did occur, however, the result would not be a nuclear explosion, because as described earlier, the material would drive itself apart before the nuclear reaction got very far. Instead, the reactor could produce a "meltdown," the consequences of which would depend on whether radioactive elements escaped into the environment.

90. What Is the Lightest Gas on Earth?

HAVE YOU EVER wondered what becomes of all the helium balloons accidentally released by disappointed children? The balloons themselves eventually burst, because as they rise, they must expand as the outside air pressure gradually drops. But what of the helium they contain? One might imagine the helium rising to the top of the atmosphere and staying there, but in fact, it is too light to remain in the atmosphere, and it eventually diffuses much farther into space, atom by atom.

That is not to say that the Earth's atmosphere is totally devoid of helium. The atmosphere, which consists of about 99 percent nitrogen and oxygen, does contain trace amounts of helium (0.00052 percent), and even less hydrogen (0.00005 percent). But these minute concentrations are presumably due only to the continuous addition of hydrogen and helium to the atmosphere from the decay of radioactive gases, such as radon, that reach the Earth's surface principally through underground cracks. To understand why the atmosphere is nearly devoid of hydrogen and helium, let's consider the distribution of molecular speeds in a gas.

The molecules in a gas have a continuous random motion, and they frequently collide with each other. As a result of these collisions, gas molecules always have a distribution of energies—some with energies much less than the average, and some with energies much greater than average. The average energy per molecule is in fact directly proportional to the gas's absolute temperature. In a mixture of two or more gases, all of them must have exactly the same temperature. Even if some of the gases start out hotter or colder than the others, the result of their mixing is to establish a common temperature in a fairly short time.

A common temperature means a common average energy for the different gases, so that molecules of the heavier gas must be moving more slowly on average than those of the lighter gas. The heavier molecules move more slowly because the energy of a molecule is proportional to both its mass and the square of its speed, so for a fixed energy, bigger mass means smaller speed. For example, in a mixture of hydrogen and oxygen gas, the sixteen-times-heavier oxygen molecules move only one-quarter as fast as the hydrogen molecules, on average. To get the idea, think of many Ping-Pong balls whizzing around the frictionless floor of an empty room. Mixed in with the Ping-Pong balls is an equal number of bowling balls, initially at rest. As a result of random collisions between balls, the bowling balls will acquire some of the Ping-Pong balls' energy. In fact, at equilibrium,

161

both types of balls will on average have the same energy, although the bowling balls will be moving much more slowly, in view of their much larger mass.

Given the molecular weights of various gases, we can easily compute what the average speed of their molecules must be for any given common temperature. For example, the gases hydrogen and oxygen have average molecular speeds of 10.4 and 2.6 kilometers per second at room temperature (note the four to one ratio). Why is hydrogen but not oxygen moving too fast to remain in the atmosphere? Recall that any object launched upward from the Earth's surface will eventually come down only if its launch velocity is less than the "escape velocity," 11.2 kilometers per second.

Both hydrogen and oxygen have average molecular speeds well below the Earth's escape velocity, yet somehow the hydrogen (and helium) atoms manage to escape. The answer to the puzzle is that there are a significant fraction of hydrogen molecules with speeds well above the average, and it is these molecules that escape into space. On the other hand, a negligible fraction of oxygen escapes into space, because there are far fewer oxygen molecules with speeds greater than the escape velocity. On the Moon, or on low-gravity planets with a low escape velocity, no atmosphere is found, because a sizable fraction of *all* gases released there would have velocities in excess of the escape velocity.

FIGURE 107. *Reminiscent of the town where all the kids are above average, hydrogen and helium escape from the Earth's atmosphere because all molecules have speeds much faster than the average some fraction of the time.*

91. What Is Your Mass When Going Close to the Speed of Light?

ONE OF THE peculiar effects predicted by Einstein's theory of relativity is that the mass of objects increases with their speed, becoming infinite as the speed approaches the speed of light. Mass, remember, refers neither to the "amount of matter," nor the size (volume) of an object; rather, it refers to a body's inertia. So the increase in mass with speed means that it gets harder and harder to accelerate a body the closer its speed gets to the speed of light. In fact, this is one way to explain why objects cannot be accelerated to or past the speed of light.

The particular equation that describes how a body's mass varies with speed predicts a very small increase in mass until a body travels at a substantial fraction of the speed of light.[1] The equation predicts, for example, that if a body's speed is 10 percent the speed of light, its mass will increase by only 0.5 percent, but if its speed is 98 percent that of light, its mass will increase fivefold. Speeds that we normally think of as very high, such as the speed of a jet aircraft or the speed of a rocket, are in fact minuscule compared with the speed of light. So clearly the predicted increase in mass with speed is insignificant for objects moving at everyday speeds—even the speed of a jet aircraft. But there are objects that do travel at speeds approaching the speed of light, namely subatomic particles. Such speeds occur naturally in cosmic rays from space, or among particles accelerated to very high speeds in a particle accelerator. So we can directly observe how much a particle's mass increases with speed (based on its energy), and we find that the prediction of relativity is correct.

Even though today's rocket ships cannot travel at anything close to the speed of light, someday a spacecraft may be able to. The obstacle for rockets seems to be an efficient energy source that can produce a sustained acceleration over a very long time. Also, the speed of the engine's exhaust needs to be extremely high (ideally the speed of light); otherwise an absurdly large fraction of the initial mass of the ship would have to be devoted to fuel. With a constant acceleration, the

---

1. The mass of a body is predicted to be $\gamma = 1/\sqrt{1-f^2}$ times its mass at rest for a body traveling at a fraction, f, of the speed of light, according to an observer watching it move past. Note that at the speed of light ($f = 1$), the equation predicts an infinite mass. At 98 percent the speed of light ($f = 0.98$), it predicts a mass increased by a factor of five—a 400 percent increase.

speed of the ship would initially increase at a constant rate over time. As the speed of light was approached, however, the same continued rocket thrust would produce less and less acceleration due to the ship's mass increase.

Interestingly, people inside the ship would *not* observe any change in their mass or that of their ship. As far as the ship's occupants would be concerned, they and their ship could be considered *at rest*, so none of the peculiar effects of relativity would apply. On the other hand, if they were to look outside and observe the universe going by, the ship's occupants would find that the masses of objects going past them were increased. The complete symmetry between the observers inside the ship and people watching the ship go by means that neither the ship's crew nor those watching the ship

FIGURE 108. *"Wait a second. Who says I'm going close to the speed of light?" thought Fred, on noticing that his spaceship scale read his normal weight.*

go past are in a "preferred" reference frame. Each observer is entitled to consider himself at rest and the other in motion. Hence each says his mass is normal and the other's mass is increased. On the other hand, just because the predicted increase in mass with speed is observer-dependent does not mean it is some kind of illusion. Either way you look at it, mass increases so as to enforce the speed limit of c.

92. What Are the Masses of Subatomic Particles?

HOW ARE THE masses of such incredibly tiny entities as electrons and protons actually measured? The masses of subatomic particles can be found using devices such as bubble chambers and mass spectrometers. The inventor of the bubble chamber, Donald Glaser, supposedly got the idea for the device by observing the rising trails of tiny bubbles in a glass of beer! Bubble chambers contain a liquid put into a "superheated" state by suddenly releasing the pressure on it. A liquid in such a state is above its normal boiling point. If the bubble chamber is placed in the path of a beam of charged particles, the disturbance to individual atoms all along the path of the particles causes the superheated liquid to boil at multiple points along these paths. If the liquid is photographed before the bubbles grow in size, you see trails of tiny bubbles created in the wake of each charged particle that entered the chamber.

The particles' paths curve in response to forces acting on the particles, and momentum can be measured from path curvature, so these pictures can be analyzed to determine the masses and other properties of the particles that created the bubble trails, much as plentary orbits can be analyzed.

The masses of neutral particles are more difficult to find than those of charged particles, since neutral particles do not leave trails in a bubble chamber. If a neutral particle takes part in reactions in which the masses of all the other particles are known, its mass can be found by measuring the energies and directions of all the other particles and reasoning that any missing mass/energy must belong to the unseen neutral particle. This

FIGURE 109. *Nettie the neutron couldn't understand why she always went to pieces when she was by herself. She was perfectly stable in the presence of others.*

same technique can be used to measure the mass of highly unstable particles that disintegrate before traveling any appreciable distance. The idea is much the same as an auditor deducing the amount of money embezzled from a company by totaling all known sources of income and expenditure. The only difference is that the "currency" used to balance the books of subatomic accounts is not money, but instead energy (and also momentum).

Another type of reaction from which particle masses can be found is the decay (disintegration) of a subatomic particle. For example, consider the decay of a neutron at rest into a proton, electron, and antineutrino. If the electron, proton, and neutron masses are known, we can find the mass of the unobserved antineutrino by measuring the energies of the proton and electron.[1] The fact that free neutrons decay into protons is a direct consequence of the fact that the

1. In practice it is not usually possible to measure the energy of the proton here, but by observing the most energetic electrons ever seen, we can deduce the antineutrino rest mass.

neutron mass exceeds that of a proton plus an electron. Conversely, free protons, being lighter than neutrons, could never decay into neutrons, no matter how much energy the protons had.[2] To see why, just imagine being shrunk to atomic size and sitting on the energetic proton before it decays. Now you see the moving proton at rest, and clearly its decay into a *heavier* neutron is energetically forbidden, since the mass before the decay would be less than the mass afterward. Oddly, neutrons in a stable nucleus do not decay. The neutron, unstable when free, can become stable when bound with sufficient energy in the nucleus, because objects have a lower mass when bound than free.

93.　How Heavy Is Light?

LET'S IMAGINE that you have an account in a bank run by a lunatic. In order to discourage big depositors, the bank pays a higher percentage interest the *smaller* your account. On accounts of $100 it pays 1 percent ($1) interest, on accounts of $50 it pays 2 percent ($1) interest, and so on. In fact, the bank pays $1 interest on any account, no matter how small, so as the size of your account approaches zero, the interest rate approaches infinity. There is a lesson here applicable to the question of the mass of a photon, a particle of light.

Most particles increase their mass without limit as their speed approaches that of light. Right at the speed of light, an ordinary particle's mass and energy would have to be infinite. This does not happen for photons, because their rest mass is exactly zero, and zero increased by an infinite percentage can be a finite number ($1 in the bank analogy). We can also conclude that photons, unlike particles with nonzero rest mass, must *always* travel at the speed of light; they can never be at rest. A photon could not have a speed less than c, because then its zero rest mass would be increased by a *finite* percentage, so that its mass and energy would both be zero—meaning the photon would not exist at such a slow speed.

How can we experimentally check whether photons do, in fact, have a rest mass of zero? Since they are never at rest, we cannot very well measure this quantity directly. Instead, the test is to see whether photons of all frequencies, which is to say all energies (see essay 29), all travel at the same speed. ("Ordinary" particles with nonzero rest mass travel at different speeds depending on how much energy they have.) A particularly precise way to check whether the speed of light in vacuum depends on frequency is to look at signals received from neutron star

2. It is possible that free protons actually do decay, but if they do, the total rest mass of the decay products cannot exceed that of the proton.

pulsars, such as the one at the center of the Crab nebula. These signals are seen in both visible light (as distinct flashes) as well as much lower-frequency radio pulses. If the speed of light were to depend on frequency, the wavelengths making up white light would take different times to reach us, which would broaden the visible pulse that we received from the pulsar—much as a group of runners who are initially bunched tightly together tend to stretch out as a race proceeds.

In fact, however, pulses from the Crab nebula are found to be extremely narrow (only about a millisecond, or 0.001 seconds wide), a fact attributed to the small size of the neutron star in essay 80. But some of the pulse width could be due to broadening caused by variation in light speed with frequency. Let's conservatively attribute the entire millisecond pulse width to such broadening. Given the known distance to the Crab nebula pulsar of 6,500 light-years, the rest mass of the photon cannot be greater than 0.04 trillionths of the mass of the electron, in order not to broaden the pulse by more than a millisecond. Based on such measurements, we can conclude that the photon's rest mass is consistent with being zero. (We can never prove something is zero, any more than we can prove that unicorns don't exist!)

So does light have mass and weight? The answer is that it all depends on your definition. As we have seen, its rest mass appears to be zero, but its mass defined as the m appearing in $E = mc^2$ cannot be zero, since the energy E is nonzero. Likewise, photons must have a weight as well, since as predicted by the theory of general relativity, a ray of light passing close to a massive body like the Sun is bent very slightly. This phenomenon can be observed during a total eclipse of the Sun, when stars near the edge

FIGURE 110. *Never having been at rest, Phyllis the photon didn't miss not having a rest mass like the other particles.*

of the Sun appear to have their relative positions slightly shifted from what they would be in the Sun's absence. The observation of the deflection of light by gravity, first made during the 1919 solar eclipse, made Albert Einstein world famous for his prediction.

94. Do Neutrinos Really Have Zero Mass?

NEUTRINOS are among the most elusive and mysterious subatomic particles. Like photons, neutrinos are believed to have zero rest mass, but unlike photons, neutrinos can pass through virtually any material as though it were almost completely transparent. At this very moment, in fact, a thousand trillion of these spooky particles are passing through your body each second. Neutrinos react with matter so weakly that in your entire lifetime perhaps only one or two will stop inside your body. They can even pass through a thickness of about 100 *light-years* of lead without interacting. Needless to say, the low interaction probability of neutrinos makes them extremely difficult to detect. It was not until about twenty years after Wolfgang Pauli suggested the concept of neutrinos in the 1930s that they were finally observed in an experiment.

Pauli first proposed the neutrino as a solution to a perplexing observation in connection with the so-called beta decay of radioactive nuclei. These decays involve the emission of an electron (or positron) from a nucleus or from a free neutron. Given the mass of the nucleus before and after such a decay, one would expect the emitted electron to have a specific amount of energy according to $E = mc^2$, where m is the decrease in nuclear mass. Instead, the electrons were found to have a continuous range of energies, up to the predicted amount. The "missing" energy was so perplexing that some scientists suggested that perhaps they had found a reaction in which energy was not conserved. Pauli, instead, suggested that an unobserved third particle, later called the neutrino (Italian for "neutral little one"), accompanied the electron, and carried off some of the energy liberated in the beta decay.[1]

Pauli's brilliant suggestion was confirmed when neutrinos were finally observed in 1956 in a nuclear reactor experiment. Aside from having a very intense source of neutrinos such as a reactor, the key to being able to observe these elusive particles is to use a huge detector filled with many tons of neutrino-sensing materials and be willing to wait a long time between neutrino interactions, since they occur so rarely. It is also extremely important to shield the detector carefully, lest other kinds of particles cause interactions in the apparatus that mimic neutrinos. Experiments designed to look for neutrinos reaching us from space

---

1. It is actually the *anti*neutrino that accompanies an electron in beta decay, and the neutrino that accompanies a positron—see essay 96 on antimatter.

often use detectors buried a mile or more underground, in order to shield the apparatus from cosmic rays.

If neutrinos have zero rest mass like photons, they must also travel at the speed of light. But it is extremely difficult to verify this fact by measuring a neutrino's speed. For example, you might think of measuring how long a neutrino takes to move a fixed distance between a pair of detectors. But if the odds that a given weakly reacting neutrino will trigger the first detector are practically infinitesimal, the odds of it triggering both detectors are essentially zero, so such direct speed measurements are not possible.[2] It is more practical to see whether the neutrino's mass is zero than to measure its speed. One way of checking on the neutrino mass is to observe the maximum energy of electrons emitted from neutron disintegration, as explained in essay 92.

FIGURE 111. *Donald's reaction was a bit extreme when he learned that trillions of neutrinos pass through his body every second.*

From this and other such beta decay experiments, we can set an upper limit on the neutrino mass. We think the neutrino has exactly zero rest mass, but all we can say experimentally is that its mass is less than 0.002 percent that of the electron.[3]

2. The speed of neutrinos has been measured indirectly through the observation of a burst of neutrinos coming from a supernova seen in 1987. Presumably the neutrinos began their journey at the same time as the supernova explosion itself. If neutrinos are massless, they should reach us at the same time as the light from the supernova.

3. There are actually two other kinds of neutrinos, also believed to be massless, which have somewhat larger upper limits on their masses, based on less precise experiments.

95.   What Are the Masses of Quarks?

IN THE EARLY 1960s Murray Gell-Mann and George Zweig independently proposed that the proton, neutron, and many other subatomic particles, previously thought to be fundamental, consist of smaller entities known as quarks. According to this zany-sounding theory, the quarks supposedly come in six "flavors." "Ordinary" particles such as protons and neutrons consist of only the "up" (u) and "down" (d) quarks, while more exotic, short-lived particles, produced in high-energy collisions, contain the "strange," "charm," "top," and "bottom" flavors—although they might just as well have been called vanilla, chocolate, strawberry, butter almond, pistachio, and maple walnut. The proton and neutron each is supposed to consist of three quarks: uud for the proton, and udd for the neutron. (For reasons unknown to me, no one ever calls the neutron a "dud," even though the order of quarks has no particular significance.)

In the three decades since the quark model was proposed, no one has actually observed a *free* quark, although many quark searches have been made, including one by the author.[1] Despite these negative findings, most physicists today believe in the quark model more strongly than ever. The strongest evidence for its validity are high-energy electron-scattering experiments, which probe the internal structure of the proton and neutron. These experiments seem to show three pointlike entities contained within the proton and neutron that have all the properties previously predicted for quarks. Perhaps the strangest of these properties is that quarks should have either $\pm \frac{1}{3}$ or $\pm \frac{2}{3}$ the charge of the electron—which was previously considered the fundamental indivisible unit of charge.

But the nonobservance of free quarks was very puzzling, and initially cast doubt on the theory. Normally, when a bound system is bombarded by a beam of particles, the bonds between the bound particles are broken, if the bombarding particles have high enough energy. Examples of processes in which bound particles are freed by outside bombardment include molecules separated into their separate atoms, atoms separated into electrons and ions, and atomic nuclei shattered into nuclear fragments. The projectile energy needed to shatter the bonds

---

1. In contrast to quarks, free electrons, protons, and neutrons are observed regularly in detectors, apart from the atoms in which they are normally bound. The particular experiment in which I participated looked for quarks among the many particles created in the high-energy collisions of pairs of protons. If any such quarks had been created, they should have left distinctive tracks in the bubble chamber we used because of their small electric charge (see essay 92).

obviously depends on their strength, which are greatest for nuclei (the smallest system), and least for molecules (the largest system). We might expect that quarks, being still smaller than nuclei, could be liberated by colliding protons or neutrons at some extremely high bombardment energy. And yet no amount of bombardment energy has been found sufficient to liberate quarks.

As a result, a theory of "quark confinement" was developed in an attempt to explain the apparent impossibility of liberating free quarks. According to this theory, the nature of the force between quarks accounts for their confinement.

Unlike either the electromagnetic or gravitational forces, which decrease with distance, the force between quarks is believed to *grow* with distance, much like the force in a stretched spring or rubber band. For example, a model of the pion (see essay 86) would be a quark and an antiquark attached by a spring. In this model, the mass of the pion is not simply equal to the sum of its constituent quark masses, because the mass-equivalent to the sizable binding energy stored in the spring must be subtracted (see essay 88).

If you were to try to pull the quark and antiquark apart, you would have to do so much work in stretching the "spring" that a new quark and antiquark would be created from this energy—and you would wind up with a *pair* of bound quarks and antiquarks. The situation

FIGURE 112. *For Ted, the gay quark, it was bad enough that he was confined with an antiquark, but he could no longer stand those euphemistic references to his "strangeness" and "charm."*

is analogous to the way a new pair of north and south poles are created if you try to saw the north pole off a magnet. Even though it seems to be impossible to liberate quarks from their confinement, estimates have been made of their individual masses. Based on theoretical calculations, the masses of the up and down quarks are estimated to be about 650 times that of the electron (which incidentally does not consist of quarks).

96. What Is Antimatter?

PHYSICISTS have found that for every sub-atomic particle there exists a kind of mirror image particle, called its antiparticle, having the opposite-sign electric charge and exactly the same mass. For example, the observed antiparticles of electrons, protons, and neutrons are called anti-electrons (or more commonly positrons), antiprotons, and antineutrons—all of which have been observed.[1] Antiparticles can be created along with their companion particles in high-energy collisions, in which some of the kinetic energy in the collisions creates the particle and antiparticle rest masses. One example of such a process would be when a proton-antiproton pair is created in a collision between protons. If a pair of protons with equal energies collide head-on, the minimum kinetic energy required to create a proton-antiproton pair is $2mc^2$, since one mc^2 worth of energy is needed to create a proton and a second mc^2 is needed to create the antiproton, which has the same mass.

Just as new matter and antimatter can be produced from kinetic energy in high-energy collisions, the reverse process has also been observed. In these "annihilation" reactions, particles plus antiparticles can create pure energy in the form of gamma-ray photons. Although antimatter has been created in high-energy particle collisions, it is hard to produce any sizable amount of antimatter, largely because of the difficulty of storing it in such a way that it does not come into contact with ordinary

FIGURE 113. *Captain Sulu's concern about the possibility of encountering antimatter was greatly accentuated when the alien extended its left hand.*

1. But some particles, such as the photon, are not distinct from their antiparticle, that is, they are their own antiparticles. On the other hand, the antineutron and the neutron are quite distinguishable, even though they are both neutral. One measure of their distinguishability is that, unlike a pair of neutrons, a neutron and antineutron can annihilate.

matter and annihilate. The only kind of storage currently possible is in dough-nut-shaped evacuated rings, where the antiparticles are kept circulating and never come into contact with the walls or air.

Antimatter can organize itself exactly like matter into atoms and molecules and, who knows? maybe even antipeople. Some scientists have, in fact, suggested that some distant galaxies could be made of antimatter rather than matter. The suggestion of antimatter galaxies may not be entirely fanciful, because the light emitted by hot antimatter would be virtually indistinguishable from that emitted by ordinary matter. One problem, however, with the idea of some galaxies being made of antimatter is that the space between galaxies is not entirely empty. If antimatter galaxies were to encounter the small amount of matter outside a nearby matter galaxy, annihilation reactions would produce gamma rays of a specific energy. The nonobservance of such gamma rays makes it unlikely that antimatter galaxies exist.

Reactions involving antimatter, while similar to those involving matter, are not completely identical in all respects. One of the differences has to do with the left or right "handedness" of certain particles in the reaction. For example, it has been found that neutrinos always spin in one direction (when viewed along their direction of motion), while antineutrinos always spin in the opposite direction.

97. Could Objects Have Negative Weight or Mass?

IF OBJECTS having negative weight existed, they would, like magic carpets, be *repelled* rather than attracted by the Earth's gravity, and rise when released. Helium balloons simulate objects with negative weight, but their rise is due to an upward buoyant force, because they are lighter than the weight of air they displace (see essay 67). How about negative mass? Remember that mass or inertia refers to the degree to which objects resist being accelerated. Evidently, the more you pushed an object with negative mass, the faster it would accelerate in the opposite direction! With the possible exception of some contrary children, there are no known examples of objects that exhibit this type of behavior.

We can, however, simulate the behavior of negative mass by again using helium balloons. While driving your car, any unsecured object will normally be "thrown" forward when you slam on the brakes, with the exception of helium balloons, which will be "thrown" backward.[1] Similarly, if you round a sharp curve to the right, objects in the car tend to be thrown to the left, whereas helium balloons will be thrown to the right. Helium balloons simulate negative mass because the air in the car moves in the expected direction in response to the car's acceleration. This air movement creates slightly different pressures around the balloon that force it in a direction opposite to the surrounding air. Still another way to simulate negative mass would be to use a lit candle in a jar. The candle flame consists of very hot gases that are, like the helium balloon, less dense than the surrounding air. Therefore, if you shove the jar forward, the candle flame will initially move forward, and then backward as the jar suddenly stops.

FIGURE 114. *Stan thought he could get his date to slide across the seat to him by making a sharp right turn, but he hadn't counted on her helium balloon.*

But could objects with negative mass or weight actually exist? Based on the fact that subatomic particles can have either positive or negative electric charges, which can give rise to either attractive or repulsive forces, you might think that mass and weight might also come in positive or negative varieties. One obvious place to look for negative mass or weight would therefore be antimatter. Antiparticles, such as the antiproton, have an electric charge opposite in sign to the corresponding particle, but they clearly do not have the opposite-sign mass, since they move in the direction they are pushed, not in the opposite direction. Could antimatter have negative weight? That is a harder question to answer experimentally, because antiparticles created in an accelerator travel at speeds close to the speed of light. Particles traveling at such high speeds would require a mere microsecond (millionth of a second) to travel a 1,000-foot distance.

On Earth, objects fall 16 feet in one second. They fall only a trillionth as much in one microsecond, since the distance fallen is proportional to the square of the time (see essay 15). Such a tiny distance of fall (or rise in the case of negative weight) is much less than the diameter of an atom, and could not be detected. In order to detect whether the weight of antiparticles is positive or negative, you

---

1. "Thrown" has been put in quotes because from the point of view of someone watching the car go past, there is no force throwing the object forward. It is only from the point of view of a car passenger that such "fictitious" forces need to be introduced.

would need to observe them over a long enough period of time to see whether they actually fall or rise an appreciable distance.

This observation can be done in principle (and maybe in practice) using charged antiparticles circulating around an accelerator storage ring, provided stray electrical forces on the particles can be eliminated. Unfortunately, neutral antiparticles, which cannot be kept at rest or "steered" around storage rings by electrical or other forces, cannot be observed long enough to see whether gravity causes them to rise or fall.

HOW
HOT
OR
COLD
IS IT?

98.　At What Temperatures Does Water Boil and Freeze?

YOUR SENSATION of hot and cold is a notoriously unreliable indicator of temperature, as you can verify with simple experiments. For example, suppose you have cold, warm, and hot bowls of water. Leave one of your hands in the hot and the other in the cold bowl for a while, and then simultaneously move them to the warm bowl. The hand that was in the hot bowl will feel much colder than the other, even though both hands are in the same temperature water. To define a temperature scale, we therefore need to rely on some physical processes independent of human sensation. Two such processes involve the boiling and freezing points of water. Suppose, for example, you place a thermometer in a pot of ice water sitting on a hot stove. You will likely find that if the pot is heated slowly, the temperature of the ice water does not depend on how long the water is heated, until virtually all the ice is melted.[1]

After the ice melts, the water temperature will steadily increase as the heat is continuously applied, until the water begins to boil. At the boiling point, the temperature again will remain constant until all the water is boiled away. The constancy of temperature during the two "phase changes" of melting and boiling make an excellent basis for defining a scale of temperature. Usually, the direction of the phase change does not affect the temperature at which it occurs: water normally freezes at the same temperature that ice melts. There are, however, exceptions: very pure water can be "supercooled" to as low as −40° Celsius without freezing, provided the cooling is done gradually in a smooth container without sharp edges. Likewise, liquids can in some special cases be "superheated" to well above their boiling points without boiling (see the description of the bubble chamber in essay 92).

According to the Celsius (centigrade) temperature scale, pure water freezes at 0° and boils at 100°, under "standard" atmospheric pressure. In the Fahrenheit

1. A slow heating ensures that all parts of the ice water are at nearly the same temperature. If the stove is on a high heat, the water in the bottom of the pot will be hotter than at the top, and a vigorous circulation will be created.

system, the freezing and boiling points are 32° and 212° respectively. These numbers may be regarded as *definitions* of the two temperature scales, so no measurements are necessary to establish them. Instead, we can use these physical processes to calibrate a thermometer. For example, if you have a thermometer without any numbers or lines on it, you can find where to put the 100° C and 0° C marks by putting it first into boiling water and then ice water.

FIGURE 115. *Professor Goldberg based his temperature scale on boiling chicken fat and cold gefilte fish.*

After making these two marks on the thermometer, you can then divide the distance between them into 100 equal divisions, showing the individual Celsius degrees. Likewise, with a Fahrenheit thermometer, you can create 180 equal divisions between the 32° and 212° marks. One hundred and 0 seem like much more "natural" numbers than 32 and 212, which might seem to make the Celsius system a more rational one. The reason for the artificial choice of 32 and 212 is that the Fahrenheit system was not originally set up based on water, but rather the temperature of the human body (close to 100), and that of freezing salt water (close to 0). But actually, both the Fahrenheit and Celsius systems have artificial elements. One example of the arbitrariness of both systems is that the boiling and freezing points of water depend on atmospheric pressure, which varies with altitude, and also from day to day. Thus, we need to define a "standard" atmospheric pressure while defining the Celsius and Fahrenheit temperature scales.

99. What Is the Temperature at the Bottom of Frozen Lakes?

HAVE YOU EVER wondered why lakes freeze from the top down, when your swimming experience tells you the coldest water always seems to be *below* the surface? The reason has to do with a most peculiar property of water. Most materials expand when heated, and contract when cooled. Water shares this property, but only if its temperature exceeds 4° Celsius. Between 0° and 4° C, water actually *contracts* when heated. As a result, water has its greatest density at a temperature of 4° C.

Consider what happens to a lake initially at some temperature well above 4° C as the air temperature slowly drops. The cooling surface water, being denser than the water below, sinks to the bottom, creating a circulation that continues until the surface temperature reaches 4° C. At this point the surface water, being as dense as water ever gets, sinks to the bottom and stays there. From now on, even when the surface water cools below 4° C, it will not sink, because it is *less* dense than the lower layers. So below 4° C, the coldest water is on the top rather than the bottom, and it is the top layer that reaches the 0° C freezing point first. The thicker the layer of ice that forms, the more of an insulating blanket it provides for the lake, and the lower the rate of heat loss through the ice. Basically, the ice coating on top prevents freshwater lakes from freezing solid in winter—a result that would occur if lakes froze from the bottom up, making the wintertime survival of fish highly questionable—except possibly for swordfish!

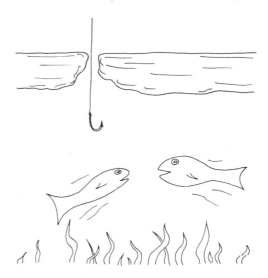

FIGURE 116. *"I sure miss the sunlight in winter."*
"Me, too, but just consider the alternative if the bottom froze first."

To understand why water contracts between 0° and 4° C, we need first to see why most materials expand when heated. Think of the atoms in a solid rod as being similar to a row of small masses connected by springs. At low temperatures, the atomic masses have very little vibration, and the springs will be at all times close to their equilibrium length. When the temperature of the rod is raised, the masses will vibrate more vigorously. But if the springs are "asymmetric," that is, somewhat easier to stretch than compress, then the maximum stretch distance will exceed the maximum compression distance. In other words, during each oscillation, the masses' average separation will exceed their equilibrium separation (favoring stretch over compression). Since the effect is more pronounced the more vigorous the oscillation, most materials therefore expand when heated. To get the idea, think of two masses connected by a spring whose thick coils do not allow it to compress at all, but do allow it to stretch. In this case, obviously, the more vigorous the oscillation of the masses, the greater will be their average separation. Thus, the asymmetry in the springlike force between atoms is why most materials expand when heated.

Molecules of ice crystals are arranged in a rather open array that leaves more space between them than for molecules crowding randomly together in liquid water, which is why ice floats, being less dense than water. Once ice melts, the water molecules are free to move throughout the liquid and fill in some of the spaces. But at temperatures near the freezing point, neighboring water molecules tend to favor certain relative orientations and positions, as in ice. This "short-range order" causes more empty space between the molecules the closer the water is to the freezing point, which is why water is less dense at 0° than 4° C. Considering that life on Earth first evolved in the oceans, and that life as we know it could not have evolved in a solid block of ice, it is possible that life on Earth owes its existence to a peculiar property of the force between water molecules.[1]

100. Why Does Hot plus Cold Not Always Equal Warm?

WHEN YOU hold hands with someone whose hand initially feels very cold, in a short time you don't notice it. That is because any two bodies initially at different temperatures will reach a common equilibrium temperature when they are brought into intimate contact. But the resulting temperature is not always what you might expect. For example, if you mix equal

1. Actually, it is possible that even if the water at the bottom of the lake froze first, an insulating ice layer would still form at the top of the lake, because once the bottom water froze, it might rise to the top, since ice is less dense than water. But this is not certain, since it is also possible the ice would adhere to the bottom.

quantities of coffee at 100° and cream at 0° Celsius, you might expect the equilibrium temperature of the mixture to be 50° C, but in fact, it will be somewhat higher. The reason is that different substances possess different "heat capacities" or "specific heats," a measure of the amount of heat required to raise or lower their temperature by 1° C.

When equal quantities of two different substances are mixed in a well-insulated container and allowed to reach equilibrium, all the heat lost by the hotter substance is gained by the colder substance. In this case the quantity with the higher specific heat will have its temperature changed less than the one with the lower specific heat. In fact, this mixing method is the standard way of determining the specific heat of a substance.

Here, for example, is a simple experiment from which you can find the specific heat of copper. Take a strainer full of copper pennies that have been in a boiling pot of water for some time (so their temperature is known to be 100° C), and quickly dump the pennies into an amount of water at 0° C that has the same mass as the pennies. Unlike the case of mixing two liquids, it takes a bit longer for the hot pennies and cold water to reach an equilibrium temperature as heat flows from the copper pennies into the water. You will know that equilibrium is reached when the water temperature stops rising. If the heat loss to the environment is negligible, you should then find the water temperature levels off at about 8.5° C. This means that the gain in temperature of the water (8.5°) will be only about 9.3 percent of the 91.5° loss in temperature of the copper pennies. If we define the specific heat of water as 1.000, then this experiment will establish the specific heat of copper to be 0.093.

Put another way, the amount of heat needed to raise or lower a piece of copper by 1° C is found, by experiment, to be only 9.3 percent the amount of heat needed to raise or lower the same amount of water by 1° C. We could also explain this observation by saying that copper heats up much more easily than water or water "retains its heat" much more than copper. So in this particular example we find that "hot" plus "cold" is still quite cold rather than warm.

FIGURE 117. *For his discovery that it is actually coldness that flows from cold bodies to hot bodies, Professor Etisoppo was awarded the prestigious Lebon Prize.*

Amounts of heat are defined in units of calories: 1 calorie is the heat required to raise the temperature of 1 gram of water by 1° C, which is why the specific heat of water is by definition exactly one. Unfortunately, the word *calorie* when used in connection with food actually refers to a *kilo*calorie, or 1,000 calories. In other words, the energy in 1 food calorie, when burned up, is enough to raise the temperature of 1 *kilo*gram of water by 1° C. Obviously, the amount of heat energy needed to heat something up depends on both its specific heat and its mass—as we have just seen, a thousand times the heat energy is required to heat 1 kilogram as compared with 1 gram of water.

If you try to verify the literal truth of this last statement experimentally, you might find it very difficult to do, because it is not easy to measure the temperature of an amount of water as small as a gram using a conventional thermometer. The insertion of a thermometer into a small quantity of water changes the very temperature you seek to measure, as the water and the thermometer bulb reach an equilibrium temperature. For example, if you insert a thermometer into various amounts of water at 100° C poured from a boiling pot, you will find lower readings the smaller the amount of water (assuming the thermometer was at room temperature prior to making each measurement). As a general rule, with systems that are small in size, great care must be taken that the very act of measurement not disturb the quantity being measured—a principle of particular importance for atomic and subatomic systems.

101.   When Should You Add the Cream to Your Coffee?

SUPPOSE YOU have just poured yourself a cup of hot coffee, when without warning, your impatient boss calls. (Self-employed or unemployed readers can imagine other urgent calls.) If you want your coffee to stay hot longer, should you add your cream right away, or add it after you come back at the end of ten minutes? You might want to experiment before reading further. For best results, use equal amounts of coffee and cream or milk, or else just use boiling water mixed with cold water if you don't want to waste the coffee and milk.

This question of whether to wait or add your cream right away can be answered if we look at what the rate of heat loss depends on for a hot object. For example, the rate of heat loss evidently depends on how much hotter an object is than its surroundings, because hot objects cool rapidly at first, and then cool more slowly. In fact, the temperature drop in a short period of time is proportional to how much hotter the object is than its surroundings.

Suppose, for example, a cup of coffee is initially 64° hotter than room temperature, and that after five minutes the temperature excess over room temperature drops by half (to 32°). What would you expect the temperature excess above room temperature to be after another five minutes? If the coffee temperature dropped as fast in the second five minutes as it did during the first five minutes, it would be exactly at room temperature at the end of ten minutes, which is clearly incorrect.

In fact, it would drop by only 16° in the second five minutes, because the rate of heat loss is proportional to the temperature excess over room temperature. By continuing this reasoning, we can see that the coffee's temperature sampled every five minutes, would be in excess of room temperature by 64°, 32°, 16°, 8°, 4°, 2°, 1°, 0.5°, . . . , and that it would reach room temperature only after an infinitely long time. (The idea is analogous to what happens to the air pressure in the tire of your car when you open the valve. Initially, the air comes out at a very rapid rate. But as the tire's air pressure approaches that of the outside air, the rate of air flow steadily drops.)

Suppose you add cream to the coffee at the end of ten minutes, when the coffee temperature has dropped from 64° to 16° hotter than the room temperature. Let's assume that the cream is at room temperature, and that you add enough cream to produce a mixture whose temperature exceeds room temperature by only half as much as the coffee.

Such a mixture will have roughly equal amounts of coffee and cream, assuming they have almost the same specific heat. In this case adding the cream will halve the excess over room temperature from 16° to 8° just prior to drinking.

Now suppose you add the cream right away instead. The coffee initially 64° hotter than room temperature is cooled by the immediate addition of the cream to 32° above room temperature. But doubling the mass of the coffee (by adding the cream) also has an important effect on the rate of its cooling. For example, a spoonful of soup evidently cools a lot faster than a bowl of soup. If we assume a simple proportionality between rate of cooling and mass, then the

FIGURE 118. *At the thermometer factory, the length of workers' coffee breaks was based on their coffee's temperature, so they always added the cream right away.*

coffee-cream mixture cools half as fast as the coffee alone. In this case it will take ten minutes (not five) for the excess temperature of the coffee-cream mixture above room temperature to be halved.

So after ten minutes the coffee-cream mixture will be 16° above room temperature rather than the 8° we found earlier when the cream was added just prior to drinking. Clearly, in this example, you would want to add the cream right away, because that has the effect of slowing the rate of cooling. Actually, the preceding result can be generalized to any amount of cream and any time of drinking: it always pays to add the cream right away, because the effect is to lower the rate of heat loss of the coffee-cream mixture. But then again, not everyone likes her coffee as hot as possible.

102.   How Much Hotter Is the Bottom of a Waterfall Than the Top?

WHAT EXACTLY is heat? At one time heat was thought to be some kind of invisible fluid that tended to flow from hot bodies to cold bodies. But this idea is inconsistent with observations, such as, for example, the seemingly endless amount of heat that friction produces when bodies are rubbed together. Heat is now understood to be a form of energy, along with kinetic, electrical, magnetic, acoustic, and nuclear energy, among other forms. In fact, heat has a close connection to kinetic energy (energy of motion).

When an object is heated, its molecules acquire some extra amount of random (disorderly) motion. The *heat content* of a body (also sometimes called its internal energy) is a measure of this total kinetic energy of all the molecules of the body. In contrast to heat, *temperature* measures the average energy per molecule. For this reason, the heat content of bodies at a given temperature is proportional to the number of molecules, or to the mass of the bodies. The cold oceans, for example, contain vastly more heat energy than a cup of boiling hot coffee—though you might have a difficult time extracting it!

When water descends some distance in a waterfall, its energy of motion (kinetic energy) increases in proportion to the distance fallen. For example, in drops of 100 and 400 meters, each gram of water increases its kinetic energy by 0.23 and 0.92 calories, respectively, if we ignore air resistance. When the water hits the bottom of the waterfall, the "orderly" downward motion of the molecules is transformed into a random disorderly motion that constitutes heat. After 100- and 400-meter drops, the water would consequently increase its temperature by 0.23° and 0.92° Celsius, respectively.

You can readily demonstrate the transformation of kinetic energy into heat by measuring the temperature of water in a half-filled thermos bottle, before and after the bottle is vigorously shaken repeatedly. Each shake might be equivalent to the water falling through a height of perhaps half a meter. So to get a temperature rise equivalent to that of a 400-meter waterfall, you will have to shake the thermos around eight hundred times. Most likely, you will generate a lot more body heat than water heat in the process!

Heat can also be produced when work is done against friction, such as, for example, when using a claw hammer to extract a nail from a piece of wood. Heating due to friction explains why small meteorites burn up upon entering the Earth's atmosphere. These messengers from space enter the atmosphere at extremely high speeds, and therefore they encounter very high air resistance. This resistance (essentially a form of friction) converts a fraction of the kinetic energy of the meteorite into heat.

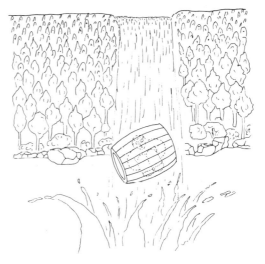

Given such examples as the heating of water in a waterfall and the heating of falling meteorites, you might wonder whether a similar heating occurs in the case of raindrops. Since raindrops fall much farther than water in waterfalls, it might seem that they should heat up considerably. This does not occur, however, because evaporation cools raindrops during their descent. Evaporation

FIGURE 119. *"Everything's cool so far,"* *thought Fred to himself two-thirds of* *the way down the waterfall.*

causes cooling because, during evaporation, only the fastest water molecules can escape the mutual attraction that water molecules have for their neighbors, so the slower-moving (colder) molecules are left behind.

103.   What Is the Lowest Possible Temperature?

HOW COLD can it get? The definitions of the Celsius and Fahrenheit temperature scales, based on the boiling and freezing points of water, give no hint of a lowest possible temperature. The idea of a lowest temperature comes from observations of the volume and pressure of gases as their temperature is changed. You are undoubtedly aware of the fact that gases, if free to do so, expand when heated and contract when cooled. For example, you can easily observe the contraction in volume of a balloon taken outside on a cold day. If we want to keep the pressure on a gas constant while its temperature is changed, we can imagine, for example, a gas in a vertical cylinder with a freely movable piston. If the enclosed gas temperature is high, experiments can easily show that the gas volume shrinks by a constant amount per degree drop in temperature as the gas is cooled. If the same rate of shrinkage continues to very low temperatures, the gas volume would shrink to zero when the temperature reached $-273°$ C. The same temperature is obtained no matter what type of gas is observed.

Similar observations may be made for high-temperature gases whose volume

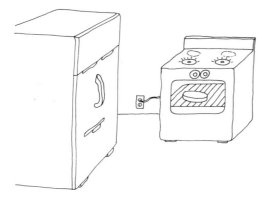

FIGURE 120. *"It's not fair!" thought the refrigerator. "How come I can't go below -273 degrees, but she can get as hot as she wants?"*

is kept fixed (the piston is locked in place) and whose pressure is observed as the temperature is lowered. In this case the pressure of a gas drops by a constant amount for each degree drop in temperature. Based on the constant rate of decrease, the gas pressure would go to zero at $-273°$ C for all types of gases.

These two kinds of observations of the variation of gas pressure and volume with temperature imply that $-273°$ C is a lowest possible temperature. We can therefore define an absolute (Kelvin) scale of temperature in which the zero on the Kelvin scale is at $-273°$ C. In the Kelvin scale, for example, water freezes at $+273°$ and boils at $+373°$ K, at normal atmospheric pressure. The experiments that imply a lowest possible temperature do not literally imply that real gases would have zero pressure and volume at 0° K. Real gases become liquids when they are cooled to a certain point, and therefore the constant rate of decrease in their volume or pressure does not hold near the liquefication point, and certainly not below it. A favorite demonstration of some science teachers is to immerse an air-filled balloon in liquid nitrogen at 72° K. This causes the nitrogen in the air in the balloon to liquefy slowly, and the balloon's size to contract dramatically. When the balloon is later removed from the liquid nitrogen, its gradual spontaneous resumption of its original size is accompanied by amusing hisses and pops.

The concept of a lowest temperature seems intuitively clear when the temperature of a gas is understood in terms of the average energy of its molecules. As a gas is cooled, the random velocities of its molecules decrease, and the molecules make less violent collisions with the container walls, resulting in less pressure on the walls. You might think that at absolute zero temperature, the energy of the molecules would be zero, and the stationary molecules would exert no pressure on the container walls. But as explained in essay 123, even at absolute zero, some small "zero point" energy is present.

104.   How Close to Absolute Zero Can We Get?

TWO WAYS to cool an object are to place it in contact with a colder object or put it into a refrigerator. (Of course, if you put something in your refrigerator after taking it out of the freezer, it will warm up rather than cool down.) Cooling by contact occurs because spontaneous heat flow is always from hot objects to cold ones. Heat never flows from cold objects to hot ones spontaneously, any more than water flows uphill, which is probably the reason we say things heat "up" and cool "down." But such "uphill" flows of heat (and water) can occur if the necessary amount of mechanical work is supplied, for example, by a refrigerator motor (or water pump).

A refrigerator (or an air conditioner) is essentially the reverse of a heat engine. In a heat engine, heat from burning fuel produces useful mechanical work, and as an unavoidable by-product, heat is expelled to the environment. In contrast, in a refrigerator, mechanical energy is consumed (by the motor) rather than produced. Also, the direction of heat flow is reversed: refrigerators expel heat from the cold interior to the hotter environment, but engines expel heat from the hot interior to the colder environment.

An air conditioner is basically the same as a refrigerator, the main difference being that with an air conditioner, heat is expelled to the outdoors rather than to the kitchen. Despite the similarities between the two devices, running a refrigerator with its door open is not a particularly effective way to improvise an air conditioner, because the heat expelled out the back of the refrigerator must exceed the heat entering the refrigerator through the open door—the difference being the work done by the motor, according to the first law of thermodynamics (another name for the conservation of energy law).

But how does a refrigerator actually work? The basic idea depends on the energy flows that occur when a material changes its state from gas to liquid or liquid to gas. For example, to vaporize 1 gram of a liquid requires a specific number of calories (its "heat of vaporization"). Likewise, that same amount of heat is liberated in the reverse process of gas condensation. These energy changes arise because the attractive forces between molecules that are present in a liquid are absent in a gas, so energy needs to be supplied to pull the liquid molecules apart during vaporization. The heat absorption that occurs during vaporization should be familiar if you have ever felt the cooling sensation when a small amount of alcohol is placed on your arm and allowed to evaporate. (Likewise, you may have observed the heat produced during condensation if you have been in a steam room and felt the steam condensing to water droplets on your body.)

Currently, one of the most common refrigerating agents is Freon (which is actually a family of manufactured chemicals), chosen because of its low vaporization temperature and chemical inertness. Despite these desirable properties, Freon is a hazard to the Earth's atmospheric ozone layer, which shields out harmful high-energy solar rays, and is scheduled to be phased out for that reason. In a refrigerator, liquid Freon is squirted out of a nozzle from one high-pressure coil into another coil at lower pressure. The sudden pressure reduction causes the Freon to vaporize, and results in absorption of heat from the surroundings. The gaseous Freon (still contained in a closed coil) then passes through a motor-driven compressor located at the back of the refrigerator. When the gaseous Freon is compressed back to a liquid state, heat is produced and ejected into the room, and the Freon continues to cycle through the coils.

FIGURE 121. *Sitting in front of an open refrigerator may feel good for a little while, but the laws of thermodynamics are against you.*

Conventional refrigerators are not able to cool below the condensation tem-

190

perature of the particular gas they rely on (− 80° Celsius for one type of Freon). The gas having the lowest condensation temperature is helium, at 4.2° Kelvin. To achieve still lower temperatures, other techniques must be used. The coldest temperatures to date have been reached using a technique in which a sample is placed in a chamber surrounded by powerful magnets that align the spins of the atomic nuclei in the sample. Once the sample is removed from the chamber, the nuclear spins no longer have any reason to remain perfectly aligned, and in the process of randomizing their directions, the nuclei absorb heat from the surrounding material. By repeating this cycle of magnetization and demagnetization many times, scientists have achieved temperatures of around 10 billionths of a degree above absolute zero (0° K). To picture the process, visualize a drill sergeant repeatedly alternating the orders "Attention!" and "At ease!" and each time draining off whatever spontaneity (heat) his soldiers show during the "at ease" phase. Pretty soon the soldiers will be at attention all the time.

105.   Is There a Highest Possible Temperature?

COULD THERE exist a highest as well as a lowest temperature? An appreciation of the fundamental nature of temperature as the average energy of molecules makes this suggestion sound reasonable, because a molecule's speed cannot exceed that of light. But in fact, there is no upper limit to temperature or energy—which you probably already realize if you have seen the cartoon for essay 103. To see why the limit on molecular speed does not impose a corresponding limit on molecular energy, we need to look at the relation between speed and kinetic energy.

Objects acquire energy when work is done on them. For example, the work done by the pull of gravity on a falling object causes both its speed and kinetic energy to increase. At speeds much less than the speed of light, an object's kinetic energy is proportional to the square of its speed. If this relationship held for very high speeds as well, there would indeed be an upper limit to the energy of an object (reached when it traveled at the speed of light), and a maximum temperature would exist.

But in fact, for high speeds, the relationship between kinetic energy and speed is more complex (see essay 93). According to relativity theory, the kinetic energy of an object becomes infinite as its speed approaches the speed of light (unless the object's rest mass happens to be zero, as in the photon's case). In effect, the

191

object's speed stops increasing, but its mass increases instead. This fact is one way of explaining how the speed of light is an upper limit, since an infinite amount of energy would need to be supplied to increase an object's speed to that of light.

Thus, as an object is heated, its molecular kinetic energy can increase indefinitely, even though the molecular speeds can never exceed the speed of light. Actually, for very high temperatures, random collisions would break the molecules apart into their constituent atoms, and at still higher temperatures even the more tightly bound atoms would be broken apart into their constituent electrons and atomic nuclei. This state of matter, known as plasma, is found in the Sun and other stars. Clearly, at some vastly higher temperature, even the very tightly bound atomic nuclei would be broken apart into their constituent protons and neutrons.

Finally, if the temperature of a substance continued to rise, even the individual protons and neutrons would break apart in incredibly violent collisions into a "quark soup." This quark soup state of matter currently does not exist anywhere in the universe. It was only at the time of the big bang, some 10 to 20 billion years ago, when all the known universe was compressed into a very small volume, that the requisite incredibly high temperatures could exist.

FIGURE 122. *"Adam, you don't have any temperature—you're going to school!"*

Given that the temperature of ordinary matter depends on the average kinetic energy of its atoms (or molecules), you may wonder whether one could define the temperature of an individual atom— ignoring its constituent particles. Actually, atoms do *not* have a temperature, since temperature is a property only of a collection of atoms. An analogy may be made to the fact that nations can have values assigned to their population or gross national product (GNP), but it makes no sense to speak of the population or GNP of the individuals comprising the nation. You might think that you could define the temperature of an atom in terms of the average energy of its electrons. But while such a temperature can be defined for the "free" electrons in a metal, it cannot be done for electrons in an atom, which must occupy well-defined energy levels.

106. What Is the Most Efficient Engine Combustion Temperature?

WHAT DO jelly doughnuts have in common with gasoline? Both are fuels for engines—your body or a car—which can convert chemical energy stored in the fuels into mechanical work. To give you an idea of the energy content of food, the energy released when you digest a jelly doughnut is actually greater than that released when a stick of dynamite is detonated—although in the doughnut case, it is released a little at a time over a much longer period! One difference between the operation of biological and mechanical engines is that in the former case the fuel is first transformed chemically for later energy release, while in the latter case chemical energy is directly converted into heat during combustion, and a fraction of that heat energy becomes available for doing mechanical work.

The efficiency of a mechanical heat engine can be defined as the percentage of heat energy that is transformed into mechanical work. For example, an engine that converts 75 out of every 100 calories burned into mechanical work is 75 percent efficient. The remaining 25 calories in this case are expelled to the environment as heat. Expulsion of "waste" heat to the environment is a property of all heat engines. As we shall see, the efficiency of any heat engine is theoretically limited to a maximum value that depends only on the temperature of fuel combustion, T_c, and that of the outside environment, T_e.

Consider a simplified heat engine operating on a two-phase cycle. In the first phase, a fuel-air mixture enters a cylinder, is compressed by a moving piston to a small volume, and is then ignited. The explosion expands the gas in the cylinder, drives the piston back, and expels the exhaust gas to the environment before the next fuel-air intake. During the expansion phase of the cycle (the "power stroke"), heat energy supplied by the burning fuel does mechanical work driving the piston back. In an idealized process, all the heat supplied during the power stroke could be converted into mechanical work.

Ideally, the amount of work done during the power stroke may be assumed to be proportional to the combustion temperature T_c, because hotter combustion temperatures cause the piston to be driven back more forcefully. During the compression part of the cycle, mechanical work is not being produced by heat energy, but instead, the piston is slowed, and it *loses* energy as it compresses the fuel-air mixture in the cylinder. It can be shown that the *net* amount of work during the entire idealized cycle (energy gain minus loss) is proportional to $T_c - T_e$.

193

This result seems reasonable, because the closer the two temperatures are, the more work you have to "give back" during the compression phase.

The maximum efficiency of an idealized engine (defined as work output divided by heat input) can be shown to be $(T_c - T_e)/T_c$, with all temperatures being in degrees Kelvin. One way to express this result is that the maximum possible efficiency is simply the percentage by which the environment temperature is below the combustion temperature. For example, if the fuel is burned at an absolute temperature $T_c = 600°$ K, and the exhaust gas expelled to an environment at a temperature $T_e = 300°$ K, the maximum efficiency is 0.5, meaning 50 percent—this being the percentage 300 is below 600.

Based on the preceding formula for engine efficiency, the way to achieve maximum theoretical engine efficiency is to raise the combustion temperature as high as possible.[1] On the other hand, practical considerations may make extremely high combustion temperatures unachievable—for example, at some pont the engine will melt! So, the theoretical limit to engine efficiency may not be a good guide to the design of real heat engines. Nevertheless, it is important to realize that the theoretical limit on engine efficiency is tied to the laws of thermodynamics, and cannot be overcome by clever technology. The fact that the laws of thermodynamics impose an upper limit far short of 100 percent on the efficiency of engines should give us a new perspective on what represents a "high" efficiency ·For example, if we were given a real heat engine with a combustion temperature of 600° K having "only" 49 percent efficiency, we should not bemoan the loss of 51 percent of the original heat energy; rather, we should marvel at the ability of technology to produce an engine 98 percent as efficient as the most efficient possible engine operating between temperatures of 600° and 300° K.

FIGURE 123. *Theoretical physicists' cars have extremely simple engines.*

1. We could also achieve higher maximum theoretical efficiency by lowering the environment temperature, but that is not something that can normally be controlled, and in any case real engines work less efficiently at low outside temperatures.

107. How Hot Is the Earth's Center?

TAKING THE temperature of the center of the Earth is no easy matter, considering that the deepest holes and mine shafts go down only a few miles. Much of what we know about the Earth's interior is found by indirect means, especially through the study of seismic waves originating from earthquakes and underground explosions. These waves, surprisingly, reveal something about the Earth's inner temperature.

Two types of seismic waves are particularly important—the S (shear) and P (pressure) waves. For a simple tabletop experiment to show the difference between S and P waves, stretch a Slinky between your hands on a table. You can create a P wave in the Slinky if you move one hand back and forth toward the other (the Slinky will elongate and contract), and an S wave if you move one hand toward and away from your body (the Slinky will undulate side to side). Both S and P waves are created in earthquakes, but in explosions that result from a sudden pulse of pressure (rather than a sideways shearing motion), only P waves are created. Seismic detectors placed at various locations can easily separate the two types of waves, based on the direction of motion of the detectors as the wave passes.

S and P waves that have a known velocity can be used to pin down the location of an earthquake by recording wave arrival times at a number of widely separated detectors. You can also work the calculation backward, and find the S and P wave velocities by observing the seismic wave arrival time following an earthquake or an explosion at a known location. Actually, the computation is quite complex, because wave speed varies with depth below the surface, which causes the waves to refract or bend rather than follow straight-line paths from their point of origin to the detector. In addition, there are a number of boundary layers in the Earth that cause waves to be reflected, and even converted from one wave type to another.

To make a model of the Earth's interior, seismologists try various hypothetical variations of material density with depth. The model then is adjusted until everyone's seismic wave observations can be fitted to the same model. The model of the Earth based on seismic studies suggests the presence of an iron core whose radius is about half that of the Earth. Other compelling arguments for an iron core are the existence of the Earth's magnetic field, and the presence of iron in many meteorites, which presumably were created with the same primordial composition as the planets. In addition, the value for the total mass of the Earth found in the Cavendish experiment (see essay 74) requires that the core consist of a material having a very high density such as iron.

Based on seismic measurements, we know that part of the core is liquid iron. This conclusion is inferred from the fact that only P waves can pass through liquids; S waves cannot. You can easily understand why only P waves can pass through liquids if you hold a butter knife vertically in a glass of water. If you move the broad part of the knife back and forth, you create a P wave, but moving it from side to side so as to slice the water will produce very little wave action (no S wave). On the other hand, if you do the same experiment with the knife stuck into a solid object, such as a Jell-O cube, both types of knife motion will send a jiggle through the cube, because both S and P waves can travel through solids.

Thus, the fact that a seismic detector placed on the opposite side of the Earth from an earthquake detects only P waves, and no S waves, tells us that the center of the Earth must have a liquid core. Actually, we believe the outer core is liquid iron while the inner core is solid iron, because of the increase of pressure with depth. The closer you get to the Earth's center, the greater the pressure due to the weight of all the outer material. The melting point of any material increases with pressure, so the Earth's highly compressed inner core is solid, even though the inner core is hotter than the liquid outer core. Based on the weight of all the outer layers, the pressure at the Earth's center has been estimated to be 3.6 million times the atmospheric pressure on the surface. Under such enormous pressure, solid iron would have to have a temperature in excess of 7,000° Kelvin. Therefore, the core of the Earth must actually be hotter than the surface of the Sun.

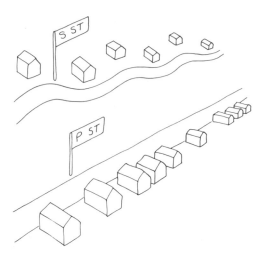

FIGURE 124. *The earthquake had a very different effect on the houses on S and P streets.*

108.   How Hot
Is the Surface of the Sun?

OBJECTS SUCH as the Sun that are so hot that
they glow reveal their temperature by their color. Think of the burner of an electric stove. As it gets hotter, the burner begins to glow more brightly, and its color changes—from deep red to bright red to orange and finally to yellow. If the temperature could be raised even higher, the burner would eventually become white, or even blue. If objects are heated only a modest amount, they won't appear to glow at all, at least not at visible wavelengths, but they will be net emitters of electromagnetic radiation as long as they are hotter than their surroundings. For example, people, because their body temperature is usually warmer than their surroundings, emit radiation primarily in the infrared region. So people "glow," though the glow can be picked up only with devices or photographic film sensitive to infrared radiation—despite the claims of "aura" readers.

Even though a glowing object such as a person, the Sun, a light bulb filament, or a stove burner may seem to have a particular color, light is actually being emitted at a variety of wavelengths, that is, in a *spectrum*. A light spectrum can be seen by viewing a glowing object through a prism that breaks the light up into its constituent wavelengths. The perceived color of a glowing object corresponds roughly to the dominant wavelength, or the "peak" of the spectrum. A spectrum can be expressed in terms of a mathematical curve whose height tells us the light intensity at each wavelength, as indicated by the curve in the cartoon. From what we know about the appearance of glowing objects, as the temperature increases, the peak of the observed spectrum must shift to shorter wavelengths, and also the overall height of the spectrum must increase (the object glows more brightly). The mathematical curve that applies to a glowing object is known as the "blackbody" spectrum. The term *blackbody* refers to an object that is a perfect absorber (or emitter) of electromagnetic radiation: all radiation that hits it is absorbed and later reemitted. But it is only at relatively low temperatures, like room temperature, that blackbodies actually appear to be black.

The blackbody spectrum for any glowing object shows an inverse proportionality between the peak wavelength and the body's absolute temperature.[1] For the Sun, whose peak wavelength corresponds to the color green, this rela-

---

1. The relationship between peak wavelength in millimeters and absolute temperature, T, is wavelength $= 2.9/T$. Of course, for this relationship to hold, the object must *have* a blackbody spectrum, which many glowing objects, such as fluorescent lights, do not.

tionship tells us that its surface temperature is about 5,700° Kelvin.[2] Consequently, a star whose spectrum has a peak wavelength half that of the Sun must have a surface that is twice as hot as the Sun. Clearly, stars that appear bluish (shorter wavelength than yellow) have higher temperatures than our Sun, and those that appear reddish have lower temperatures. (It makes you wonder about our everyday association of red and blue representing "warm" and "cold" colors.

FIGURE 125. *The blackbody nature of the Sun was discovered by the astronomer Kent C. Toogood.*

Apparently, the complexions of people and stars respond rather differently to the effects of heat!)

The theory behind the shape of the blackbody spectrum, developed by Max Planck at the turn of the century, was a milestone on the road to the present-day quantum theory. Planck imagined solid objects to consist of an arrangement of atomic masses connected by "springs." As an object is heated, the masses vibrate more vigorously, and emit radiation at the frequency at which they vibrate. Planck found that in order to get agreement with the observed spectra, he had to make what was then a bizarre assumption, namely that the energy of the vibrating atoms was *quantized*. Specifically, he postulated that the atoms could vibrate only with an energy that was an integral multiple of some value—the value being proportional to the vibration frequency. Planck's postulate of energy quantization was not fully understood until Einstein suggested that atoms can emit electromagnetic radiation only in the form of discrete photons whose energy is proportional to the frequency of light emitted.

2. In addition to the continuous blackbody emission spectrum, the Sun and other stars also have a *discrete* line spectrum dependent on their temperature and the particular elements they contain. The sun, incidentally, appears yellow rather than green because for a blackbody spectrum the average wavelength exceeds the peak wavelength.

109.   How Hot Is the Interior of the Sun?

THE CENTER of the Sun is believed to have a temperature of around 20 million degrees Kelvin (or Celsius—it hardly matters at such high temperatures!). Clearly, the evidence for the Sun's interior temperature is less direct than that for its surface temperature, since the interior cannot be observed in visible or any other wavelength light. The interior temperature is estimated using a model for the Sun's energy generation based on several nuclear fusion reactions. By running the model on a computer and fitting it to the observed surface properties of the Sun (or any other star), the central temperature can be calculated.

The primary nuclear fusion reaction in the solar model, known as the p-p chain, involves combining four protons (hydrogen nuclei) to make one helium nucleus and other particles that have a great deal of energy. Energy is liberated because the final particles are about 0.7 percent lighter than four hydrogen nuclei, and this decrease in mass provides the energy. As its name implies, the p-p chain reaction accomplishes the hydrogen-to-helium conversion in a series of steps. A series or chain is necessary because of the extreme unlikelihood of four protons colliding at one point due to their random motions. Even having two protons get close enough to react in the first step of the p-p chain is unlikely, owing to their electrical repulsion. It is only at extremely high temperatures that some protons have enough energy so that, in incredibly violent collisions, they get close enough for the strong nuclear attractive force to overwhelm their repulsion. (A pair of protons can be thought of as two individuals in a love-hate relationship, who always fight until they get very close, at which point their mutual passion takes over.)

Surprisingly, the fusion reaction actually begins at a temperature that is too low for the protons to make contact. Instead, through the quantum process known as "tunneling," discussed in essay 55, a small fraction of the most energetic protons manage to react, even though according to classical physics their energies are not quite high enough to overcome their repulsion. At this temperature, we can say the hydrogen has reached its "kindling point," and the reaction can proceed spontaneously.

On Earth the extraordinarily high temperatures created in nuclear fusion reactions make it difficult to sustain fusion in a controlled way. Regrettably, it is so far only in the uncontrolled release of energy in the H-bomb that humans have been able to harness fusion energy to date. Attempts to release fusion energy in a controlled way are stymied by the fact that the extreme heat released tends to blow the fuel apart and stop the reaction. In the core of the Sun, this self-termination of the fusion reaction does not occur, because the enormous weight of the Sun's outer layers supplies just enough inward pressure on the core to counter-act the outward pressure due to the released energy. During most of the life of the Sun, these inward and outward pressures will be in stable equilibrium.

FIGURE 126. *The neutrino knew the real temperature of the Sun's core, but it wasn't telling—or at least it wasn't telling what the scientists wanted to hear.*

The most direct check on the Sun's interior temperature, and on the correctness of the solar models, is made possible by the neutrinos produced as a by-product in the fusion reaction. Since the Sun (and virtually everything else) is almost transparent to neutrinos, they travel out from the core immediately, whereupon some vanishing small fraction of these solar neutrinos can be detected on Earth. Observations of neutrinos confirm the basic correctness of the solar models, even though the number of neutrinos is only about a third of what the models predict.

This puzzling discrepancy could mean that the solar core temperature is slightly lower than we think it is, or perhaps something happens to the neutrinos before they reach us. Recent experiments indicate that the latter explanation is probably correct. If neutrinos, for example, have a small nonzero mass, it is predicted that some of the solar neutrinos could be transformed into another type of neutrino before leaving the Sun, in which case they wouldn't register in the detectors. The idea that neutrinos, without disintegrating or reacting, could simply change into another type of particle is as Kafkaesque as your metamorphosis into a giant bug. But this possible process for neutrinos, actually observed for one other type of particle, is a further illustration of the eeriness of the quantum realm.

110. How Hot or Cold Can Stars Get?

ASTRONOMERS have found, by observation, that heavier stars tend to be hotter. The reason is that the more massive a star, the greater its core temperature must be to provide the necessary outward pressure to counteract its stronger gravity. Higher core temperatures also cause stars to burn their fuel faster, and hence live shorter lives. As a result of their extremely high core temperatures, the most massive stars (the so-called blue giants) burn their fuel at such a furious rate that they live perhaps a mere million years, which is just a "blink of an eye" as far as star lifetimes go.

At the other extreme, the lowest-mass stars have very low temperatures, and therefore live much longer, since they spend their fuel at such a miserly rate. These "brown dwarfs" emit so little light that astronomers have not seen any of them! Our galaxy might well have vast numbers of brown dwarfs that are too faint to be seen, which would be one possible solution to the "dark matter" mystery (see essay 83). Some astronomers believe that other stars have planets that may harbor intelligent life. If they are right, it is likely that neither the hot blue giants nor the tepid brown dwarfs would be the best candidates. Stars much hotter than our Sun burn out too fast for life to evolve, while stars much colder than our Sun would likely not provide enough warmth, unless a planet were exceptionally close to such a sun—perhaps too close for a stable orbit.

The observed connection between a star's mass and its temperature does not imply that the temperature of a star is strictly determined by its mass. Many stars heat up as they get older, even while losing mass. It is, in fact, only during the hydrogen burning stage, occupying the bulk of a star's lifetime, that the core temperature stays relatively constant. After a star exhausts most of the hydrogen fuel in its core, it lacks the necessary outward radiation pressure to counteract the inward crush of gravity. The resultant gravitational contraction creates high enough pressures and temperatures at the core to ignite the helium produced in hydrogen fusion.

Helium burning requires a core temperature of 200 million degrees, compared with the 20 million degrees required for hydrogen burning. When helium nuclei fuse, they create carbon nuclei plus energy. For massive stars, a core contraction again occurs once the helium has been consumed, leading to still higher central pressures and temperatures, which are eventually high enough to ignite the carbon nuclei. This process can repeat itself several more times, with a gravitational collapse being halted each time, once the ash from the previous reaction is ignited at a higher temperature than the previous reaction. Eventually silicon nuclei are ignited at 2.7 billion degrees, producing iron nuclei. At this point, no further fusion reactions can save the star from further core collapse into a black hole, because iron nuclei, being the most stable, do not liberate energy when they fuse, but rather consume it (see essay 87).

FIGURE 127. *Professor Kowalski's astronomy class ponders the question of whether intelligent life exists in the universe.*

The core temperatures needed to burn hydrogen, helium, carbon, and other nuclei are all based on theoretical calculations. The reason that the temperature needed to achieve fusion is higher for heavier nuclei is that their higher number of protons create a stronger electrical repulsion than in the case of light nuclei. Heavy nuclei must therefore collide more violently in order to get close enough to fuse. At the other extreme of temperatures, the coldest stars in the universe would be the "black dwarfs," the dead burned-out cinders of stars too small to become black holes, neutron stars, or anything else exotic. Black dwarfs eventually cool to the temperature of surrounding space.

111. How Cold Is Space?

HOW CAN we define the temperature of empty space? Actually, space is not empty, but is filled with a remnant of the electromagnetic radiation that was present near the time of the big bang. When the universe was a million years old—a mere 0.01 percent of its present age—it is believed that the expanding universe, opaque until that time, suddenly became transparent to light, allowing the light to separate from the matter and shine forth.

The temperature of the universe at that early time is believed to have been approximately 3,000° Kelvin, which is the highest temperature at which neutral hydrogen atoms can exist intact. During the subsequent expansion of the universe, this initial burst of electromagnetic radiation (light) should have by now cooled to about 3° above absolute zero. This 3° remnant from the big bang is called the "cosmic background radiation."

In the early 1960s, some fifteen years after the big bang theory was first proposed, a pair of scientists, Arno Penzias and Robert Wilson, accidentally discovered the existence of this cosmic background radiation. They had been trying to perfect microwave antennas for communication, and they could not seem to get rid of an ever present background noise that appeared to come from all directions. After ruling out such possibilities as a defect in their equipment or pigeon droppings in their receiving antenna, they concluded that their signal was not random noise at all, but rather the "last faint whisper" of the big bang.

The evidence that supported this interpretation was twofold. First, the signal was nearly uniform in all directions, unlike virtually any man-made signal. Second, the temperature of the cosmic background radiation could be measured by observing how much radiation was present at different wavelengths, and fitting the spectrum to a blackbody shape. Once the spectrum had been shown to have a blackbody shape, the temperature could immediately be found by using the inverse relation between temperature and peak wavelength, as explained in essay 108. Experimentally, the greatest amount of cosmic background radiation (the peak of the spectrum) is found at a wavelength of about 1.1 millimeters, which means that its temperature is 2.7° K—quite close to the theoretical prediction. The existence of an isotropic (same in all directions) background radiation of just about the predicted temperature is the single most important evidence supporting the big bang theory.

Recent observations of the cosmic background radiation show that it is not quite uniform, but that it is slightly colder in one direction in space and slightly warmer in the opposite direction by 0.12 percent. This variation in temperature with direction can be easily explained if the solar system and the galaxy is traveling through space relative to a reference frame moving with the

FIGURE 128. *"We are 95 percent certain that the signal we have discovered is the radiation left over from the big bang that created the universe. Of course, we have not yet ruled out the 5 percent probability of its being due to pigeon poop in our antenna."*

universal expansion. Only in a reference frame moving right along with the expansion would the temperature of incoming radiation be equal in all directions. In other reference frames, such as ours, the radiation temperature appears hotter if you move through space in a certain direction, and colder if you move in the opposite direction. The temperature variation is a consequence of the Doppler shift, which causes a change in observed frequency (also wavelength) depending on your speed relative to a source of waves (see essay 46).

Aside from the nonuniformity in the cosmic background radiation due to our motion through space, the measured radiation otherwise appears nearly uniform. In fact, until the recent discovery of tiny temperature variations at the level of 0.00001°, cosmologists had been worried that the radiation might be *too* uniform. The near uniformity in the cosmic background radiation implies that the early universe was extremely "smooth": it had very little variation in the density of its matter and radiation. But only if there are *some* initial variations in the ancient background radiation, perhaps revealing gravitational "seeds" of early matter, can we understand how the universe evolved to its present "clumpy" state.

112.   How Hot Is the Hottest Superconductor?

ELECTRICAL resistance retards the flow of electric current in a manner similar to the way rusty pipes impede the flow of water. Even the best electrical conductors, such as copper, offer some resistance to electric current. Electrical resistance is the result of collisions between moving electrons (making up the current) and relatively fixed atoms in the material, which are typically ordered in some kind of regular arrangement or "lattice." Because of electron-atom collisions, energy is transferred to the lattice, which is therefore heated by the passage of current. In some applications, such heating is desirable. Light bulbs, toasters, and electric heaters could not work without it. But in many other applications, such as computers, motors, and power transmission lines, resistive heating leads to wasted energy or malfunctions.

In view of such problems associated with electrical resistance, the phenomenon of superconductivity has long been an area of practical as well as purely scientific interest.[1] Superconductivity refers to the property of certain materials to conduct electricity without any resistance whatsoever. A current created in a loop of superconducting wire will still be present a year later, even if the power

1. Isn't our universe super! It has superfluids, supernovae, supercooling, superheating, and superconductors, without being in the least superfluous.

source is disconnected. In 1911 Kammerlingh Onnes first discovered superconductivity by accident, when he measured the resistance of mercury. Imagine Onnes's shock when he found that mercury's resistance suddenly dropped to zero when its temperature was lowered below 4.2° above absolute zero. He undoubtedly must have thought a wire leading to his instruments had come loose. Since Onnes's discovery, many other materials have been discovered to exhibit superconductivity, but only at extremely low temperatures. Until 1986 no material was found to be superconductive above 20° Kelvin.

Then, in the year 1987, pioneering work by Georg Bednorz and Alex Muller focused the search for superconductivity on a new class of ceramic materials. Many physicists jumped into what had been a somewhat dormant field, and the race for still higher-temperature superconductors was on, with the record, at the time of this writing,

FIGURE 129. *Unable to find any room-temperature superconductors, Fred fell for the salesman's pitch for the super-duper conductors.*

at 164° K. The ultimate hope is to find a material showing superconductivity at room temperature, around 300° K, which would allow superconductive devices to be built without requiring expensive refrigeration.

But even if that hope remains unfulfilled, an important barrier has already been broken. Materials showing superconductivity at temperatures above the boiling point of liquid nitrogen (77° K) can easily be cooled by that relatively cheap substance. This milestone makes many technological applications economically viable now, although many more applications will require superconducting materials that can be made into flexible wires, which is difficult with ceramics.

A theory explaining superconductivity was not put forth until four decades after the phenomenon was discovered. In this BCS theory (named after Nobel laureates John Bardeen, Leon Cooper, and Robert Schreiffer), electrons do not flow through a superconductor singly but rather in pairs, each member of which moves in the opposite direction from the other. The electron pairs are formed when one moving electron slightly deforms the crystal lattice, and this deformation travels in a wavelike manner to other parts of the crystal, causing it to attract an electron moving in the opposite direction. Each electron in the bound pair is essentially immune to energy loss in collision with atoms of the material, because the random collisions are not energetic enough to break the pair bond if the temperature of the material is sufficiently low.[2]

In an imperfect analogy, a single marcher can easily lose energy in collision with other stationary people on a field, but a row of marchers with locked arms can march across the field unimpeded. Unfortunately, the BCS theory is not able to explain superconductivity at the relatively high temperatures now observed, and another Nobel prize probably awaits anyone who does develop a successful theory.

113.   How Much Global Warming?

HAVE YOU ever noticed how hot a car can get on a sunny day when you leave it with all the windows rolled up? You are, in this case, observing the greenhouse effect. In a locked car or a greenhouse, the glass is transparent to sunlight, but opaque to the infrared radiation produced by the warmed interior. The resulting imbalance between incoming sunlight and outgoing heat radiation causes the interior to heat up. "Greenhouse gases" in the atmosphere operate in much the same way, since they, too, are transparent to incoming sunlight, but partly block the infrared waves that the warmed Earth radiates back into space. The effect of the greenhouse gases is to raise the Earth's surface temperature, until it radiates as much energy as it receives. Can the reader guess which atmospheric gas is primarily responsible for the Earth's greenH_2Ouse effect?

For billion of years, the Earth has benefitted from a *natural* greenhouse effect. It can be shown, for example, that the presence of natural greenhouse gases in the atmosphere have kept the planet's surface 33° Celsius warmer than it would be without its atmosphere. In effect, the atmosphere acts like an insulating blanket that keeps the warmth in. How do we know what the surface temperature would be without an atmosphere? Start with the fact that the Sun's energy warms the planet, which then radiates energy back into space in proportion to the *fourth* power of its surface temperature—meaning if you double the absolute surface temperature, it radiates sixteen times as much. Obviously, there must be some equilibrium surface temperature at which the Earth radiates as much into space

2. Low temperatures are required because at high temperatures, the lattice vibrations have enough energy to break the bonds between electron pairs when one electron of the pair collides with the lattice.

as it receives from the Sun. That equilibrium temperature, calculated from the known amount of solar energy reaching Earth, turns out to be $-18°$ C or 0° Fahrenheit—which is what the planet's temperature would be in the absence of an atmosphere.

Although the natural greenhouse effect has allowed life to flourish on Earth, the primary concern of scientists today is with a man-made addition, which might substantially increase the average global temperature. The main culprit among the gases added by human activities is carbon dioxide—presently only 10 percent of the amount of atmospheric water vapor, but growing at a significant rate. CO_2 gets added to the atmosphere primarily through the burning of fossil fuels, and secondarily through the clearing of forests—since plants absorb carbon dioxide.

The primary scientific debate over the greenhouse effect concerns the extent of global warming that would result from a given increase in CO_2 emissions. This greenhouse warming cannot be directly measured, because the effect is a long-term one, and there are other unknown causes of long-term temperature fluctuations. In other words, while the recent increase in atmospheric CO_2 is well established, the extent of global warming it causes is not. The primary tool for answering the global warming question has been the use of global climate models. These models divide the atmosphere above Earth's surface into a three-dimensional grid of cells, assume a set of initial conditions, and allow the system to evolve on a powerful computer, according to the known laws of physics.

A number of scientists have created such models, which significantly differ in their predictions. The range of predictions for the average global temperature increase during the next century is currently between 1.5° and 4.5° C (2.4° to 7.2° F). There are many reasons for this threefold uncertainty range, the most important being the effects of clouds, which can have opposite effects depending on whether they are at high or low altitudes.

To have confidence in the ability of global climate models to predict the future, we might want to see how well they do in "predicting" the present global climate (given the past). The global temperature over the past one hundred years shows considerable annual and decade-scale fluctuations. Some scientists claim to see a rise in global average temperature of 0.5° C during this time—although that temperature rise is superimposed on much larger, apparently

FIGURE 130. *A long-range climate predictor at work.*

random variations. Most of the global climate models are, however, in reasonable agreement with such a temperature increase, based on the CO_2 increases to date. Thus, the greenhouse effect is likely to cause problems in the future, but it remains to be seen how serious they will be, and how much and at what cost they can be ameliorated by intervention.

114.   Nuclear Winter or Nuclear Summer?

MOST PEOPLE are not particularly concerned about what the weather would be like following a nuclear war. But in 1983 a group of scientists suggested that the climatic aftermath of a nuclear war could produce even more devastation that the direct effects of the war. Their "nuclear winter" hypothesis was based on the idea that vast amounts of dust and smoke would be thrown up in the air as a result of the explosions and fires—perhaps 100 million tons in some estimates. This dust and smoke would in effect create an "anti-greenhouse" effect. Incoming solar radiation would be blocked by the opaque dust and smoke, but infrared radiation from the warm planet surface would pass through unhindered into space, causing the Earth's surface to cool.

Obviously, the extent of the cooling and its duration would depend on how much dust and smoke were created, and how long they stayed in the atmosphere. In the original nuclear winter study, scientists suggested that the average global temperature could drop well below freezing even if the war occurred during the summer, and that recovery to normal temperature could take months or even years. When these predicted climatic effects were combined

FIGURE 131. *Nuclear winter or nuclear summer? Martin couldn't decide which wardrobe to bring to the bomb shelter.*

with radioactive fallout and other known effects of nuclear weapons, many people felt that a nuclear war raised the real prospect of the extinction of mankind, if not all life on Earth. But it now seems that such dire predictions involved rhetorical overkill.

More recent work on the climatic aftermath of a nuclear war, applying the same global climate computer models that are used to study the greenhouse effect, predict that, in a large-scale war, the maximum temperature drop might be around 12° Celsius in midlatitudes for a summer war. A war in the wintertime would lead to less severe temperature drops (since it is already cold), and in either case recovery to near normal temperatures would probably be a matter of weeks or months, rather than months or years. For this reason, incidentally, you could not cure the global warming problem with a "small" nuclear war, whose climatic effects would not be as long lasting as those associated with the greenhouse effect. Also, the climatic aftermath of a nuclear war would be extremely uncertain, depending as it would on many unknowns, such as how much dust and smoke would be created, and how high they would be lofted.

In view of such uncertainties, some scientists have suggested that a "nuclear summer" might be just as possible as a nuclear winter. They point in particular to the possible formation of high-altitude cirrus clouds whose water vapor would create a greenhouse effect and warm the planet's surface. Whether it be nuclear summer or nuclear winter following a war (or even "nuclear springtime"!), we cannot say that the climatic effects of a nuclear war would surely be negligible. Undoubtedly, there could be a catastrophic disruption of agriculture on a worldwide scale, although perhaps as much due to economic and social chaos as climatic conditions.

Certainly, parts of the world even now faced with near starvation could find themselves faced with complete disaster after a nuclear war. Many estimates have been made of the number of casualties, but usually these are made by groups with particular agendas. One need not do such a study—with all its questionable assumptions—to realize that a large-scale nuclear war would be an unprecedented catastrophe for humanity, though probably not the extinction event suggested in the doomsday scenarios.

HOW
FAST
IS IT?

115.   How Fast Should You Jump in a Falling Elevator to Survive?

SUPPOSE YOU were riding in an elevator whose cable had just broken. Could you possibly save your life by jumping off the floor just before the elevator hit bottom? Of course, your state of weightlessness during the fall would make it rather difficult to jump off the floor, but let's not worry about that for now. Suppose that the elevator, at the moment of impact, is moving downward at 96 feet per second— a speed it would attain after three seconds of free fall.

Unless you are a track star, it is unlikely that you can jump higher than about 3 feet off the ground, which corresponds to an upward takeoff speed of about 14 feet per second. Even if you could push off at this speed just before the elevator impact, your net downward speed would be 96 minus 14, or 82 feet per second. Thus, by jumping prior to impact, you would probably not avert death or serious injury.

But suppose you had a device that could propel you upward at 96 feet per second relative to the elevator. If you activated the device just before impact, your speed relative to the ground would be *zero*! Could such a mechanism actually save your life? That depends entirely on one crucial factor, which has so far not been considered, namely the time of acceleration. If the device propelled you upward in too short a time (causing too many g's acceleration), the effect on your body might be little different from that of the elevator impact itself.

On the other hand, if you had a device similar to the ejection seat on military jets, and it did not subject you to too many g's, you could survive. Of course, the device would need to be equipped with sensors that could measure the elevator's downward speed and eject you upward at exactly that speed just prior to impact. Considering all the complexities, it might be easier to design elevators so that their cables don't break!

How about a slightly less ridiculous idea, namely ejection seats for cars that

213

could be activated by computer just prior to a collision? Conceivably, these could allow you to escape injury in certain types of crashes for which air bags would be ineffective. Again, the ejection would have to be at the same speed as the car but in the opposite direction, in order to leave the occupants at rest relative to the ground. Unfortunately, if such an ejection mechanism were activated by the force of the collision itself (as is the case with air bags), precious little time would be available to blow the roof of the car and propel the occupants upward. In fact, it seems likely that the time would be so marginal that the occupants would have to experience a prohibitive number of g's during the upward acceleration.

A much better alternative might be to use sensors to detect an impending collision one or two seconds in advance, and activate the ejection system, which could then operate with fewer g's acceleration. On the other hand, if we could build cars smart enough to sense impending collisions, we ought to be able to design them to avoid collisions in the first place,

FIGURE 132. *Joe found that he always had to wait less for the freely falling elevator.*

thereby eliminating the primary piece of hardware causing most collisions—the nut behind the wheel.

116.   At What Speed Should You Walk to Get Least Wet in a Rainstorm?

AT WHAT speed should you walk or run through a rainstorm if you are caught without an umbrella and you want to get the least wet? Let's make some simplifying assumptions in order to figure this out. First, let's approximate your shape by a box, say 6 feet tall by 2 feet wide by 1 foot deep. Next, let's assume that the rain is falling straight down at some constant speed.[1]

When you walk forward 100 feet, say, the front of your body sweeps through a volume $6 \times 2 \times 100$ feet, and all the raindrops occupying that volume will hit your front. This result does not depend on either your speed or the speed at which the rain descends. How about the rain hitting the top of your flat head? The number of raindrops landing on your head is proportional to the amount of time your head is exposed, so it is inversely proportional to your speed in the case of a vertically descending rain. In a more realistic approximation of a human shape, most surfaces would be somewhere between the two extremes of strictly horizontal and vertical, but this does not matter. It is always best to spend the shortest possible time in the rain, since for the mostly vertical parts of your body the time does not matter, and for the mostly horizontal parts the shorter the time the better.

If the rain is descending obliquely, then it may not be best to run as fast as you can. Suppose, for example, the wind is blowing from behind you, in the direction you are headed. In this case the optimum strategy is to walk or run at the same speed as the wind, so that you see the rain falling directly downward. The vertical portions of your body will then not get wet at all. Of course, the top of your head willl get wetter at this speed than if you go faster, but since your front has a much larger area than your head, this speed is probably close to the optimum—unless you care more about not getting your head wet than your front.

How can you tell what speed the rain is descending if you are caught

FIGURE 133. *Although the significance of the ritual was unknown, the tribe loved to run in a circle in a downpour while carefully adjusting the angle of their rain catchers to avoid having raindrops hit the tube walls.*

in a rainstorm? Let us suppose you are sitting comfortably in your car, watching the rain streak your side window. If the wind is blowing directly toward the window, you will see the raindrops leaving vertical streaks. As you drive your car, the

1. Raindrops or other objects that fall through great distances eventually reach a "terminal velocity" when the upward, speed-dependent force of air resistance just counters gravity.

rain streaks will no longer be vertical, but will make an angle with the vertical that increases with the speed of the car.

Suppose you drive at some fixed speed, say 20 miles per hour, and observe that the oblique rain streaks move downward by x inches for every inch they move sideways. If x is 1 inch, the rain streaks will make a 45° angle with the vertical, and the speeds of rain and car must therefore be equal. In general, the rain must be descending at x times the speed of the car. If you actually try to measure the rain's speed of descent using this method, be sure to have a friend watch the raindrops and do the measuring while you watch the road![2]

The idea that raindrops descending vertically will appear to descend at an oblique angle when you move through the rain implies that if you try to catch raindrops in a tube without their hitting the walls of the tube, you need to tilt the tube in the direction in which you are moving. If you substitute telescopes and starlight for tubes and raindrops, this situation is analogous to "stellar aberration," in which stars seen perpendicular to the plane of the Earth's orbit appear to move in tiny circles during the Earth's path around the Sun. As discussed in essay 42, stellar aberration proves that the Earth orbits the Sun, rather than the other way around.

117.　How Fast Does Electricity Travel in Wires?

ELECTRONS, the carriers of electricity in conductors, move through wires at a snail's pace, typically 0.1 millimeters per second. At that rate a given electron would take perhaps fifteen hours to travel from the wall outlet to your bed lamp. This "drift velocity" of the electrons can be measured, based on the amount of electric charge that passes through the wire per unit time, namely, the current.

Fortunately, you do not have to wait fifteen hours for your bed lamp to go on or off when you throw the switch. When the switch is thrown, electrons all along the wire nudge their neighbors with a "signal velocity" equal to the speed of light, so that electrons start or stop flowing through your bed lamp perhaps a ten-billionth of a second after you throw the switch. The signal velocity of electricity in wires can easily be measured by sending a short electric pulse through a wire, and

2. Also, don't expect to get an especially accurate result, because for streamlined cars the airflow around the car's windshield alters the speed of the raindrops as they hit the side window.

using a device such as an oscilloscope to measure the short time delay for the pulse to travel the length of the wire.

One way to understand the reasons for the very low drift velocity and very high signal velocity is to use a simple model for electron conduction in a wire. Think of the fixed atoms in a wire as being similar to a very large number of nails in a board. Tilt the board by a small angle and release BBs at the top end of the board. As the BBs (representing electrons) make numerous random collisions with the nails, they give up their energy to the nails, and slowly stagger down the length of the board—a motion analogous to the slow drift of individual electrons through a wire. The average speed of the BBs down the board can easily be increased by increasing the angle of the board, just as the drift speed of electrons in a wire can be increased by applying a higher voltage across the ends of the wire.

To what does the electron signal velocity correspond in our nail board model? If we start with a horizontal board and BBs all along its length, the speed at which BBs begin coming off the lower end once the upper end has suddenly been raised is a measure of the signal velocity.[1] This nail board model shows why the signal velocity can be so high even though the drift velocity is extremely low.

Electrons moving through a wire also have a third kind of motion besides the drift and signal velocities, namely a "thermal velocity" missing in our nail board analogy so far. As with molecules randomly moving in a gas, the free electrons in a conductor have a random motion characteristic of the particular temperature. At room temperature, the electrons in a wire have an average speed of 118 kilometers per second. If you want to think of electron flow in a wire using the nail board analogy, picture BBs whizzing randomly around at blindingly high speeds on a very slightly tilted board, while they simultaneously slowly drift down the board at a snail's pace.

FIGURE 134. *Rick never made it when he tried to get to his bed before the electricity stopped flowing after he turned out the light.*

Actually, the nail board analogy, though it may have intuitive appeal, fails to explain many important features of electron conduction, especially why certain

1. One flaw in the nail board analogy is that the BBs all along the board don't nudge each other the way electrons do when those at one end start moving. BBs don't move until they are hit by other BBs. Electrons, on the other hand, "feel" electrical repulsion from far away, and start to move as soon as another electron approaches them. It is this "communication" from one electron to the next that travels at the signal velocity.

materials are conductors while others are insulators and still others are super-conductors. For this purpose, we must use quantum mechanics, which explicitly recognizes the wave nature of the electron.

So, to address the question raised by the cartoon: how long *do* you have to make it to your bed after you throw the switch? Even though the electrons stop flowing through the lamp filament a mere ten-billionth of a second or so after you throw the switch, you might have as much as a tenth of a second while the filament is still hot enough to emit light—still not long enough to make it to your bed.

118. How Fast Can Chemical Rockets Travel?

ROCKETS RELY on the principle of action and reaction, or recoil. A rocket pushes against the ejected gases from fuel combustion, which push back on the rocket and propel it forward. We can see the relevant variables for describing the performance of rockets by analogy with a person sitting at rest on frictionless ice. Clearly, if you threw an object while on a frictionless surface, you would recoil in the opposite direction. Your recoil speed would be equal to the speed of the object times its mass expressed as a fraction of your own.

For example, if the object's mass were 1 percent of yours, you would recoil at 1 percent of its speed, thereby conserving momentum in the process. Clearly, if you wanted to achieve a higher recoil speed, you would need to either throw a more massive object or throw a given object faster. (Actually, in practice, if you threw a more massive object, you might not be able to throw it as fast as a lighter object.)

An analogy somewhat closer to the rocket situation involves firing a machine gun on frictionless ice, in which case your recoil speed would increase by a constant amount for every bullet fired. The main difference between the recoils of a rocket and a machine gun is that rocket engines eject the hot gases continuously rather than in bursts, and so a rocket's recoil speed increases steadily—although not at a constant rate, since its mass continually decreases as the fuel empties.

The two relevant variables that determine the final speed a rocket can achieve after burning all its fuel are essentially the same two variables that determine your recoil speed when you throw an object on ice. In the case of the rocket, the two key variables are the "exhaust speed" at which hot gases are expelled, and the "fuel mass fraction," that is, the total mass of the fuel expelled, expressed as a fraction of the rocket's total initial mass. In order to achieve the highest possible speed for a single-stage rocket, both the exhaust velocity and the fuel mass fraction should be as large as possible.

There are, of course, practical limits to both variables. The maximum exhaust speed of gases is determined by the maximum rate at which energy can be released in chemical reactions. And if you increase the fuel mass fraction close to a value of one, you then have little mass left for the payload, or for the body of the rocket itself. Still another approach to achieving high speeds is the use of multi-stage rockets in which parts of the rocket body that no longer contain fuel are jettisoned—leaving a smaller-mass rocket to be accelerated forward.

The problem of reaching much higher exhaust velocities than achieved by present-day rockets will likely not be solved by improved chemical fuels, since there are limits to the amount of energy per kilogram that chemical reactions can liberate. Nuclear reactions, which can emit a million times more energy per kilogram than chemical reactions, are one possible way of achieving higher exhaust velocities.

The ultimate exhaust speed, of course, would be the speed of light—but don't expect to propel your rocket to high speed by shining a flashlight out the back! Flashlights convert only the tiniest fraction of their mass into light energy before the batteries go dead. Rather than ejecting light, we could imagine a spaceship that recoils from external light striking it. In friction-free space, with a moderately large solar sail, this tiny steady force could allow the ship to attain respectably high speeds during the months and years of a space voyage.

FIGURE 135. *Stranded in space, Sally, the ship's flatulographer, wondered how she could get back.*

119. How Fast Do Subatomic Particles Travel in Accelerators?

TODAY'S PARTICLE accelerators have been called the "cathedrals" of our age—so awesome is the feat of their construction, and so far from everyday concerns is their purpose. Particle accelerators are devices for producing high-energy beams of subatomic particles such as protons or electrons. Such particle beams are used to probe the structure of matter at its most fundamental level. For a given design, the higher the energy of the particle beam, the larger the accelerator must be.[1] The Superconducting Super Collider (SSC) that would have cost over $8 billion would have been the world's largest accelerator. The SSC would have accelerated protons toward each other at speeds a mere 0.3 meter per second below the speed of light, that is, 99.9999999 percent of c, inside a ring of about 50 miles in diameter.

Accelerator experiments usually observe particles created when the primary beam smashes into a stationary target, or collides with a beam circulating in the opposite direction. You might think that the energy gain using colliding particles is only a factor of two over collisions in which one particle hits another at rest. But in fact, colliding beams allow experimenters to observe *much* higher-energy collisions, owing to the relativistic increase of mass with speed discussed in essay 91.

For example, protons in the SSC would move at speeds so close to the speed of light that they would be 22,000 times more massive than protons at rest. If such speedy protons hit a stationary target, they are like 22,000-pound trucks hitting 1-pound pigeons. In contrast, if two oppositely circulating proton beams collide, the collision is like a head-on collision between two 22,000-pound trucks. Although the kinetic energy is only twice as much in the latter case, the energy available to create new matter is vastly greater. In a head-on collision of two trucks (or protons), *all* the kinetic energy may be used to create new matter, which can be at rest after the collision. On the other hand, in a collision of a truck with a pigeon (or an ultrahigh-speed proton with a stationary proton), the mov-

---

1. Circular accelerators contain their particle beams in large evacuated rings using strong magnetic fields that bend the beams into circles. In general, for a given magnetic field, the radius of curvature in a particle beam's path is proportional to the particle momentum. Thus, to achieve high momentum or speed with a circular accelerator requires the circle to have a large diameter.

ing truck loses very little energy in the collision, and hence very little is available to create new matter. (Of course, in the case of colliding trucks, unless they are traveling at close to the speed of light, it is heat rather than new matter that is created.)

The colliding beams in the supercollider would have enough energy to create secondary particles of up to twice 22,000, or 44,000, times the mass of a proton—if such massive particles exist. A primary purpose in building the SSC was precisely to look for such high-mass particles, which cannot be produced in accelerators having lower energy. In order to get information about what happens in these collisions, we need ways to find the identity, direction, and speed (or energy) of any new particle that is created. A number of techniques have evolved for measuring particle speeds, one of which is analogous to using timed sequences of traffic lights to control and monitor car speeds. Devices known as "velocity selectors," for example, allow particles that

FIGURE 136. *"I know it's a lot cheaper than the supercollider, but have we seen any new particles created this way yet?"*

have only a narrow range of speeds to pass through them. By adjusting the velocity selector to a particular speed, we can monitor how many particles have that speed by using electronic counters similar to Geiger counters. Particle speeds can also be directly measured if we use pairs of such scintillation counters placed some distance apart, and note the short time difference between the electric pulses produced in the two counters.

120. Might There Be Faster-Than-Light Particles?

THE SPEED of light in vacuum, c, is considered by most physicists to be the fastest possible speed. One rationale for c as a universal speed limit is that it would take an infinite amount of energy to accelerate a particle up to the speed of light (see essay 105). On the other hand, light itself obviously does not have infinite energy. It is only nonzero-mass particles that would require infinite energy to be accelerated to the speed of light. Photons (and presumably neutrinos) move at the speed of light only by virtue of the fact that they have zero rest mass.

The existence of objects that do travel at the speed of light has suggested to some physicists the idea that the speed c may perhaps not be so much a limiting speed, but instead a way of dividing all moving objects into three clearly defined speed categories. The three categories, and the Greek roots of the words, are tardyons ("slow"), luxons ("light"), and tachyons ("swift"). Tardyons are particles that cannot attain the speed of light; luxons are particles such as photons, and perhaps neutrinos, that always move at the speed of light; and tachyons are hypothetical particles that always travel faster than light. Thus, in this scheme, the speed c is a *two-way* barrier. The speed of most known particles (tardyons) can never exceed it, while the hypothetical tachyons can never go slower than c.

As explained in essay 93, massive particles have sublight speeds, while zero-mass particles must have the speed of light. The equation for the mass of a particle given in the footnote to essay 91, when applied to tachyons having speeds greater than light, requires their mass to be imaginary! "Imaginary" is here being used in the mathematical sense of the word, namely that the square of the mass is a negative number. The concept of imaginary mass has in many eyes doomed tachyons to the realm of the unthinkable. However, some physicists have suggested that these bizarre entities might actually exist, and have even proposed ways to look for them. The most straightforward technique for finding tachyons is to search for them among the many secondary particles produced in high-energy accelerator collisions. If we use, for example, the time-of-flight method for finding particle speeds (see previous essay), we can see if any of the emitted particles have speeds in excess of the speed of light. Another technique would be to look for particles produced with an imaginary mass, using "missing mass" experiments. The mass of any unobserved or "missing" particle in an interaction can be found if all the other particle energies, directions, and masses are known. In looking for tachyons, we would calculate the *square* of the missing mass from the equations for energy and momentum conservation, and see if it is ever negative.

FIGURE 137. *It wasn't the points he'd get for speeding that concerned Eddie as much as how he'd explain the imaginary mass on his license.*

To date, none of the tachyon searches have proved positive, which implies one of (at least) three possibilities: (1) tachyons do not exist, (2) they are not abundantly produced in the reactions examined, or (3) the detectors used are inadequate. Still another possibility is that tachyons do exist, and in fact are all around us, but do not interact with ordinary matter.

If tachyons are more than just a figment of some physicists' imaginations, their imaginary mass is not their strangest property. According to one interpretation, the equations of relativity predict that faster-than-light particles could actually be used to send information backward in time! Yet even this bizarre property is not conclusive grounds for rejecting the tachyon hypothesis, because we can change the time order of tachyon transmission and reception simply by reinterpreting the two processes. In fact, such a reinterpretation can also be given to antimatter, which can be regarded as ordinary matter moving backward in time. To understand what is meant by "reinterpretation," just think about the high degree of symmetry between the processes of transmission and reception of signals, such as sound waves. Suppose, for example, you speak, causing your vocal cords to vibrate, and the resulting sound impinges on my eardrums, causing them to vibrate. The reinterpreted time-reversed sequence has my vibrating eardrum create the transmitted sound that causes your vocal cords to vibrate. This situation is, of course, unrealistic, because we assume that the sound of your speech affects nothing but my eardrums, but for subatomic processes the symmetry between transmission and reception is quite real.

121. Does the Earth Really Rotate?

THE DAILY movement of the Sun across the sky and the nightly rotation of the stars give evidence for the twenty-four-hour rotation of the Earth on its axis. Ancient peoples were much more aware of celestial phenomena than we are, but they thought that the Earth was at rest while the Sun, Moon, and stars rotated about it. What evidence is there, in fact, that our current view is correct? Presumably, if we took a space journey to another planet, we could look back at the Earth and *see* it rotating against a starry background, much as we can now see some other planets rotating when viewed on consecutive nights through a powerful telescope. But what evidence can we point to for our planet's rotation that does not require us to leave the planet?

One indirect piece of evidence is the Earth's equatorial bulge. The fact that the Earth's diameter is 44 kilometers greater at the equator than along a north-south axis is a direct consequence of the planet's rotation and the resulting centrifugal force. The Earth's rotation rate is too small for our bodies to sense directly, but there are other observations that show it is the Earth, and not the heavens, that rotates.

The most direct of these is the Foucault pendulum seen in some museums. You can get the idea by suspending a pendulum from your fingers while swinging it. The pendulum will swing back and forth in a fixed plane. If you now start to rotate about an axis or walk in a small circle while the pendulum swings, it will appear to you as though the plane of the pendulum swings is rotating. Actually, the swings occur roughly in a fixed plane, but your perspective rotates. In exactly the same way, the plane of swing of a pendulum at the north pole would appear to rotate once every twenty-four hours, as a result of the Earth's rotation. We are imagining the pendulum to be at the north pole only because it is much easier to understand what happens there, since the direction of gravity and the axis of rotation coincide. If the same observations are made at the equator, the plane of a pendulum does not appear to rotate at all, and at latitudes intermediate between the pole and the equator, the rotation also occurs, but with a period greater than twenty-four hours. The apparent rotation of the plane of the Foucalt pendulum is direct evidence for the Earth's rotation.

Still another piece of evidence for the Earth's rotation is the Coriolis force, which, like the more well-known centrifugal force, is a "fictitious" force in a rotating system. The seemingly strange motions caused by the Coriolis force can be attributed to the Earth's rotation while a projectile is in the air. But do not think that this means you can travel somewhere by jumping up, and have the Earth rotate underneath you! By jumping up, you do not lose your rotational motion about the Earth's axis. (For exactly the same reason, if you jump up in the aisle of a train moving at 60 miles per hour, it will not move out from under you, and cause you to land behind the point you left the floor.)

FIGURE 138. *Not having much to do, the Eskimos liked to stand around in a circle at the North Pole playing with their Foucault pendulum.*

The effect of the Coriolis force was observed in World War I, when artillery shells would often miss their targets in a systematic way. Shells fired along a southerly direction tended to land to the west of their target. We can most easily see why by imagining an artillery piece fired from the north pole. An artillery shell aimed right at the target would hit it only if the Earth were not rotating. But due to the Earth's rotation, the target moves eastward with the Earth while the shell is in flight, so the shell lands to the west of the target. The same effect occurs for shells fired south from other Northern Hemisphere latitudes, because points on the Earth's surface travel in circles of greater and greater size as you move toward the equator. Thus, the sideways (easterly) velocity a shell gets when it is fired southward will be less than that of its target point, and the shell will always tend to land to the west of the target, if it lands above the equator—assuming the gunners don't know about the Coriolis force and have perfect aim.[1]

122. What Is the Earth's Speed through Space?

AT ONE TIME, it was believed that the Earth was at rest in space, while the Sun, planets, Moon, and stars all revolved around it. Surely, it was thought, people would fall off the Earth if it did move through space. Nowadays, when people routinely ride in high-speed vehicles without falling out, such ideas seem laughable. In fact, if the motion of a vehicle such as a jet airplane is completely uniform (constant speed in a straight line), there is no sensation of movement whatsoever. Were it not for vibrations and engine noise, you might conclude your plane was on the ground at rest.

Just over a century ago, Albert Michelson and Edward Morley thought they did have a way to measure the absolute speed of the Earth through space. They reasoned that such motion would make light signals appear to travel faster in some directions than in others. After a series of repeated trials involving light signals reflected from mirrors, Michelson and Morley failed to detect any effect whatsoever due to the Earth's motion, even though their apparatus was extremely sensitive, and should have detected the effect if it had been present.

This negative finding by Michelson and Morley was extremely perplexing at the time. It was not until Einstein developed his relativity theory almost two dec-

1. For example, consider an artillery shell fired southward from the north pole. (All directions from the pole are southward!) If the range of the shell is 60 miles, it lands at a point on the Earth that is traveling in a circle of radius 60 miles and circumference 377 miles. Suppose the shell is in the air for 86 seconds, or 1/1,000 of a day. In that time, the Earth rotates $1/1,000$ of a revolution, and the target point moves east by $377/1,000 = 0.377$ miles, which is how much the shell misses the target.

ades later that the Michelson-Morley experiment was fully understood.[1] In fact, the unmeasurability of absolute motion through space is one of the key pillars underlying Einstein's theory of relativity.

According to relativity, each of two uniformly moving observers can consider herself to be at rest and the other to be in motion. In other words, there is no preferred reference frame that can be said to be absolutely at rest in space. Recent satellite observations, however, of the cosmic background radiation—a remnant of the big bang—reveal that this idea of the impossibility of measuring absolute motion in space needs to be qualified.

When observers look at the wavelength distribution of the cosmic background radiation, they find a peak wavelength of the spectrum. The wavelength is, however, slightly direction-dependent. This result is exactly what would be predicted if the Earth were moving through space relative to the uniform "sea" of cosmic background radiation, because such motion would create a Doppler shift in wavelength that would alter the peak of the spectrum. Based on this variation with direction, we can conclude that the Earth is moving through the universe at 0.12 percent of the speed of light, or 370 kilometers per second, in the direction of the Virgo cluster of galaxies. Taking into account the Earth's motion around the Sun and the Sun's motion around the galaxy, the figure for our galaxy's speed through space is about 600 kilometers per second.

At first thought, the observation of an absolute motion of the Earth through universal space would seem to violate the underlying premise of relativity. But the conflict with relativity theory is only an apparent one, because we can define such a "preferred" reference frame only for each point in space moving with the overall expansion of the universe. Thus, the "preferred" reference frame in our region of space is in relative motion with respect to the "preferred" reference frame in a remote region of space. In other words, despite the presence of the cosmic background radiation, it is still impossible to define a single preferred reference frame at rest in space everywhere.

FIGURE 139. *The Earth speeds through space toward the Virgo cluster of galaxies.*

1. According to Einstein, the negative finding of the Michelson-Morley experiment did not play a role in the development of relativity theory. Instead, he claimed that the germ of his idea was the following thought experiment he imagined as a young boy. Einstein visualized what a light wave might look like to someone moving with it. Apparently, such a light wave "surfer" would see the light wave at rest. Since no one had ever observed such a thing in nature, Einstein concluded that it must be impossible to catch up to a light beam.

123.　What Is
the Slowest Possible Speed?

ACCORDING TO classical physics, no reason exists why objects cannot be absolutely at rest. But as we shall see, quantum mechanics predicts that the speed of a *confined* particle must exceed some minimum value. An essential feature of quantum mechanics is the existence of the so-called wave function, whose value tells where a particle is likely to be found.[1] If a particle is trapped inside a box, the associated wave function must also fit inside the box, which requires that it vanish at the edges of the box. This requirement sets a limit on the longest possible wavelength as twice the width of the box—which is quite analogous to the situation for waves on a plucked guitar string, as seen in essay 60. Based on the existence of a maximum wavelength, the minimum speed of a particle can be shown to be inversely proportional to both the mass of the particle and the width of the box containing it.[2]

Applying this relationship to a billiard ball confined to a 4-foot-wide pool table gives an astonishingly tiny minimum speed. A ball with that minimum speed would travel a distance equal to the width of a proton in a time equal to the age of the universe! Although the minimum speed may be insignificant for billiard balls, such is not the case for subatomic particles. For example, in the case of an electron confined to a box of atomic size, we find a minimum speed of 2,200 kilometers per second. (Apparently, electrons, like some caged animals, just cannot sit still when confined.)

While quantum mechanics predicts a minimum speed for a confined particle, it does not predict the direction of motion. For this reason, we often refer to the minimum speed as an *uncertainty* in speed. Moreover, the equation for minimum speed tells us that the uncertainty in the electron's speed is inversely proportional to the size of the confining box, which we can refer to as the uncertainty in the particle's position.

This inverse relationship between uncertainties in speed and position, which is one form of the Heisenberg uncertainty principle, tells us that the price of more exact information on the position of an object is an unavoidable degradation of information on its speed, and vice versa. The coupling of the two uncertainties makes it impossible to predict exactly the motion of a particle, because

1. More specifically, the probability of finding a particle at a given point is proportional to the square of the magnitude of its wave function at that point.

2. The minimum speed is $h/2mL$, where h is Planck's constant, m is the particle's mass, and L is the width of the box. Given the incredibly tiny size of h, the minimum speed will be negligible unless m or L is very tiny.

such a prediction requires that both position and speed be exactly known at some initial time. In everyday life, such limitations have little practical significance, because the size of the two uncertainties is so small for objects of ordinary mass, but that is not the case for tiny masses. Thus, missiles follow well-defined trajectories, but not electrons confined to an atom. Theoretically, not only is such a trajectory unobservable, but an atomic electron literally doesn't follow one. Atoms, most definitely, are not miniature solar systems.

Quantum mechanics involves other uncertainties besides those described above. There is also the uncertainty of *when* any individual atom will undergo a transition from one state to another, even though quantum theory does allow us to calculate the probability of the transition. Some physicists, including Albert Einstein, have been greatly bothered by the probabalistic nature of quantum mechanics. Normally, we use probabilities as a way of accounting for conditions of which we are ignorant, such as in gambling or weather forecasting. The idea that a fundamental theory of physics should deal in probabilities, rather than exact predictions, meant to Einstein that quantum mechanics was incomplete, and that a future theory would be needed to restore deterministic predictions. According to a well-known remark attributed to Einstein, "God does not play dice." Most physicists today do not share Einstein's conviction about the incompleteness of quantum mechanics. If the quantum mechanical view is correct, nature is fundamentally unpredictable in certain respects, and the best we can do is make probabalistic predictions.

FIGURE 140. *If God did play dice, wouldn't he be completely bored?*

124.   At What Speed
Do the Continents Drift Apart?

IMAGINING THE Earth's continents to be anal-
ogous to pieces of a gigantic jigsaw puzzle, Alfred Wegener in 1924 proposed a
theory of continental drift. He based his theory largely on the close match between the shape of the eastern coastline of South America and the western coastline of Africa. For many years most geologists ridiculed this idea, since no
plausible mechanism was known for the large-scale motion of continents. But
the theory of "plate tectonics," advanced in the 1960s as an updated version of
continental drift, has now become well-established. According to this theory,
the Earth's surface, or crust, consists of seven large and around twenty smaller
plates that slowly move on the underlying layer known as the mantle.

The boundaries of the plates do not generally coincide with the boundaries of
the continents, although they nearly do in some cases. A pair of adjacent plates
can move past each other laterally, which is likely to cause many earthquakes at
the boundary as plates stick and slip, or else the plates can move toward or away
from each other. At places where plates move away from each other, such as the
mid-Atlantic, new crust is created as liquid material from the mantle fills in the
gap. Places where plates move toward each other often become mountainous, as
in the case of the Himalayas—the result of the Indian plate's colliding with an
Asian one.

How did the theory of continental drift or its modern incarnation, plate tectonics, go from a ridiculed idea to a well-established theory? Aside from the close
fit of the continental shapes of South America and Africa, many other pieces of
evidence slowly began to accumulate. For example, the geology, flora, and fauna
of the African and South American continents show striking similarities between the two continents that are hard to explain unless they were at one time
connected. Furthermore, when geologists date rocks on the two continents, they
find on each one a reasonably sharp dividing line, based on the ages of the rocks.
On one side of the line rocks are 2 billion years old, and on the other side they are
550 million years old. The dividing lines on each continent match up perfectly if
the continents are joined together as suggested by the fit of their coastlines. In
the same way, you can tell when two pieces of a jigsaw puzzle belong together
when the color patterns match as well as the shapes.

Perhaps the strongest piece of evidence for the theory of plate tectonics,
which won over the skeptics in the 1960s, is based on observations of the magnetization of the seafloor near the mid-Atlantic. As the seafloor continually
spreads, due to the separation of two huge plates, new molten material fills in the

gap. As this molten material solidifies, it tends to be slightly magnetized based on the direction of the Earth's magnetic field at the time of solidification.

It is now known that the Earth's magnetic field has reversed itself many times during Earth's history. This series of magnetic reversals has been coded into a pattern on the mid-Atlantic sea floor much like the pattern on a piece of magnetic tape or disk. The pattern can be read by planes flying over the mid-Atlantic with sensitive magnetometers that register small deviations from the ambient field. Places where the contribution to the magnetic field from the seafloor is "normal" (same sign as the Earth's present field) are shown on a map in white, and places where it is "reversed" are shown in black.

The crucial observation that proved that new crust is being created continuously in the gap between the separating mid-Atlantic plates was the *symmetry* in the pattern of white and black stripes about the mid-Atlantic ridge. The symmetrical pattern strongly implied that the material of the ocean floor at equal distances from either

FIGURE 141. *"You're telling this congressional committee you want airfares to have an automatic rate adjustment based on continental drift?"*

side of this ridge originated at the ridge line, and solidified at the same time as it began to spread apart. This pattern of symmetrical stripes provided a detailed record of the separation of the two plates over time. Based on the known times of Earth's magnetic reversals, we can conclude that the Atlantic Ocean is currently widening at approximately 3 centimeters per year.

HOW
OLD
IS IT?

125. How Is Time Measured?

CALENDARS have been around as long as humanity has had a need to keep track of time. For our agriculturally based ancestors, keeping track of the time of year was far more important than keeping track of the time of day, so it is not surprising that accurate calendars were developed long before accurate clocks. Even so, it was not until the year 1582 A.D. that our present-day calendar was established. Prior to that time, the European calendar was based on the one developed under Julius Caesar, in which an extra day was added every fourth (leap) year on the assumption that the year is exactly 365.25 days long.

But in fact, the length of the year is approximately 365.2422 days. This discrepancy of 0.0078 days per year, if it is unaccounted for, causes the seasons to shift slowly through the year. This slow shift of the seasons under the Julian calendar was corrected in 1582 by Pope Gregory XIII, who defined our present calendar, which requires that a leap year be added every fourth year *except in even-century years that are not divisible by four hundred*. According to this crazy-sounding rule, the year 2000 will be a leap year, but 1700, 1800, and 1900 were not. It is easy to show that the Gregorian calendar reduces the problem of "drifting seasons" to negligible proportions.[1]

The earliest clocks were based on sundials and astrolabes, which are devices that tell time by the stars. To tell time indoors or on cloudy days, people initially relied on sand hourglasses, slow-burning candles, or water clocks. Mechanical clocks were not invented until Galileo's discovery that the period of pendulums is nearly independent of the size of their swing (see essay 18). The central time-keeping elements of watches and clocks today usually consist of quartz crystals or electronic circuits, both of which have a precisely defined vibration frequency that can count off the seconds or microseconds.

1. This prescription means that the fraction of years that are leap years is 0.2425, namely ¼ minus ³⁄₄₀₀ (so as to exempt the three out of four even-century years not divisible by 400). The preceding rule for leap years would be exactly correct if the year had 365.2425 days, which differs by only 0.0003 days per year from the actual number. As a result of a discrepancy of 0.0003 days each year, the Gregorian calendar will accumulate a seasonal drift of only one day after 3,333 years elapse—a tolerably small error.

The most accurate clocks today are based on the fixed frequency of light emitted from the cesium atom. These atomic clocks are believed to be accurate to one second in 1.6 million years. In fact, the accuracy of the atomic clock is greater than that of the Earth itself. Originally, the length of the second was defined in terms of the length of the day (one day = 86,400 seconds), which for most practical purposes we continue to use. However, we can now measure the second so precisely based on atomic vibrations that we can chart the slowing down of the Earth's rotation. If the second were still defined in terms of the length of the day, the time meant by one second would slowly grow as the Earth slowed down—and we could then say that time literally isn't what it used to be.

It could be argued that the disagreement between clocks based on atomic vibrations and clocks based on the Earth's rotation does not automatically allow us to say which clock keeps the correct time. But there is no known reason why atomic vibrations should gradually speed up over time, and there is a very good reason why the Earth's rotation should slow over time, namely tidal friction. So our preference for a clock based on atomic vibrations over one based on the Earth's rotation is well justified.

FIGURE 142. *Atomic vibrators give the best sec's.*

126. What Is Your Age versus Your Spaceship Twin?

ONE OF THE strange predictions of the theory of relativity is that moving clocks run slow. The word *clocks* here refers to any processes or systems that evolve in time, not just mechanical or electronic clocks. So all biological, physical, and chemical processes are affected in the same way. One might even say that when a moving system is seen by an observer watching it move past, time itself runs slow. This effect, known as "time dilation," leads to large time slowdowns only for objects traveling at speeds approaching the speed of light.

For example, a clock in a spaceship going at 98 percent the speed of light would be seen to run at a fifth its normal rate, according to someone observing the ship go past. Theoretically, right at the speed of light, time would come to a standstill. At ordinary speeds—even the 600 miles per hour of a jet aircraft—the time dilation effect would be extremely small. This is not to say the effect is too small to measure. Extremely sensitive clocks taken aboard jet aircraft do, in fact, slow down relative to clocks left behind on the ground, by exactly the amount predicted by relativity theory.[1]

Besides being checked using ordinary clocks, the predictions of time dilation have also been checked by observing the half-lives of various unstable elementary particles. For example, particles known as muons decay with a half-life of 2.2 microseconds (millionths of a second), but when they are moving at 98 percent the speed of light, they live five times longer, and hence travel five times farther, just as predicted by relativity.[2] When scientists design new particle accelerators, unless the time dilation predicted by relativity is taken into account, the accelerators will not work as designed, as the muon example illustrates.

Time dilation, however, occurs only when you observe a relatively moving system, such as a spaceship passing Earth. No time dilation effect is seen when the spaceship riders look around their ship, because for them the ship may be considered at rest. Earth observers might be tempted to explain this nonobservation by saying that the spaceship riders do not notice time running slow because their brains are running slow! But the spaceship riders can make the

FIGURE 143. *A twin pair o' ducks*

same claim about events on Earth, which they perceive as running slow. The two sets of observers are completely symmetrical, so each says her time seems to be normal and the other's time is running slow. This is the essence of the "twin

1. In addition to the effect of motion, however, in this case part of the time difference results from the effect of gravity on clocks, which varies according to the clock's altitude.

2. The factor by which time intervals expand for any given speed is the same factor γ described in footnote 1 of essay 91.

235

paradox," whereby each of two twins—one on Earth and the other in a moving plane or spaceship—might be expected to say the other's time runs slow.

In view of the symmetry between the twins, it might seem paradoxical that a clock taken on a jet aircraft should run slower than a twin clock on the ground: why can't jet plane observers regard themselves as being at rest and the ground as moving? This paradox is resolved if we realize that the symmetry between two observers holds only if they are moving uniformly (at constant speed in a straight line). The jet plane, since it accelerates at takeoff, turns around, and decelerates on landing, is clearly moving nonuniformly, so in this case we should no longer expect a complete symmetry between observers.

Symmetry would also break down in exactly the same way if you took a space flight to a distant star while your twin stayed behind on Earth. In fact, if the spaceship's speed were high enough, a million years might elapse on Earth and only one year aboard the spaceship. The required speed in this case would be 0.1 millimeters per second below the speed of light. Thus trips into the future are not simply science fiction—provided you don't mind your time travel being strictly one-way!

127.　How Old Is the Universe?

INFORMATION ON both the age and size of the universe comes from the same source, namely Hubble's law—which states that galaxies are rushing away from us at speeds proportional to their distance from us. But great uncertainty exists in the value of the proportionality constant between galactic distances and speeds. This constant allows us to translate the relative speeds given by Hubble's law (such as "galaxies are moving twice as fast when twice as far away") to absolute speeds (such as "300 kilometers per second"). There is no law giving the proportionality constant—it can be found only by observation. One source of uncertainty is due to the great difficulty in measuring the distances to the farthest galaxies; another is the unknown rate of slowing down of the universal expansion—the deceleration caused by the gravitational attraction of everything in the universe for everything else.

If there was very little matter in the universe, the resultant low gravity would lead to little deceleration in the expansion. In this case the age of the universe in years would simply equal its observed size in light-years. The reason for this relationship is that at the edge of the observable universe (13 to 20 billion light-years away), galaxies are receding at the speed of light. Therefore, if there is no deceleration, that is, constant-speed expansion, the matter now at the edge of the universe was all at one place 13 to 20 billion years ago. In fact, according to Hubble's law, all the matter in the universe would have been at one place at one time—the time of the big bang.

On the other hand, if the expansion is appreciably slowing down, previous expansion speeds were greater than those occurring now. Thus, it would have taken less time for the galaxies at the edge of the observable universe to reach their present distances than had the expansion been at constant speed. In general, the greater the deceleration caused by gravity, the younger the present age of the universe must be. For a large enough value of the deceleration, we would find that the universe would be closed. In other words, for any greater deceleration, the universe would reach some maximum size and then collapse, leading to the "big crunch." Given the uncertainty introduced by the unknown deceleration, the age of the universe is usually estimated to be between 10 and 20 billion years, and it is sometimes quoted simply as 15 billion years.

Whether or not the deceleration is, in fact, enough to close the universe depends entirely on the amount of matter in the universe. The critical density of matter needed to just close the universe is the equivalent of three hydrogen atoms per cubic meter of space. The luminous matter that we actually observe is roughly a hundredth of this critical value. But based on well-observed gravitational effects attributed to dark matter, the amount of unseen matter in the universe could well be a hundred times that of the visible matter—in which case the actual density of matter would appear to be reasonably close to the critical value.

If, in fact, the universe is closed, ultimately leading to a big crunch, our estimate of the age of the universe would refer only to the time since the most recent big bang. One can imagine an endless series

FIGURE 144. *"Now, tell me again that part about what you were doing the day before you created the universe."*

of big bangs and crunches in an oscillating universe of possibly infinite age. Some physicists have even suggested that after each cycle, the constants of nature and even the laws of physics undergo drastic changes—the ultimate recycling program! How much time do we have before the big crunch begins? That is very difficult to say, because we don't even have proof that the expansion is decelerating at a fast enough rate to lead to an eventual collapse, and, in fact, the present best estimate says it is not.

128. How Old Are the Stars?

OUR SUN IS believed to be a middle-aged star about halfway through its estimated 10-billion-year lifetime. There are, however, some stars believed to have lifetimes thousands of times shorter, and others thousands of times longer, than our Sun. The longest-lived of these stars, born when the galaxy was formed, would now be the merest infants.

The key factor in determining the lifetime of a star is its mass at the time of its formation out of the interstellar gas and dust of the galaxy. The greater a star's initial mass, the hotter its core temperature must get in order to create the internal pressure needed to keep the star from collapsing under its own gravity. Hotter stars necessarily burn their fuel faster, and hence live shorter lives. We can estimate stellar lifetimes from the rate at which stars burn their fuel, and the mass of the fuel available for burning. The relevant mass is somewhat less than the entire mass of the star, since the nuclear reactions that power the star take place only in the hot inner core.

Astronomers trying to judge the ages of various stars have to rely on mathematical models that describe the birth, life, and eventual death of stars, since even the shortest-lived stars live for millions of years—far too long to follow their evolution by direct observation. Stars are born in the "stellar nursery"—the dust-rich plane of the galaxy—when a cloud of dust and gas begins to collapse due to its own gravity. The cores of stars ignite by themselves once the collapse causes sufficiently high central temperatures to initiate fusion reactions. Such star formation continues to occur today. For example, a dark cloud of interstellar gas and dust in the constellation Orion is believed to be one such place where star formation is now occurring.[1]

Once its core does ignite, a star spends most of its middle years generating energy by converting hydrogen at its core into helium—for a length of time that depends on its mass and central temperature. The post–hydrogen burning life of a star also depends dramatically on the star's mass. Following their hydrogen burning stage, stars such as our Sun are believed to go through the "red giant" and "white dwarf" stages, and eventually become burned-out cinders ("black

1. As explained in footnote 2 in essay 79, astronomers don't actually observe stars being formed.

dwarfs") The terms *red giant* and *white dwarf* remind us that such stars are much larger or smaller than most red or white stars.

Stars much heavier than our Sun are believed to have hot enough core temperatures to fuse a whole series of nuclei—each the "ash" of the previous fusion reaction—until iron is formed. The chain abruptly ends when iron, the most stable nucleus, is formed. At this point, without the heat and radiation pressure from nuclear fusion, the star's outer layers undergo gravitational collapse. The collapse becomes an explosion when the outer layers crash into the dense, fantastically hot inner core. The resulting supernova explosion blows off the outer layers, and leaves a core in the form of a black hole or neutron star. Although these various stages in the life cycle of one star cannot be observed, the theory of stellar evolution can be checked by observing whether the relative numbers of stars at various stages of their evolution match the theory's predictions.

FIGURE 145. *The supervisor in the stellar nursery was forever berating her staff for allowing the newborns to become completely covered by dust.*

Estimating the age of a particular star is relatively easy if the star is at a well-defined stage toward the end of its life, such as the red giant stage. But it is not so easy if the star is in the hydrogen burning stage that lasts most of its life, because we cannot see inside the star to learn the fraction of hydrogen that has been consumed (or the amount of helium created). In contrast to the dramatic changes that occur toward the beginning and end of stars' lives, their long middle age is relatively uneventful.

129. How Old Are Atoms?

VIRTUALLY ALL objects in the everyday world show signs of age. In the microscopic world of atoms and subatomic particles, however, matter neither rusts nor rots. Processes such as rust, decay, and other indications of age all involve chemical changes or rearrangements of atoms, but no changes in the nature of the atoms themselves. We do speak of radioactive "decay" of unstable atomic nuclei, but the word *decay* applied to atomic nuclei may convey a misleading impression. Unlike the decay we see in the everyday world, the decay of a nucleus is a sudden, unpredictable event with no precursors. Individual nuclei about to decay are, as far as we know, absolutely identical to newly created nuclei. At the most fundamental level, the identity, or equivalence, of any two electrons or any two nuclei of a given element guarantees that matter contains no "memory." It is precisely because radioactive nuclei contain no memory that the fraction decaying in any given year stays constant in time, which is the basis for radioactive dating.

We can use radioactive dating to determine the age of materials based on the total fraction of radioactive atoms that have already decayed (see next essay). But dating the age of a piece of material is not the same as finding the age of the atoms of which the material is composed. Atoms represent the ultimate level of recycling; the atoms of which your body is made were at one time part of many other objects. At one time, in fact, the atoms of your body were probably part of another star. But the atoms of our world have not been around since the beginning of creation.

Immediately following the big bang 10 to 20 billion years ago, the universe was far too hot for atoms to exist. If any atoms were to form spontaneously then from collisions of their constituent particles, their subsequent violent collisions with other particles would immediately break them apart. It was not until an estimated million years following the big bang that hydrogen and helium atoms could form, when the universe cooled to an estimated 3,000°. Even today, these two elements are believed to comprise 98 percent of the atoms in the universe by mass—although a negligible fraction of the atoms on the Earth.

FIGURE 146. *The lab at the center of a star where the elements are cooked up.*

When was the rich variety of elements we see around us formed? According to the present theories of stellar evolution, all the heavy elements were "cooked up" in a series of nuclear fusion reactions that power the stars. When any given nucleus, such as carbon, is formed as the "ash" of one fusion reaction, that same nucleus can serve as the fuel for a subsequent reaction once the kindling temperature is reached. In this way, all the elements up to iron get successively cooked up in the cores of stars.

The elements heavier than iron, whose production consumes energy rather than produces it, are formed only during supernova explosions. Thus, from the presence of heavy elements on Earth, we can infer that much of the matter making up our solar system was at one time part of some other star. The atoms of which our world is made are therefore certainly older than the age of our solar system—4.6 billion years.

130. How Does Radioactive Dating Work?

RADIOACTIVE nuclei decay at a rate that is virtually unaffected by any pressures or temperatures encountered on Earth. This relative independence of most radioactive decay rates from outside environmental conditions is what makes radioactive decay so useful as a clock to measure the age of events in the distant past. The relative independence of nuclear decay rates on outside temperature and pressure is due to the high energy needed to change the structure of the atomic nucleus compared with the energies needed to change atoms. Therefore, extreme temperatures beyond those found on Earth are required to affect nuclear processes.

Any given element, such as uranium, has various isotopes, which, by definition, differ in the number of neutrons contained in the nucleus. For example, all uranium nuclei have 92 protons, but the uranium-235 isotope has 143 neutrons, while uranium-238 has 146 neutrons. (The numbers 235 and 238 represent atomic weight, the sum of the number of neutrons plus protons.) All radioactive (unstable) isotopes decay according to the radioactive decay law, which is based on the assumption that individual nuclei have no "memory" and are completely identical.

As a result of this lack of memory, a constant fraction of nuclei decay in any given year. In other words, unlike the situation with human mortality, nuclei that have "been waiting" to decay for a long time are not more likely to decay than others. As a result, all nuclear decays can be characterized by a half-life—the time required for half of a sample of radioactive nuclei to decay. At the end of two half-lives, half of the remaining half will have decayed, and at the end of N half-lives, only $1/2^N$ of the initial amount will remain. Apropos of the cartoon for the next essay, a radioactive cat would have to be lucky indeed to live for as long as eighteen half-lives. Only one cat in $2^{18} = 262,144$ would live that long.

Fortunately, we can easily measure the half-life of a long-lived isotope without waiting for half the nuclei to decay. For example, if we can determine how many nuclei are originally present, we can find the half-life merely by counting how many decays occur in a short time interval—say one hour—even if the half-life is a billion years. We must use nuclei with half-lives of millions or billions of years in order to date events in the Earth's history, because if the half-life is much shorter than this, not enough of the original radioactive isotope will still be around to use for dating purposes.

The radioactive nuclear isotopes that give rise to a nuclear decay are known as the "parent" nuclei, and the nuclei into which they decay are known as the "daughters." Clearly, as the number of parent nuclei declines over time, the number of daughter nuclei (initially zero) will grow. Actually, in practice, some number of nuclei identical to daughter nuclei may originally be present, so we need to make a further distinction between "original daughters" and "radiogenic daughters" (born from radioactive decay).

FIGURE 147. *Serious dating errors can result if you fail to distinguish between the original and radiogenic daughters.*

In order to use radioactivity as a means of dating rocks or other materials, we need to have some means of estimating what fraction of the daughter isotope is original and what fraction is radiogenic. It is also important to have some assurance that the system is closed, so that we know neither parent nor daughter nuclei were removed or added through means other than radioactive decay. Serious dating errors can result if either parent or daughter nuclei are added or removed without our being aware of the fact, or if we confuse the original and radiogenic daughters.

● ● ● ● ●

131. How Old Is the Earth?

ESTIMATING THE age of the Earth has long been the province of scientists and theologians. Some of these estimates have been remarkably precise, though not necessarily accurate. For example, around 1650, based on his analysis of the Bible, Archbishop Ussher calculated that God created the world on Sunday, October 23, 4000 B.C. During the eighteenth and nineteenth centuries, however, many scientists began to suspect that the Earth was far older than the Bible seemed to suggest. One interesting nineteenth-century calculation of the age of the Earth was made by Lord Kelvin, who used his estimate of the rate of heat loss from the Earth's interior to find how far back the Earth would have been a molten mass, which it presumably was at the time of its creation. Kelvin's best estimate was that the Earth could not be more than 400 million years old—a figure now believed to be less than a tenth the true age. Kelvin did not know that heat is continually being supplied to the Earth's interior through the decay of radioactive nuclei, so it actually cools at a much slower rate than he assumed.

Ironically, radioactivity, which caused Kelvin's estimate to be in error, now offers the most reliable means for finding the age of the Earth. The best radioactive nucleus for this purpose is uranium, in view of its long half-life and relative natural abundance. Natural uranium consists mostly of the isotope uranium-238, but about 0.7 percent is uranium-235, the isotope used to make nuclear bombs. Both uranium isotopes progress through a chain of successive radioactive decays, and eventually reach stable lead. Uranium-238 eventually decays into lead-204 with a half-life of 4.5 billion years, and uranium-235 eventually decays into lead-207 with a half-life that is about one-sixth as long (713 million years).

The difference in the two uranium isotope half-lives causes the relative amounts of the two parent and daughter isotopes found in nature to vary slowly over time. For example, 4.5 billion years ago (one half-life of uranium-238), there would have had to have been twice as much uranium-238 around as now. But at the same time there would be over sixty-four times as much uranium 235, because 4.5 billion years represents over six half-lives of uranium-235, and after six half-lives the amount now left would be only $\frac{1}{2}^6 = \frac{1}{64}$ the earlier amount. Just as the amount of uranium increases as we go back in time, the relative amounts of lead-204 and lead-207 must *decrease*, since some fraction of the present lead is the result of uranium decay. You could say that the method is similar to finding out how long a returning college student has been home from the ratio of clean socks in his drawers to dirty socks under the bed.

FIGURE 148. *Very lucky radioactive cats have 18 half-lives.*

If we assume that *all* the lead now found in nature is the result of uranium decay, we can use the known uranium half-lives to estimate the age of the Earth, based on the observed uranium-lead ratio. For example, at present, the ratio of uranium-235 to lead-207 is $\frac{1}{214}$. This number implies that nearly eight half-lives must have passed since the uranium began decaying, because at the end of eight half-lives, the uranium would be $\frac{1}{2}^8 = \frac{1}{256}$ its original amount (slightly less than $\frac{1}{214}$). Eight half-lives of uranium-235 would be 5.7 billion years—which is an estimate of the age of the Earth on the assumption that *all* the lead-207 found in nature resulted from uranium-235 decay. Clearly, if we assume, more realistically, that some lead-207 were present originally, we will get a *younger* age of the Earth, because not as much uranium-235 would have had to decay to produce the lead we now find. (This is equivalent to the assumption that some dirty socks were left under the bed years ago by another brother.)

How can we find how much of the lead we see in nature is the original daughter, and how much is radiogenic? You might think we could use rocks lacking uranium ore to estimate the amount of the original-daughter lead isotopes present at the Earth's creation. But unfortunately, we have no way of knowing how much lead may have been removed from such rocks over the ages. We can, however, estimate the amount of the original-daughter lead isotopes by studying uranium-free meteorites presumed to consist of the original matter from which our solar system formed. When the original daughter is subtracted from the present amounts of lead-204 and lead-207 found in nature, and the relevant uranium decay for each type of lead is used to find the age of the Earth, both calculations yield exactly the same number: 4.6 billion years, the currently accepted age of the Earth.

132.   Why Do Carbon Atoms Provide Some of Our Best Recent Dates?

WHAT MAKES the element carbon so useful for radioactive dating? The most common stable isotope of carbon (carbon-12) has six protons and six neutrons in its nucleus. Carbon-14, on the other hand, with eight neutrons and six protons, is radioactive, with a half-life of 5,730 years. Obviously, that half-life is far too short for any primordial carbon-14 present at Earth's creation still to be around, since 8 million half-lives would have elapsed during the Earth's 4.6-billion-year existence—so not even a single atom would now be left. Yet carbon-14 does exist in nature, as a result of the continual bombardment of the Earth's atmosphere by cosmic rays from space. The continual creation of new carbon-14 nuclei, and their subsequent decay, imply that there must exist some equilibrium level of carbon-14 in the atmosphere.[1]

Although the carbon-14 half-life is far too short to be useful for dating events throughout most of Earth's history, it is well suited for dating events in Earth's recent history—say the last 50,000 years. When living organisms assimilate carbon from the atmosphere, the ratio of carbon-14 to carbon-12 atoms they absorb is just the equilibrium ratio in the atmosphere. After that initial assimilation, the radioactive carbon-14 decay causes the ratio of the two carbon isotopes to gradually change in favor of stable carbon-12, since the number of these atoms does not decrease with time. For example, 5,730 years (one carbon-14 half-life) after a plant dies, its remains will contain only half as much carbon-14 relative to carbon-12 as the atmosphere contains.

Even if some carbon should leave the sample due to chemical processes, the ratio of carbon isotopes would be almost unaffected, because chemical processes distinguish only very slightly between different isotopes of an element. Unlike other radiometric methods that require you to keep track of the amounts of both parent and daughter nuclei, the carbon-14 dating method requires only that the amount of parent carbon-14 be measured relative to the stable carbon-12 isotope.

The two conditions required for reliable carbon-14 dating are (1) a constant atmospheric production rate (so that the equilibrium concentration of carbon-14 in the atmosphere is known), and (2) an assimilation time of carbon-14 by living organisms that is very short compared with the half-life. The first condition will be satisfied only as long as the cosmic ray bombardment rate is roughly constant over time. There are some indications that this may not be true, which may be a source of some error in ra-

FIGURE 149. *"I don't know, I think they ought to call the offspring of unstable radioactive nuclei 'sons.'"*

diocarbon dating—perhaps by 15 percent over the last 20,000 years. The second condition of sufficiently rapid assimilation of carbon-14 by organisms is, however, usually satisfied.

---

1. Although that equilibrium was disrupted during the period of atmospheric nuclear testing, it has now been largely restored.

245

Radiocarbon dating has proved extremely useful to geologists, historians, anthropologists, biologists, climatologists, and art historians. A large variety of carbon-based materials have been dated using the technique, including manuscripts, mummy cloths, paintings, wood, charcoal, and bone. By dating such materials, relatively precise dates can be attached to many historical artifacts—assuming the correction is made for varying levels of carbon-14 in the atmosphere.

Relatively recent geological events can also be dated using the radiocarbon method, including the retreat of the last continental glaciers, and accompanying climatic changes. The climate history can be gleaned from small bubbles trapped in old ice, which can be examined for their ratio of carbon to nitrogen. A high value of this ratio signals abundant bacterial respiration into the atmosphere, and hence presumably a warm climate. By correlating the ratio of carbon to nitrogen (indicating temperature) with the measured carbon-14 to carbon-12 ratio (indicating age), scientists can estimate temperatures at various times in the past.

133.   When Was the North Pole a South Pole?

THE EXACT mechanism by which the Earth produces its magnetism remains unknown. Presumably, a "dynamo effect" is created as a result of flows in the Earth's liquid iron core. This term refers to some arrangement whereby electrical currents create a strong magnetic field from a weak one, via positive feedback. One clue to the mechanism for producing the Earth's magnetism lies in the fact that the field reverses sign at irregular intervals. On average, the magnetic reversals occur at intervals of about 250,000 years. A reversal may now be overdue, since the last one occurred about 700,000 years ago.

The dates of reversals can be established by examining layers of seafloor sediments, and looking at the polarity of magnetization frozen in sedimentary rocks at the time they solidified. If we can estimate the rate at which sediments are deposited, the dates of magnetic reversals can be found. These data on seafloor sediments show that a reversal of the Earth's magnetic field is preceded by a "sudden" drop in the strength of the field lasting 2,000 years, followed by a reversal perhaps 20,000 years later. Such drops in the strength of the Earth's magnetic field could be quite hazardous to life, since the Earth's magnetism acts to deflect much of the cosmic radiation from space that would otherwise reach the Earth's surface.

Although the cause of magnetic reversals is unknown, one suggestion is that they may be due to the occasional impact of large asteroids. Support for the asteroid impact theory of magnetic reversals comes from two sources. First, large meteorite impacts are often associated with tektites—small glassy objects of various shapes, presumably melted by the high temperatures of the impact. The layers of seafloor sediments that show magnetic reversals often also show tektite concentrations at just the times of those reversals. Second, the pattern of major temperature drops over the past 200 million years also appears to coincide with the pattern of magnetic reversals.

A large asteroid impact would have a profound climactic effect on Earth, due to the large volume of dust injected into the atmosphere and the resulting temperature drop associated with the blockage of sunlight. It has been estimated that sea level would drop by about 10 meters, due to the expansion of the polar ice caps. The redistribution of some of the Earth's water toward the polar rotation axis would cause the Earth's rotational speed to increase—just as a figure skater increases her rate of spin when she moves her arms in. Of course, in the case of the Earth, the increase in rotational speed would be very slight, perhaps only one part in a million, because the mass of water moved close to the axis would be only about a millionth of the Earth's mass. Nevertheless, a one-part-in-a-million speedup of the Earth's spin amounts to one extra rotation in every million days, or 3,000 years.

FIGURE 150. *Magnetic reversals make for trying times for navigators.*

Such a change in spin could wreak havoc in the Earth's core. The Earth, with its liquid interior, is similar to an uncooked egg, which can easily be distinguished from a hard-boiled egg when the two are spun. Like the uncooked egg, the Earth with its liquid interior does not rotate as a solid object. A speedup of rotation at the Earth's surface would cause a slippage relative to the liquid iron core, and a resulting disruption of the flows that produce the Earth's magnetic field, causing the field to drop to very low levels. According to theory, it would take some time for the field to reestablish itself, and it would be a matter of chance whether the new field would have the same or opposite sign as the original field.

134. How Long Has It Been since the Last Mass Extinction?

THE TERM "dinosaur" is often used pe-joritively to refer to a person who is hopelessly out of touch with his present-day environment. But the real dinosaurs adapted *very* successfully to their environment, and they lived on this Earth perhaps twenty times as long as we have, so far. True, the dinosaurs did die out abruptly 65 million years ago, according to the fossil record, but they were far from alone. Paleontologists have found that all large animals died out, as well as many tiny plants and animals in a fairly short span of geological time—an event we refer to as a mass extinction. The cause of this mass extinction has been attributed to the collision of a 10-kilometer-diameter asteroid with the Earth. An asteroid of this size not only would have produced enough dust to lower the Earth's temperature drastically, but also would have generated so many nitrogen oxides that essentially pure nitric acid would have rained down over much of the Earth's surface.

The fact that we are now here to theorize about this matter obviously means that some of humanity's ancestors managed to survive the mass extinction. It is not known why some mammals managed to survive, while dinosaurs did not, but plausibly this might be because very large creatures, like dinosaurs, were far less numerous than small mammals, for reasons having to do with the food supply. Presumably, many small animals also died along with the dinosaurs, but not in sufficient numbers to end all the mammal species.

The evidence for the connection between the last mass extinction and a large asteroid impact was discovered by Luis Alvarez and his son Walter Alvarez, who found a very thin layer of iridium in sedimentary rock in many places throughout the world. Iridium, an element that is very rare on Earth, is much more abundant in meteorites. The difference in iridium abundance on Earth and in meteorites apparently has to do with iridium's affinity for iron. As the elements of the early molten earth sorted themselves out by density, most of Earth's iron found its way to the core, taking most of the iridium with it and leaving very little on the surface.

The Alvarezes' key finding was that in a 1-millimeter-thick layer of sedimentary rock dated 65 million years ago, iridium was three hundred times more abundant than at either earlier or later times (higher or lower rock layers). This extremely thin layer contained other elements also found in meteorites, and in relative amounts that are the same for rocks throughout the world but *only* in that thin layer. Moreover, the numerous species of fossilized organisms found in the same sedimentary rock show an abrupt extinction within 1 millimeter of the iridium layer.

The Alvarezes were able to calculate the 10-kilometer diameter of the hypothesized asteroid based on the 1-millimeter thickness of the worldwide iridium layer. From that thickness, we can easily find the total volume and mass of iridium deposited. Then, assuming that the asteroid had an iridium abundance equal to that found in other meteorites, we can easily compute its mass and diameter based on the amount of iridium it deposited worldwide. You might find it far-fetched that a localized asteroid impact would lead to a *uniform* layer of iridium worldwide, but that is precisely what would have occurred if the impact was sufficiently violent for much of the vaporized material to ascend to the stratosphere, where it could reside for years and spread equally through the stratosphere before returning to Earth.

Following the Alvarezes' discovery, other scientists uncovered evidence that mass extinctions may be *periodic* events. Looking over the last 250 million years, they found evidence in the fossil record

FIGURE 151. *Sol's dark companion was hurt that her existence was kept a secret, so every once in a while she would throw a tantrum.*

for eight extinction events (with varying severity) spaced at 26-million-year intervals. An explanation proposed for this periodicity involves a hypothetical dark companion star to our Sun, appropriately named Nemesis, after the Greek god for vengeance. Nemesis supposedly orbits the Sun with a 26-million-year period, and consequently its average distance from the Sun is nearly a hundred thousand times greater than the radius of the Earth's orbit, according to Kepler's law. Presumably, when Nemesis is near its perihelion (the point of closest approach to the Sun), it passes through the Oort "cloud"—a distant spherical shell of comets surrounding the Sun—and it unleashes a shower of comets (or asteroids) in our direction. The failure of astronomers to have seen Nemesis does not mean it does not exist, since a small dark companion star to our Sun at an enormous distance could easily escape notice.

135. How Old Is Life
on Earth?

SCIENTISTS use fossils to study extinct forms of life on Earth. Most of the familiar fossil specimens occur in rocks dated less than half a billion years old, and these tell us little about the emergence of life, which is now believed to go much further back in time. The remains of the earliest known life-forms are the stromatolites, which are observed in rocks as layered structures of calcium and silica compounds. The layering presumably records daily or seasonal growth variations. Two lines of evidence have convinced researchers that tiny stromatolites are indeed the remains of living organisms. First, they exhibit a laminated structure consistent with certain living bacteria found in coastal areas around the world. The second, more convincing line of evidence is based on the carbon-13 to carbon-12 isotopic ratio contained in fossil stromatolites. (Neither carbon isotope is radioactive, so the observed ratio does not change over time.)

Isotopes of a given element behave almost identically in chemical reactions. Nevertheless, there are very small differences in their chemical reaction rates caused by their small mass differences. These differences in reaction rates make one isotope of carbon in CO_2 more likely to be photosynthetically absorbed by an organism than another, by perhaps a few parts in a thousand. This alteration by photosynthesis of the natural environmental ratio of carbon-13 to carbon-12 can be seen in living organisms. The fact that stromatolites show exactly the same carbon-13 to carbon-12 ratio as found today in photosynthesizing organisms indicates that they are probably the remnants of living organisms.

The oldest stramatolites are those found in western Australia in sediments radioactively dated as 3.6 billion years old. In fact, the oldest preserved rocks on Earth, in Greenland, go back even further to 3.8 billion years ago, and these also show an altered carbon-13 to carbon-12 ratio. Given that the age of the Earth is believed to be 4.6 billion years, life appears to have originated relatively early in Earth's history.

During the very early years following the Earth's formation out of the matter that coalesced to form the solar system, the planet would have been an exceedingly inhospitable place for life. In fact, it seems quite likely that up until 4.0 billion years ago, any life that might have spontaneously arisen would have been soon destroyed by the conditions that then existed—especially oceans of molten rock, a high-pressure atmosphere, and the flash heating by constant asteroid bombardment. Large asteroids are believed to have bombarded the early Earth much more frequently than at present, which is to be expected, given that many large chunks of matter in the solar system would not yet have coalesced into planets and moons.

A record of early asteroid impacts is preserved in the craters of the Moon, some of which have been dated based on returned lunar rock samples. These lunar rock datings confirm that early asteroid impacts on the Moon, and presumably the Earth as well, were far more frequent and involved far more energetic collisions than occur now. In fact, the largest of these asteroids, the size of a small planet, would likely have sterilized the entire Earth—primarily through evaporation of the oceans due to the heat energy created by the impact.

Given the observed dating of lunar craters, it appears that it was not until 4.0 billion years ago that the last of these life-sterilizing impacts is likely to have occurred, which leaves an open "window" of time for the first appearance of stable life on Earth between 3.8 and 4.0 billion years ago. Apart from supernatural explanations, the fact that life on Earth seems to

FIGURE 152. *"Honey, do you remember that movie* The Invasion of the Body Snatchers?*"*

have appeared so soon after conditions for stable life were favorable would seem to imply either that spontaneous generation of life is likely throughout the universe, or that what happened on Earth was a highly improbable but unique event. An alternative possibility that the "seeds" of life drifted to Earth from interstellar space also cannot be ruled out. And now, some 4 billion years later, those primitive life-forms have evolved into beings who can reflect on all this. We live in a wild, wonderful, and even wacky universe.

Bibliography

RECOMMENDED PHYSICS TEXTBOOKS

Elementary Level

P. G. Hewitt. *Conceptual Physics*. 7th ed. New York: Harper Collins, 1992.

More Advanced Introductory Level

D. Halliday, R. Resnick, and K. Krane. *Fundamentals of Physics*. New York: John Wiley & Sons, 1992.

P. Tipler. *Physics for Scientists and Engineers*. New York: Worth Publishers, 1990.

R. Serway. *Physics for Scientists and Engineers*. Philadelphia: Saunders College Publishing, 1990.

RECOMMENDED ASTRONOMY TEXTBOOKS

W. J. Kaufmann, III. *Universe*. New York: W. H. Freeman and Company, 1991.

M. A. Seeds. *Horizons: Exploring the Universe*. Belmont, Calif.: Wadsworth Publishing Company, 1989.

RECOMMENDED PHYSICS DEMONSTRATION BOOKS

R. Ehrlich. *Turning the World Inside Out and 174 Other Simple Physics Demonstrations*. Princeton, N.J.: Princeton University Press, 1990.

R. D. Edge. *String and Sticky Tape Experiments*. College Park, Md.: American Association of Physics Teachers, 1981.

RECOMMENDED BOOK OF PHYSICS BRAINTEASERS

J. Walker. *The Flying Circus of Physics with Answers*. New York: John Wiley & Sons, 1977.

RECOMMENDED BOOKS OF SCIENTIFIC CARTOONS

L. Gonick. *The Cartoon Guide to Physics*. New York: HarperCollins Publishers, 1991.

S. Harris. *Einstein Simplified: Cartoons on Science*. New Brunswick, N.J.: Rutgers University Press, 1989.

S. Harris. *You Want Proof? I'll Give You Proof!* New York: W. H. Freeman and Company, 1990.

J. Gribbin and K. Charlesworth. *The Cartoon History of Time*. New York: Penguin Books, 1990.

Index

About the Author and the Illustrator

Robert Ehrlich, professor of physics at George Mason University, delights in making physics interesting to students and the general public. He is the author of *Turning the World Inside Out and 174 Other Simple Physics Demonstrations* (1990) and three other books.

Gary Ehrlich has a degree in architectural engineering and currently works as an acoustical consultant. He also illustrated *Turning the World Inside Out and 174 Other Simple Physics Demonstrations*.